# Creating Exhibits That Engage

# AMERICAN ASSOCIATION FOR STATE AND LOCAL HISTORY BOOK SERIES

### ABOUT THE SERIES

The American Association for State and Local History Book Series addresses issues critical to the field of state and local history through interpretive, intellectual, scholarly, and educational texts. To submit a proposal or manuscript to the series, please request proposal guidelines from AASLH headquarters: AASLH Editorial Board, 2021 21st Ave. South, Suite 320, Nashville, Tennessee 37212. Telephone: (615) 320-3203. Website: www.aaslh.org.

### ABOUT THE ORGANIZATION

The American Association for State and Local History (AASLH) is a national history membership association headquartered in Nashville, Tennessee, that provides leadership and support for its members who preserve and interpret state and local history in order to make the past more meaningful to all people. AASLH members are leaders in preserving, researching, and interpreting traces of the American past to connect the people, thoughts, and events of yesterday with the creative memories and abiding concerns of people, communities, and our nation today. In addition to sponsorship of this book series, AASLH publishes *History News* magazine, a newsletter, technical leaflets and reports, and other materials; confers prizes and awards in recognition of outstanding achievement in the field; supports a broad education program and other activities designed to help members work more effectively; and advocates on behalf of the discipline of history. To join AASLH, go to www.aaslh.org or contact Membership Services, AASLH, 2021 21st Ave. South, Suite 320, Nashville, TN 37212.

# Creating Exhibits That Engage

## A Manual for Museums
## and Historical Organizations

*John Summers*

ROWMAN & LITTLEFIELD
*Lanham • Boulder • New York • London*

All photos are by the author, unless otherwise noted.

Published by Rowman & Littlefield
A wholly owned subsidary of The Rowman & Littlefield Publishing Group, Inc.
4501 Forbes Boulevard, Suite 200, Lanham, Maryland 20706
www.rowman.com

Unit A, Whitacre Mews, 26-34 Stannary Street, London SE11 4AB

British Library Cataloguing in Publication Information Available

**Library of Congress Cataloging-in-Publication Data Available**

978-1-4422-7935-3 (cloth)
978-1-4422-7936-0 (paper)
978-1-4422-7936-7 (electronic)

♾™ The paper used in this publication meets the minimum requirements of American National Standard for Information Sciences—Permanence of Paper for Printed Library Materials, ANSI/NISO Z39.48-1992.

Printed in the United States of America

# Dedication

This book is respectfully dedicated to the people, institutions, and organizations that have helped to shape my understanding of the fascinating world of museum exhibits.

The Fleming College Museum Management and Curatorship program, the Ontario Museum Association's Certificate in Museum Studies program, and the University of Toronto Faculty of Information's Master of Museum Studies program have all afforded me the opportunity to teach aspiring and emerging museum professionals. Their faculty and staff have been supportive throughout my teaching and writing. My students have been a constant source of inspiration and energy, and the need to organize my thoughts in order to teach them has greatly aided the development of this book.

The Antique Boat Museum in Clayton, New York, and its former executive director, John Mac-Lean, offered valuable work experience on exhibit projects and the creative freedom to explore new ways to communicate with visitors, and both opportunities were and are appreciated. The Regional Municipality of Halton and its former director of planning and chief planning official, Ron Glenn, allowed me to integrate the writing of this book with my job as manager of heritage services and curator, and the region has generously given permission for me to incorporate into the book work first undertaken for that organization.

My colleagues in Heritage Services, particularly Karla Corrigan, Claire Bennett, Megan Wiles, and Meredith Leonard, have helped shape my thoughts and ideas about exhibit development through their work on projects we have carried out together and the many meetings and discussions those have entailed. Claire's experience with traveling exhibits was of great assistance in preparing Appendix 2. Courtney Murfin, Mary-Kate Whibbs, and Lindsay Marlies Small have generously shared their insights into the nature of exhibit text, and Courtney also made a significant contribution to the chapter on interpretive planning. Barbara J. Soren, an audience researcher and evaluation consultant who specializes in working with cultural and community organizations, agreed to be interviewed for the evaluation chapter. In addition to those noted above, Dr. Carl Benn, Professor Deb Scott, Joel Stone, Megan Meloche, Maureen Marshall, and Sarah Munro were all kind enough to read and comment on the manuscript at various stages in its development.

Finally, and most importantly, neither this book nor the work and life experiences that have gone into creating it would have been possible without the patient and unstinting support of Wendy Cooper, my wife and fellow museum professional, to whom I shall be forever grateful.

# Contents

**Part I:   Context, Audience, and Process**

**Part II:   Concept Development**

# List of Illustrations

# Foreword

Collectively, the artifacts held by museums represent the cultural memory of humankind and of the world we live in. Since their origins, it has been the task of public museums to research those collections and then engage wider audiences with the knowledge and understanding they have uncovered. In so doing, we all gain a greater understanding of the world we live in, and our place in it.

Today, the basic challenge of engaging the wider public remains the same, but rapid societal change means that audience expectations of the museum experience are expanding exponentially. Museums must either rise to the demands posed by changing audiences, by developing experiences that respond to visitors' evolving needs and expectations, or face slow but inevitable extinction. While the task is scary, it also provides remarkable opportunities for museums to support audience engagement with their collections in ways that were not possible before. And this applies to small- and medium-sized museums as well as to large, well-funded ones. Regular change, social interaction, and opportunities to participate are central to modern audience demands and can turn people from one-off visitors into regular users of their local museum.

Small- to medium-sized institutions make up a substantial majority of museums in the United States, Canada, and United Kingdom (and no doubt elsewhere). Often dependent on a few, if any, paid staff and a core of volunteers, how can they possibly find the resources to transform themselves (and then keep changing) as audiences expect? The answer lies in building their own skills base, and this book by John Summers helps to show the way. John brings more than thirty years of practical experience to bear both in developing museum exhibits and in training others to do so. As he says, "Every exhibit development project is an adventure," but, with this book, he provides a very experienced hand to support you on the journey.

Yes, as he also says, it is a "nuts-and-bolts guide to how to do it step by step," suited to the resources of small- to medium-sized museums. But the book is much more than that. It gives the people who work in small- to medium-sized museums the confidence to experiment and innovate because they can know the basic underpinning will hold. Three issues come through clearly (and reflect my own sometimes bitter experience also). First is to have a sense of the big picture from the outset, and how everything fits together to create the visitor experience. Second is seeing the project from the visitor's point of view. Finally comes the importance of thinking time. Together these can assure you are rightly confident in the project before committing serious money—but also that the project has the potential to truly hold a contemporary audience, "creating stories that connect the artifacts and artworks in your collections with the visitors who walk through your doors."

⋆ ⋆ ⋆ ⋆ ⋆

Graham Black, professor of Museum Development, Nottingham Trent University, UK, and author of *The Engaging Museum: Developing Museums for Visitor Involvement.*

# Preface

All across North America, almost every day of the year, visitors walk through the doors of museums to experience exhibits. For members of the public in figure 0.1, an exhibit can be the beginning of a journey that can offer new insights and a memorable social experience. For the museum staff working with the exhibit model in figure 0.2, the moment the visitor encounters the exhibit is the end of an institutional journey during which the exhibit was planned, designed, fabricated, and installed. *Creating Exhibits That Engage: A Manual for Museums and Historical Organizations* will lead you from the first concept for the exhibit up to that moment. As someone who is interested in museums, you have been a consumer of exhibits. By following the process outlined here, you

**Figure 0.1** Visitors entering the museum.

**Figure 0.2** Staff planning an exhibit.

can become a producer of museum exhibits too. The whole book is about the answers to two simple questions: (1) What is a good exhibit? and (2) How do I make one?

In *The Engaging Museum: Developing Museums for Visitor Involvement*, Graham Black says, "The role of museums in the twenty-first century is as it has always been, to seek contemporary ways to engage audiences with their collections."[1] I do not think, at this date, you would be likely to find many who would dispute this statement, but how do you pull it off? Black goes on to say, "It is as if budding and existing curators and exhibition designers are expected to know by magic how to most effectively put objects in cases or on open display in a way that will engage visitors directly with them."[2] That is where this book comes in.

It is my hope that the information presented here will be useful to anyone involved in developing exhibits, in any capacity and at any size of institution, but this book is particularly addressed to the staff, volunteers, and supporters of small- to medium-sized museums and related organizations such as local historical societies. At the "small" end of the scale, this includes museums with one full-time or one part-time or even no professional staff. By "medium-sized," I mean museums that have at least three to four professional staff including a curator, an educator, a collections manager, and a manager or director. I hope it will become evident as you work through the process that the number of staff and the size of the budget and/or museum are not the most important factors for success when creating exhibits. As you may have seen in the course of your own museum visits, lots of staff and a large budget are in themselves no guarantee of an excellent exhibit, just as a small staff and a modest budget are not necessarily barriers to creating a first-rate visitor experience.

I received my museum studies training and early museum experience in Canada, worked for a decade in the United States, and returned to work again in Canada. Throughout this cross-border career, I have found more similarities than differences between museums of similar size on both sides of the border, particularly when it comes to creating exhibits. Good exhibits, the ones that visitors remember and tell their friends about, have many things in common no matter where they are created or viewed. Having begun my museum career as an interpreter of historic foodways,

I'm tempted to call this an exhibit cookbook. A recipe in a cookbook is an infinitely customizable method. Once you know how to make yeast bread dough, you can make as many variations of the basic loaf as you want to. The same is true for exhibits. Whether your exhibit budget is $1,000 or $100,000 or more, you need to determine what you will say, and to whom, and by what means, and how you will know if you have succeeded. That is the exhibit recipe for which your particular circumstances are the ingredients. The steps in this book can be adapted to a wide range of topics and easily scaled for different sizes of project. For example, depending on the resources available to you, interpretive planning and the work of the interpretive planner (see chapter 7) can be either a lens through which to view the exhibit development process, a role temporarily filled by a member of the museum's staff or a contract professional brought into the project.

A quick online search for books about exhibits will reveal that there are many titles already on the market. Why do we need another? A number of the published books are about large-scale, high-profile projects at international institutions. There are almost as many on art exhibits. There are titles on trade and consumer show exhibits and any number of coffee-table books featuring the work of particular designers and design firms. There are also reference-oriented works featuring chapters on exhibit-related topics by different authors. Many of these books are about exhibits as end products, but far fewer are about how to create them, and fewer still provide a nuts-and-bolts guide to how to do it step by step that is suited to the resources typically available in small- to medium-sized institutions. There is no formula that will automatically produce a good exhibit. If there were, and I had it, you would be paying a lot more for this book. There is, however, a method and a process you can follow that will greatly increase the likelihood that you will be able to create one. That's what you're holding in your hands now.

Don't be put off by credentialism or feel that you aren't qualified to create exhibits if you do not have a design degree or are not an architect. Exhibits are about more than just graphics and well-drawn plans. At their heart, they are about something you probably already do every day at your museum: creating stories that connect the artifacts and artworks in your collections with the visitors who walk through your doors. The formal design process is just one part of exhibit making, and in some ways not the most important part. The most important qualification you can have is a strong desire to create compelling visitor experiences.

Once you have worked on an exhibit project, you will never walk through a museum the same way again. I have often had students in my exhibit planning and design course tell me that after taking it they look at exhibits in a new light. They spend more time thinking about how the graphic panels are attached to the wall and how the interactives were built than they do taking in the content. You will also probably start finding typographical errors and other mistakes, but I will leave it up to you whether you bring them to the museum's attention or not.

This book is the product of three decades of experience in museums, during which I have worked as a historical interpreter, curator, manager, fabricator, designer, and teacher of exhibit planning and design. Work as a curator has given me an understanding of artifacts. Work as an interpreter has given me sympathy for visitors and a keen sense of audience. Work on developing exhibits has brought these two together, and work as a manager has shown me the importance of creating and leading the right team to realize the project. In those decades I have seen the change in exhibit production from a situation in which you typically hired a designer and then stood back and waited for the results, to the present day, when advances in technology mean that the whole design and production cycle, from concept to finished graphic panels and casework, can be brought in-house for less than the cost of a moderately priced car.

This book and my teaching are informed by having done this work myself, from researching and developing concepts, to hiring and managing designers and fabricators, to creating content and programming, to purchasing materials and fabricating in the workshop. Without for a moment claiming to have all the answers about how to create the perfect exhibit, I will share ideas, techniques, and approaches that I have found to work well and also be candid about the ones that did not.

If you want to know what is involved in making exhibits, this book will show you the scope of a typical project. If you need to create an exhibit, the steps outlined here will lead you through from beginning to end. Even if you are just hiring contract professionals to create some or all of an exhibit, the information in this book will help you to understand their perspective on the project and lead to a more effective working relationship.

*Creating Exhibits That Engage: A Manual for Museums and Historical Organizations* is organized into four sections: (1) Context, Audience, and Process; (2) Concept Development; (3) Design Development; and (4) Fabrication. Part I explores different types and styles of exhibits, what makes a good exhibit good, who is involved in exhibit development, the audience for exhibits, and the exhibit development process. Part II discusses the development of the exhibit's big idea, front-end, formative, and summative evaluation, the exhibit brief and request for proposals, interpretive planning, writing exhibit text, and the all-important budget.

Part III outlines the stages in developing a design, including visual design principles, graphics, typography, accessibility and universal design, the use of gallery models, digital imaging, working with color, design software, shop drawings, and selecting artifacts and images. It also explores the principles and processes of curating exhibits. Part IV presents the materials, tools, and techniques of fabrication in both the graphics studio and the workshop, and it covers the later stages of an exhibit project including installation, close-out, and project archiving.

The part and chapters are presented in generally the same order in which they would occur in an exhibit project. Each concludes with a Chapter Checklist, which is a summary of the key steps and concepts in that stage of the exhibit development process. Four appendices address institutional exhibit planning, traveling exhibits, a sample request for proposals, and some proven design strategies.

Museum exhibits are fascinating to visit and even more interesting to create. Existing in three dimensions, and making use of color, sound, light, space, and time, exhibits shape a story that shares the artifacts and historic materials in our collections with visitors.

I am a curator at heart, and I am as interested in artifacts as I was when I first began to work in museums, but the most satisfying moments of my working life have been when I see visitors engaging with an exhibit I helped to create. When I overhear them exclaiming in surprise and delight, or sharing with others in their group, or see them just deeply and quietly engaged with what is on display, I know that the museum has reached out and successfully established a connection with them through the medium of an exhibit. I hope that this book will inspire and help you to plan and design your own.

John Summers
Burlington, Ontario

## Notes

1. Graham Black, *The Engaging Museum: Developing Museums for Visitor Involvement* (New York: Routledge, 2005), 267.
2. Black, *The Engaging Museum*, 271.

*Part I*

# Context, Audience, and Process

# Chapter 1

*The Nature of Exhibits*

**Exhibits: It's What We Do**

How important are exhibits to museums? To borrow a phrase from the retail sector, "Exhibits R Us." They are the place where the visitors meet the stuff. Simply put, "Museums are not museums without exhibitions."[1]

As well as its unique content, each exhibit usually has a distinctive style and a typical method of presentation. Styles come and go, and sometimes that is for the better. For example, I for one hope that all those orange-and-brown 1970s exhibits with super-graphics painted on the wall never come back. Like most styles, exhibit styles also recur every so often—how many times has the fashion world rediscovered black? Examples of almost every historical exhibit style can be found in museums today. Some are strongly associated with particular historical periods, such as cabinets of curiosities in the Renaissance, the severe, white-walled art museums of the Modernist era in the early twentieth century, or the naturalistic streetscapes of the 1970s and 1980s.

**Figure 1.1** Visitors viewing an exhibit.

Some are old styles in new clothing. Visible storage installations and glimpses into vaults are really just a version of the original eclectic and interpretation-free cabinets of curiosity and *Wunderkammer*. Displays of mounted specimens can be seen in exhibits of tools and hardware as well as in natural history displays. Indoor streetscapes originated with the nineteenth century's great fairs, such as the 1893 World's Columbian Exposition in Chicago. Its Liberal Arts Building showed reduced-scale facades from typical national buildings from participating countries. Streetscape exhibits have been used to interpret automobiles, western towns, and, at the Canadian Museum of History (formerly the Museum of Civilization), an entire country from coast to coast.

All of these modalities have their strengths and relevance to particular topics and audiences, and they are all tools in the exhibit maker's toolbox. Individual exhibits may make use of several styles within the same show.

The museums where you go to see those exhibits are full of staff who believe in what they do. Educators, curators, interpretive planners, designers, and their colleagues are often profoundly knowledgeable in their fields and deeply committed to their work. Volunteers, from docents to board members, give generously of their time. Their institutions have vision statements that embody lofty goals, and staff and institutions alike are mission driven. And it is not enough to just do good programs or exhibits. When we go to museum and cultural sector conferences today, we are increasingly enjoined to be relevant and truthful not just to history but to the world around us, and to be fully engaged with all of our communities. In addition to their traditional core function of artifact-based collection, research, and interpretation, museums are exhorted to involve themselves in issues ranging from climate change to social justice.

Museum workers live in a world of measurement and assessment. Grant applications require logic models to show how your project will change the world. We set learning objectives and earnestly and self-critically evaluate whether we have done our job well and whether our audience has learned what we wished them to. There is much talk of "outcomes" and "effectiveness."

All of this is well and good, and we should set these goals and develop the tools to tell us if we have reached them. Yet this earnestness can sometimes lead us astray when it comes to exhibitions. Museum blogger Ed Rodley reminds of this when he says, apropos of how long it takes to develop museum exhibits, "And a lot of it [the time taken to develop an exhibit] will be spent in testing and evaluating and making sure it addresses the formal education frameworks and standards that govern so much of what we do nowadays. And in all that measuring, I often remember the sociologist W. B. Cameron's quote that 'not everything that can be counted counts, and not everything that counts can be counted.'"[2]

## The Exhibit as a Social Space

Diagrams with circles representing visitors and artifacts and arrows that show information traveling between them can be a useful conceptual tool, but only to a point. Mechanistic ideas of the "transmission" of information only go so far in explaining what happens in an exhibit. A more useful concept is the structuralist idea of *bricolage*.[3] In a theoretical context, bricolage refers to the act of assembly, of uniting previously discrete and disparate elements. In an exhibit context, bricolage means that our visitors bring who they are to an exhibit and unite it with some portion of what's on display, and out of that, they assemble their experiences.

In educational terms, this is known as a "constructivist" approach, one that emphasizes process over product: "What is important for adopting a constructivist agenda is recognizing that measuring (a term itself associated with experimental design approaches) the extent to which visitors or learners have mastered standard subject content may be irrelevant to understanding the interesting and rich ways in which visitors have made meaning from exhibitions."[4]

"Supported Interpretation" goes beyond constructivist exhibits by offering particular resources that visitors may, at their discretion, use. For example, in an art exhibit, works might be accompanied by images of symbols employed by the artist with brief explanations rather than discussing the symbols in a conventional text panel. The exhibit presents the work and the visual references and leaves the rest up to the visitor. This approach "anticipates visitors' needs to know and embeds appropriate resources in the exhibition interface that they may choose from to support their interpretations. By connecting visitors with art in this way, a[n] S[upported] I[nterpretation] exhibit provides for personalized meaning-making rather than conveying authoritarian knowledge or leaving visitors to fend for themselves."[5]

As John Falk and Lynn Dierking note in *The Museum Experience Revisited*, "Many museum professionals fail to fully appreciate that visitors actively create and make meaning of their own museum experiences."[6] As with a work of literature, where the author's writing and the reader's experience of it are related but not identical, museum visitors (readers) cannot help but perceive our (author's) exhibits (works) through different eyes.

We can learn a great deal about our visitors through demographic data and audience profiles, but we do not have a clue about the personal information and experiences they will bring to our museum. What this means for exhibits is that we need to leave them some space. We can set learning objectives, and we can evaluate what visitors take away, but our definition of success should not necessarily be a 100 percent correspondence between the two.

Exhibits are not school, and as Sue Allen points out in a thought-provoking article about learning at San Francisco's Exploratorium, "We expect these institutions [science centers] to provide a hugely diverse visiting public with entertainment, the freedom to choose their own path, follow their personal interests, do their own inquiry, and create their own meanings. Yet at the same time we want our museums to be respected educational institutions."[7]

Whether it is part of your plan or not, museums and their exhibits are social spaces, and the interactions that arise within them are as much between visitors and those they are visiting with as they are between visitors and displays.[8] Precisely because they are not ordered and controlled classroom settings, exhibits can be effective learning environments.[9] We must remember, however, that the learning will not take place through rows of desks and lectures. In her book *What Makes Learning Fun? Principles for the Design of Intrinsically Motivating Museum Exhibits*, author Deborah L. Perry quotes museum evaluator Randi Korn: "After hours of conversations with museum visitors, I started to realize that there is a gulf between the visitor experience from the visitor perspective and the visitor experience from the museum practitioner perspective. . . . [Learning] is our obsession, and it seems to be the single framework we use to develop exhibits."[10]

If you were to ask me to name some museum exhibits that have stayed with me long after I visited, I would give you the following rather eclectic list: seeing Edward Hopper's 1942 painting

*Nighthawks* in person for the first time at the Art Institute of Chicago; being below decks aboard the submarine USS *Nautilus* at the Submarine Force Library and Museum in Groton, Connecticut; viewing the paintings executed on the walls of Dr. James MacCallum's summer cottage by Canadian Group of Seven painters Tom Thompson, Arthur Lismer, and W. E. H. MacDonald at the National Gallery in Ottawa, Ontario; standing next to one of the Difference Engines in an exhibit about Charles Babbage at the Science Museum in South Kensington, London; and visiting an exhibit called *Boats and Boating in the Adirondacks* at the Adirondack Museum in Blue Mountain Lake, New York.

The force of the experience of these exhibits has lingered long after I was there, but I could not tell you many specifics about the exhibits or what they might have been trying to teach me. In fact, if I had been administered an evaluation questionnaire at the end of those exhibits, I'm not sure I would have provided much useful information to the interviewer. I might well have shown up in the survey as a visitor for whom the exhibit's stated learning objectives were not met, but these exhibits and their artifacts clearly made a big impact nonetheless.[11] I may not have read all the details of Edward Hopper's biography, but for me the alienation, anomie, and inherent strangeness of the modern condition flowed palpably from the four figures in the diner as I stood in front of the painting. I could not tell you how the Difference Engine worked, but I understood its importance as a transformative technology, and I was struck by its massive yet precise physicality, the way it seemed to be a cross between a watch and a steam engine.

The point of this example is that those experiences have stayed with me, perhaps because of the exhibit's stated objectives and perhaps in spite of them. The intensity of the impact of these artifacts on me particularly might mean that I'm simply at heart a curator and an object worshipper, but it might also suggest that the job of exhibits is to bring visitors into contact with authentic objects and then step back to leave them some space for their own experiences.

As Kathleen McLean notes in her article "Museum Exhibitions and the Dynamics of Dialogue": "Like other cultural and educational media, exhibitions are about people communicating with each other. How this conversation takes place, and who is responsible for conversing with whom, will depend on museum missions and the visions of exhibit creators, administrators, visitors and their constituencies."[12] All of the evaluation and measurement in the world will not reveal exactly what the visitors in figure 1.2 are thinking as they begin to explore the Stonehenge site. My memories of the experience of taking my then-young son through a John Singer Sargent exhibit at the Museum of Fine Arts Boston are much stronger than my recollection of any of the particular works on display. I was seeing him see the paintings, so the exhibit experience in this case wasn't purely or even mainly between me and the art but rather between the two of us as visitors.

I am not arguing against learning objectives and exhibits with goals, for they are important and powerful tools for shaping effective exhibits. Like all such implements, however, they must be used judiciously, and we must not let them overshadow other and equally important parts of exhibit making. We will examine the means used to create exhibits and shape visitor experiences in chapter 4 (The Big Idea), chapter 5 (The Brief and Request for Proposals), and chapter 6 (Evaluation).

"Only connect," said novelist E. M. Forster, "only connect the prose and the passion."[13] That should also be our goal for an exhibit. The object of exhibits should be to both teach and delight, and if some visitors learn and others are (only) delighted but do not meet the stated learning objectives, we have still done a good day's work.[14]

**Figure 1.2** Visitors viewing an orientation presentation.

**Why Everyone Should Try Designing an Exhibit, at Least Once**

They say that "experience starts when you begin," and that is certainly true of making an exhibit. Working on one individual part is not the same as seeing the whole project come together. Exhibits take place in both space and time and do not cohere unless they are actively designed and not simply put into a gallery with no thought about what kind of visitor experience they offer. We have all seen exhibits that just looked like a bunch of things in a room and did not offer a meaningful experience. When you have to combine the materials of the exhibit through design, you begin to understand how to shape all of the resources into a visitor experience. That is why it is better if the exhibit text can be written right in the layout instead of a separate essay. That is why the person who works with the images should also have a chance to work on the text. That is why the images should be in the layout when you write your text, and why you should either have the artifacts themselves or images of them in front of you when you write and design.

Going through the exhibit development process even once will enrich your understanding of how all the parts of an exhibit fit together. Even if you never make another exhibit, you will have a greater appreciation of what is involved in doing so, and you will better be able to spot a good exhibit when you see one.

## Who Should Make Exhibits?

Irrespective of the size of the museum in which you work, the answer to the question "Who should make exhibits?" is "as wide a range of people as possible." As Anne Ackerson and Joan Baldwin note in a post on their blog "Leadership Matters: Thoughts on 21st Century Museum Leadership," opening up the exhibit development process can have benefits beyond just making better exhibits.

> Create an atmosphere where all ideas are welcome. If you're creating new exhibit space, make sure your volunteers, docents and guards are at the table. And by that I don't mean gathering the frontline staff together for their opinion, I mean inviting them to the big-girl table. After all, they watch and interact with visitors every day. Listen to them. What can they tell you about how visitors behave in your galleries or historic house? . . . But the most important thing about listening from the bottom up is that it creates an atmosphere of equity in your organization. Everybody speaks and everybody listens. Disrupters are heard. Push back is important. You are the connector, you learn from your staff.[15]

For project managers and institutional leaders, the thought of all of those people getting involved may sound like a recipe for chaos and long, complicated meetings. To old-school museum workers, and particularly curators, this might sound like a bad idea, for it can challenge long-held assumptions about curatorial authority. This attitude is changing, however, and a 2002 article from the Smithsonian's Office of Policy and Analysis identifies a trend that began in the 1980s away from the linear, curator-centered model of exhibit development.[16] Notwithstanding this, I still have students every year from institutions where the curator creates exhibits in isolation, and where exhibits are created first and educators are invited in later.

For the small- to medium-sized museums that are the majority of North American institutions, the gains from opening up the exhibit development process to the whole institution far outweigh the drawbacks. In order to create an exhibit that truly serves a museum's audiences and achieves its institutional goals, all of the perspectives represented within the museum need to be involved. Public program staff cannot do their jobs properly if they are only brought in at the end and told to make up a program to go along with the finished exhibit rather than being involved from the beginning of the process.

Curators cannot ensure the historical and scholarly integrity of the exhibit if they are not there at the table from the beginning. Members of the board cannot truly support the project and help to find resources to carry it out if they are not partners in the process. Marketing and front-of-house staff cannot do their best to promote the exhibit if they do not feel a sense of ownership. Community members and volunteers also have a stake in how the museum makes exhibits. To be sure, not everyone needs to be at every meeting, but the process of developing an exhibit should be embraced by the whole museum.

How much of the development of an exhibit should you do yourself, and when should you hire the work out? The answer depends both on the scope of your project and the skills and ambitions of your staff. The services on offer from consultants range from a complete turnkey exhibit to specific elements such as graphic production. If you are just beginning exhibit development, you could start with a turnkey project and gradually assume more of the responsibility as your experience grows.

You could also decide to contract for the parts of the exhibit where you are not able to purchase the necessary equipment, or will not use it enough to make it a worthwhile investment. When you do hire service providers to help develop your exhibit, never miss an opportunity to ask questions, look over their shoulder, and learn from them.

## What Is a Good Exhibit?

Do you know who has the best answer to this question? Our visitors. Here is what they said in a 1984 study in which visitors to the Natural History Museum London "compared old and new exhibits and, in their own words, described what they thought contributed to the 'ideal' one":

1. It makes the subject come to life.
2. It gets the message across quickly.
3. You can understand the point(s) it is making quickly.
4. There's something in it for all ages.
5. You can't help noticing it.
6. It allows you to test yourself to see if you are right.
7. It involves you.
8. It deals with the subjects better than textbooks do.
9. The information is clearly presented.
10. It makes a difficult subject easier.
11. It gives just enough information.
12. It's clear what you're supposed to do and how to begin.
13. Your attention isn't distracted from it by other displays.[17]

A 1986 focus group at a zoo produced similar observations. When visitors were asked what contributes to a positive learning experience in a museum, they said:

1. It is memorable.
2. It's an experience that involves your senses.
3. You are gently guided to make discoveries.
4. It is a personal experience.
5. You get lots of opportunities to investigate and make observations.[18]

It is worth noting that most of the visitors' answers do not deal with fact-based knowledge acquisition or the achievement of learning objectives. Maybe when we evaluate exhibits we should be evaluating for the perceived quality and character of the visitor experience as much as for whether they have learned what we wanted them to learn. For example, "Well, I think I learned what the museum wanted me to learn" does not show up in the list above. Nor did any of the visitors surveyed say, "I wanted the exhibit to make me feel like I was back in grade 10 Algebra just before the big test."

**Twenty Ways to Make a Good Exhibit**

As I hope you will learn as you work through this manual, there are many ways to make a good exhibit. Before we begin to explore them in detail, I want to share with you some guiding principles for exhibit making.

1.  Have fun when you make the exhibit, and chances are that your audience will have fun when they visit it.
2.  Let yourself (and your institution) come through. Don't be afraid to have a point of view.
3.  Design the exhibit for the kids (but don't pander to them) and everyone will have a good time. It is surprising how often design for younger audiences is just good design.
4.  There is no such thing as a "permanent" exhibit, and ten years should be the maximum an exhibit is on display. Begin planning for renewal as soon as you put the exhibit in.
5.  Engage your whole institution when you make the exhibit and everyone will learn, including the visitors.
6.  Get the exhibit off the walls and out into the gallery. An exhibit is a story told in three dimensions.
7.  Aim for the slow reveal. Do not give it all away as soon as someone walks into the gallery.
8.  Ask (lots of) questions and provide some answers, but do not provide them all. Remember to leave some room for your audience, intellectually as well as physically, so that they can respond, engage, and leave their mark.
9.  Exhibits are like poetry: they should both teach and delight. Err on the side of delight if you can.
10. As you shape the story of the exhibit, remember that the history of failure is as instructive (and often more interesting) than the history of success.
11. Make a good white model of your gallery space, and use it throughout the project. Take it to every planning meeting.
12. Teach, but teach gently. Remember, it goes with delight. Visitors will learn what and if they want to, and it is okay if they do not.
13. Humor can have its place, but use it well, and make sure the joke is on you and not the visitors.
14. No clip art is allowed in your graphic design for the exhibit. None of any description. Why? Because it looks like clip art.
15. Use as little stock photography as possible, especially the kind that really looks like stock photography.
16. Out-of-copyright material is a gift, so use it. Make friends with your scanner and find out what it can do for you.
17. Tread lightly with goals, objectives, and learning outcomes. Visitors are not nails, and the exhibit is not a hammer.
18. Exhibit design is a creative process that can have a didactic outcome, but a purely didactic process will not necessarily produce a creative outcome.
19. Remember that sooner or later, every museum visitor needs to sit down, have a drink of water, and go to the bathroom.
20. Never forget that most of your visitors are casual visitors, in every sense of the word. They should be glad they came to see you after their exhibit experience.

## Chapter Checklist

1. Exhibits are the most visible part of the work of museums.
2. Exhibits are about the interaction between visitors as much as the interaction between visitors and artifacts.
3. Exhibits should be evaluated on the degree to which they engage visitors as well as whether specific learning outcomes are achieved.
4. To understand exhibits you have to participate in making them.
5. The whole institution should be engaged in exhibit making.
6. If you want to make exhibits that work for your visitors, ask your visitors what makes exhibits work for them.

## Notes

1. Kathleen McLean, "Museum Exhibitions and the Dynamics of Dialogue," in *Reinventing the Museum: Historical and Contemporary Perspectives on the Paradigm Shift*, ed. Gail Anderson (Lanham, MD: AltaMira Press, 2004), 193.
2. Ed Rodley, "Natural's Not in It," posted in the blog "Thinking About Museums" on December 17, 2012, at http://exhibitdev.wordpress.com/2012/12/17/naturals-not-in-it, 1–4; William Bruce Cameron, *Informal Sociology: A Casual Introduction to Sociological Thinking* (New York: Random House, 1963), 13.
3. Nasrulla Mambrol, "Claude Levi Strauss' Concept of Bricolage," at https://literariness.wordpress .com/2016/03/21/claude-levi-strauss-concept-of-bricolage/. Accessed March 2017.
4. George Hein, "The Challenge and Significance of Constructivism," keynote address delivered at the Hands-On! Europe Conference, London, November 15, 2001, and published in *Proceedings, Hands On! Europe Conference, 2001* (London: Discover, 2001), 35–42, http://george-hein.com/papers_online/ hoe_2001.html. Accessed July 2018.
5. Pat Villeneuve, "Building Museum Sustainability through Visitor-Centered Exhibition Practices," *The International Journal of the Inclusive Museum* 5, no. 4 (2013): 40.
6. John H. Falk and Lynn D. Dierking, *The Museum Experience Revisited* (Walnut Creek, CA: Left Coast Press Inc., 2013), 105. Similarly, "[Lisa C.] Roberts makes a compelling argument about the evolution of museum learning from traditional models of information transfer and the acquisition of knowledge to active and visitor-centered meaning-making . . . arguing that the real strength of museums is the setting-up of exhibitions and visitor experiences such that visitors can create their own story lines . . . and construct their own meanings." Lisa C. Roberts, *Knowledge to Narrative: Educators and the Changing Museum* (Washington, DC: Smithsonian Books, 1997), cited in Deborah L. Perry, *What Makes Learning Fun? Principles for the Design of Intrinsically Motivating Museum Exhibits* (Lanham, MD: AltaMira Press, 2012).
7. Sue Allen, "Designs for Learning: Studying Science Museum Exhibits That Do More Than Entertain," *Science Education* 88, no. S1 (2004): S17–S33. Published online in Wiley InterScience at www.interscience .wiley.com, reference number DOI 10.1002/sce.20016.
8. "Although people chose to visit a museum for a variety of reasons, for the most part museum visits tend to be driven by a social agenda. In fact, for most folks, visiting a museum is, first and foremost, a social experience. 'We wanted to spend time together as a family' or 'We wanted to show the museum to our out-of-town friends' or 'It's a place I can hang out with my friends' are all commonplace reasons given for visiting museums." Perry, *What Makes Learning Fun?*, 11.
9. Henrik Zipsane, "Why Museums Are Valid Learning Environments," blog post on the Electronic Platform for Adult Learning in Europe (EPALE) at https://ec.europa.eu/epale/en/blog/why-museums-are-val id-learning-environments. Accessed September 2016.
10. Perry, *What Makes Learning Fun?*, 12.
11. According to the Heath brothers, my visit was a "sticky" experience. Chip Heath and Dan Heath, *Made to Stick: Why Some Ideas Survive and Others Die* (New York: Random House, 2007), 3–24.
12. McLean, "Museum Exhibitions and the Dynamics of Dialogue," 209.

13. "Only connect! That was the whole of her sermon. Only connect the prose and the passion, and both will be exalted, and human love will be seen at its height. Live in fragments no longer. Only connect, and the beast and the monk, robbed of the isolation that is life to either, will die." E. M. Forster, *Howard's End*, chapter 22, https://en.wikiquote.org/wiki/E._M._Forster.

14. Sir Philip Sidney, *The Defence of Poesy* (1583), http://www.bartleby.com/27/1.html; https://www.poetry foundation.org/resources/learning/essays/detail/69375. Accessed September 2016.

15. Anne Ackerson and Joan Baldwin, "Is Your Museum an Idea Factory?," posted in the blog "Leadership Matters: Thoughts on 21st Century Museum Leadership" on October 2, 2016, at https://leadershipmat ters1213.wordpress.com/2016/10/02/is-your-museum-an-idea-factory/?wref=tp.

16. "The Making of Exhibitions: Purpose, Structure, Roles and Process," Smithsonian Institution Office of Policy and Analysis, October 2002, 12. Accessed October 2016 at http://www.si.edu/content/opanda/ docs/rpts2002/02.10.makingexhibitions.final.pdf.

17. Beverly Serrell, *Exhibit Labels: An Interpretive Approach* (Walnut Creek, CA: AltaMira Press, 1996), 46. She cites a 1984 study (M. B. Alt and K. M. Shaw, "Characteristics of Ideal Museum Exhibits," *British Journal of Psychology* 75) in which visitors to the Natural History Museum London "compared old and new exhibits and, in their own words, described what they thought contributed to the 'ideal' one."

18. Serrell, *Exhibit Labels*, 46–47.

# Chapter 2
## *Audience*

### Getting to Know Your Audience

Do you find that when you meet someone new at a social occasion they often remark on how interesting it must be to work in a museum? Most days, they are right. Most days, there is no job I would rather have. We are fortunate to have the opportunity to do work about which we care deeply, but in a way we are also cursed. Like Jimmy Stewart and Doris Day in Hitchcock's 1956 film *The Man Who Knew Too Much*, we suffer from the curse of knowledge.[1] The more you know about a given subject, the harder it can be to communicate, because the more you know, the further away you are from the audience with which you need to communicate.

This means, paradoxically, that the more time you spend making exhibits the harder it may become to meet the needs of your audiences. All of us who create exhibits need to be careful not to "museum-splain" by condescending or talking down to visitors. The most memorable idea I've ever read about museum visitors is also the most concise: "The museum visitor is not an empty vessel, waiting to be filled with our wisdom."[2]

There are two antidotes to museum-splaining in exhibit development. The first, which is up to you, is to see as many exhibits as you possibly can, particularly those on subjects about which you know almost nothing. It is good to be reminded, from time to time, of what the general visitor's experience can be like. For example, if I were to visit an exhibit about the history of algebra, I would be that visitor, the one who has no background knowledge, is not sure where to go first, and probably will not try the interactives for fear of looking foolish. If I emerge from that exhibit having felt welcomed, learned something, and had a positive experience, then that is one well-designed exhibit, because it engaged a nonspecialist visitor in a meaningful way.

### The Visitors' Bill of Rights

The second antidote to museum-splaining is to be ever mindful of your audience, and work as hard as you can to keep their perspective in front of you as you develop the exhibit. A great place to start is with the Visitors' Bill of Rights, which lays out eleven things that visitors expect to get from their experience of a museum exhibit.[3]

None of these points are about the content of the exhibit. This underscores the crucial role of the visitor's personal experience in determining whether their exhibit experience is a good one or not. You could create an exhibit with well-researched content and engaging interactives, but unless you have also given consideration to these fundamental elements of the visitor's experience, all of your hard work could come to naught.

**The Visitors' Bill of Rights**

1.  COMFORT: Meet my basic needs. Visitors need fast, easy, obvious access to clean, safe, barrier-free restrooms, [water] fountains, baby-changing tables, and plenty of seating. They also need full access to exhibits.
2.  ORIENTATION: Make it easy for me to find my way around. Visitors need to make sense of their surroundings. Clear signs and well-planned spaces help them know what to expect, where to go, how to get there, and what it's about.
3.  WELCOME/BELONGING: Make me feel welcome. Friendly, helpful staff ease visitors' anxieties. If they see themselves represented in exhibits and programs and on the staff, they'll feel more like they belong.
4.  ENJOYMENT: I want to have fun! Visitors want to have a good time. If they run into barriers (like broken exhibits, activities they can't relate to, intimidating labels) they can get frustrated, bored, [and] confused.
5.  SOCIALIZING: I came to spend time with my family and friends. Visitors come for a social outing with family or friends (or [to] connect with society at large). They expect to talk, interact, and share the experience; exhibits can set the stage for this.
6.  RESPECT: Accept me for who I am and what I know. Visitors want to be accepted at their own level of knowledge and interest. They don't want exhibits, labels, or staff to exclude them, patronize them, or make them feel dumb.
7.  COMMUNICATION: Help me understand, and let me talk too. Visitors need accuracy, honesty, and clear communication from labels, programs, and docents. They want to ask questions and hear and express differing points of view.
8.  LEARNING: I want to learn something new. Visitors come (and bring the kids) "to learn something new," but they learn in different ways. It's important to know how visitors learn and assess their knowledge and interests. Controlling distractions (like crowds, noise, and information overload) helps them too.
9.  CHOICE AND CONTROL: Let me choose; give me some control. Visitors need some autonomy: freedom to choose and exert some control, touching and getting close to whatever they can. They need to use their bodies and move around freely.
10. CHALLENGE AND CONFIDENCE: Give me a challenge I know I can handle. Visitors want to succeed. A task that's too easy bores them; [a task that is] too hard makes them anxious. Providing a range of experiences will match their wide range of skills.
11. REVITALIZATION: Help me leave refreshed, restored. When visitors are focused, fully engaged, and enjoying themselves, time stands still and they feel refreshed: a "flow" experience that exhibits can aim to create.

So, we need to be mindful of our visitors' basic needs, and careful of the tone of voice in which we address them. What else should we take into account when we are creating exhibits? It would help us to know something about them, both the visitors and the nonvisitors (or, to put it more positively, the "not-yet-visitors"). Most institutions now collect statistical and demographic data through their point-of-sale systems, such as age ranges, group sizes, zip codes, and postal codes. As this data builds up, it can help identify trends and patterns. For example, perhaps 60 percent of your casual visitors come from the same three areas in the city. Is that related to advertising? Traffic and transit? The demographics of those areas as they relate to the content and themes of your exhibits?

Modern marketing practice divides consumers into segments and develops strategies and products to match their particular needs, and in the last two decades the museum and cultural sector has done the same. Some institutions segment their audience in terms of their degree of engagement with the subject matter. The Dallas Museum of Art uses four groups, from least to most comfortable with the museum's content and presentation: Tentative Observers; Curious Participants; Discerning Independents; Committed Enthusiasts.[4]

Another example of market segmentation can be found in the tourism sector. In 2012 the Ontario Tourism Marketing Partnership developed segments that guide the development of tourism products such as museum exhibitions in a report titled "Applying Consumer Insights to Attract North American Visitors." They use twelve audience segments: Aces; Connected Explorers; Family Memory Builders; Knowledge Seekers; Mellow Vacationers; Nature Lovers; Outgoing Mature Couples; Pampered Relaxers; Solitaires; Sport Lovers; Up and Coming Explorers; and Youthful Socializers.[5]

## Motivations for Visiting

Gathering and analyzing this demographic data and considering these segments can provide a baseline for understanding the audience for your exhibit, but it does not tell the whole story. In the words of researcher and museologist John Falk, "The reductionist ways in which museum visitors have typically been studied, beginning with a focus on 'who' visits the museum, have long prevented us from truly understanding the museum visitor experience."[6]

Christy Coleman, CEO of the American Civil War Museum, makes the same point in her provocatively titled blog post "Are History Museums 'Stuck on Stupid?'" "Often what's missing in all this [visitor] research is understanding what truly motivates people to connect with the past. Regardless of ethnicity, creed, age, origin or nationality, people, i.e., our visitors, want meaningful connections. They want to explore history in full context of their lives. They want to clearly see how the issues they grapple with daily have a genesis or flow that may provide answers or direction to solving issues most perplexing. Most importantly, our visitors want to connect to other people."[7] For the female visitor in figure 2.1, her encounter between visitor and museum object is a private transaction in a public space, but it is also taking place in the context of a tour group that will likely discuss it among themselves.

According to educator and museum consultant Barbara J. Soren, "Four factors that are considered central to understanding the complexities of museum-going are:

\* \* \* \* \*

Demographics that are descriptive, but not predictive, of museum-goers/nongoers, such as education, income, occupation gender, race/ethnicity;

Psychographics, by which is meant the psychological and motivational characteristics of individuals, such as attitudes toward leisure and learning;

Individual experiences, interests, and cultural background including perceptions about museums;

Environmental factors, cues, and experiences within an individual's surroundings that influence museum-going, such as word-of-mouth recommendations and advertising."[8]

\* \* \* \* \*

**Figure 2.1** Visitor meets artifact in gallery.

John Falk and coauthor Lynn D. Dierking revolutionized museums' understanding of the importance of their audience with their 1992 book, *The Museum Experience*, and its 2013 edition, *The Museum Experience Revisited.*[9] For Falk, what is most important to understand about museum visitors is not their basic statistical or demographic details: "The museum visitor experience cannot be adequately described by understanding the content of museums, the design of exhibitions, by defining visitors as a function of their demographics and psychographics or even by understanding visit frequency or the social arrangements in which people enter the museum."[10] It is, rather, what visitors perceive that the museum affords, and whether it meets what he calls "the visiting public's identity-related needs and desires."

Over hundreds of detailed post-visit interviews with visitors, he has found that these can be grouped into five categories:[11]

\* \* \* \* \*

Explorers: Visitors who are curiosity driven with a generic interest in the content of the museum. They expect to find something that will grab their attention and fuel their curiosity and learning.

Facilitators: Visitors who are socially motivated. Their visit is primarily focused on enabling the learning and experience of others in their accompanying social group.

Professionals/Hobbyists: Visitors who feel a close tie between the museum content and their professional or hobbyist passions. Their visits are typically motivated by a desire to satisfy a specific content-related objective.

Experience Seekers: Visitors who are motivated to visit because they perceive the museum as an important destination. Their satisfaction derives primarily from the mere fact of having been there and done that.

Rechargers: Visitors who are primarily seeking a contemplative, spiritual, and/or restorative experience. They see the museum as a refuge from the work-a-day world or as a confirmation of their religious/spiritual beliefs.

\* \* \* \* \*

As of 2013, when *The Museum Experience Revisited* was published, Falk and Dierking had added two new categories reflecting new museum and exhibit forms, though they caution that these have not yet been fully researched.

\* \* \* \* \*

Respectful Pilgrims: Individuals who visit museums out of a sense of duty or obligation to honor the memory of those represented by the institution/memorial.

Affinity Seekers: Visitors motivated to visit a particular museum or more likely a particular exhibition because it speaks to their sense of heritage and/or Big "I" identity or personhood.

\* \* \* \* \*

Unlike fixed data points, such as race, address, age, or level of education, these categories represent motivations that can be adopted by a variety of visitors under different circumstances. For example, a visitor who is a Professional/Hobbyist when visiting an exhibit on their own is more likely to be primarily a Facilitator when the grandchildren are along on the trip.

What do you do with all this information, and how can it shape the development of your exhibits? If you do an online search for "audience segmentation," it will yield a large number of typologies, so much so that you might long for the old days when museums just did what they wanted to without worrying about the visitors so much. Do you have to make a separate exhibit for each audience, and if you do, does that mean that no other audience will enjoy it? What if your museum only has one gallery? What if research shows that the Outgoing Mature Couples and the Experience Seekers do not want the same experience?

Not to worry. Falk and Dierking advise: "The goal should not necessarily be to develop different kinds of exhibitions . . . for each type of motivation, but rather to insure that someone with a particular motivation, or combination of motivations, can find ways to use your exhibitions . . . to meet their varied needs. Designing exhibitions . . . that are open-ended, allowing for multiple entry points and different outcomes, is critical."[12]

So, you still get to mount the exhibits that are important to your museum, you just have to do so in a way that facilitates a range of approaches and expectations on the part of your visitors. No problem! Before we get to how to do that, though, we are going to look more closely at what happens and when during exhibit development.

## Chapter Checklist

1. The more time you spend making exhibits the further away you are from the perspective of your audience, and the harder you need to work to keep it in front of you.
2. Visitors have many motivations for visiting your museum and its exhibits, but the desire for meaningful connections and experiences is a part of almost all of them.
3. Rather than trying to design different exhibits for each audience, you should try to create open-ended exhibits that a wide range of visitors can use to meet their own needs.

## Notes

1. Chip Heath and Dan Heath, *Made to Stick: Why Some Ideas Survive and Others Die* (New York: Random House, 2007), 19–21.
2. Marsha L. Semmel, director, Office of Strategic Partnerships, IMLS, writing in the Foreword to John H. Falk and Lynn D. Dierking, *The Museum Experience Revisited* (Walnut Creek, CA: Left Coast Press Inc., 2013), 7. The same point is made by Carla Yanni in the Introduction to *Nature's Museums: Victorian Science and the Architecture of Display* (Princeton, NJ: Princeton Architectural Press, 2005), 9: "Visitors in museums were not empty vessels waiting to be filled with ideology." Similarly, Jones et al. say in *Framing Marginalised Art: Developing an Ethical Multidimensional Framework for Exhibiting the Creative Works by People Who Experienced Mental Illness and/or Psychological Trauma*, by Anthony G. White: "Visitors demand respect. They bring with them rich life experience and are not empty vessels waiting to be filled with knowledge." The Cunningham Dax Collection, 2010. Accessed October 2016 at http://www.academia.edu/2587955/Framing_Marginalised_Art_Developing_an_Ethical_Multidimensional_Framework_for_Exhibiting_Creative_Works_by_People_Who_Have_Experienced_Mental_Illness_and_or_Psychological_Trauma.
3. Judy Rand, "The Visitors' Bill of Rights," in *Reinventing the Museum: Historical and Contemporary Perspectives on the Paradigm Shift*, ed. Gail Anderson (Lanham, MD: AltaMira Press, 2004), 158–59. The Visitors' Bill of Rights first appeared in "The 22-Mile Museum, or a Visitors' Bill of Rights" in *Curator: The Museum Journal* 44, no. 1 (January 2000): 7–14.
4. Randi Korn & Associates, Inc., "Levels of Engagement with Art, 2008 Study, Prepared for the Dallas Museum of Art," 16, at https://www.dma.org/sites/default/files/file_attachments/dma_310864.pdf. Accessed October 2016.
5. OTMPC Traveller Segment Profiles at https://www.tourismpartners.com/en/research/traveller-segment-profiles. Accessed October 2016.

6. John H. Falk, "Understanding Museum Visitors' Motivations and Learning," 109, at http://slks.dk/filead min/user_upload/dokumenter/KS/institutioner/museer/Indsatsomraader/Brugerundersoegelse/Ar tikler/John_Falk_Understanding_museum_visitors__motivations_and_learning.pdf. Accessed October 2016.
7. Christy S. Coleman, "Are History Museums 'Stuck on Stupid?,'" posted on September 23, 2016, in the blog "Museum Revolution" at http://museumrevolution.com/history-museums-stuck-stupid/. Accessed October 2016.
8. Barbara J. Soren, "Meeting the Needs of Museum Visitors," in *The Manual of Museum Planning*, second edition, ed. Gail Dexter Lord and Barry Lord (Lanham, MD: AltaMira Press, 2001), 55.
9. John H. Falk and Lynn D. Dierking, *The Museum Experience* (Washington, DC: Whalesback Books, 1992); John H. Falk and Lynn D. Dierking, *The Museum Experience Revisited* (Walnut Creek, CA: Left Coast Press, 2013).
10. Falk, "Understanding Museum Visitors' Motivations and Learning," 111.
11. Falk and Dierking, *The Museum Experience Revisited*, 47–49.
12. Falk and Dierking, *The Museum Experience Revisited*, 63.

# Chapter 3

*Workflow*

**The Exhibit Development Process**

So you are ready to create an exhibit. Where do you start? I have found it useful to divide exhibit projects into five stages: concept, design, fabrication, installation, and postopening. The next book you read about exhibit development might have four stages, or seven, but whether you are doing the entire project in-house or working with out-of-house contractors on some or all of the elements, the exhibit will follow the same general steps from initial idea to finished exhibit. How many stages you go through, and how they are implemented, will depend on your particular circumstances, including the size of institution; the size, composition, skills, and experience of the project team; the scope and complexity of the project; the division between in-house and out-of-house resources; and finally the project budget and timeline.

Figure 3.1 outlines the stages in exhibit development, but the reality of your particular project will always be more complex than a flowchart. For example, the five stages follow each other in order, but there are iterative links between them, particularly concept and design, where changes made in one stage will need to be referenced back to the other and vice versa. Depending on the size of your team, the scope and schedule of your project, and the spaces in which you do your work, there will also be overlap between stages such as design/fabrication and fabrication/installation. On a really tight schedule, you may be fabricating some elements before others are completely designed. Some components, particularly interactives, will have to be designed, fabricated, and tested before they can be approved, and if that is the case then any required changes might affect the design and even the concept. The details of the stages will also depend on your institution's approval processes and whether or not you are working with an outside contractor or contractors.

You will notice that there is no single stage called "budget." That is because although a budget is developed at the beginning, you will be reviewing, estimating, and possibly adjusting your costs all the way through the project. You will rough out a budget at the concept stage, refine it in design, spend a lot of it during fabrication, and analyze what you have done during postopening. We'll look at exhibit budgets in more detail in chapter 9.

Concept and design are the idea phases. They are the place for creativity, vigorous discussion, and great ideas that occur to you in the middle of the night. At this point in the project, changing your mind is relatively cheap, typically requiring only some additional meeting time to discuss and implement. For this reason, it is important to keep the project confined to these two stages until you are absolutely satisfied with where you are going because by the end of the design stage the window of opportunity for major changes will be pretty much closed. You can make

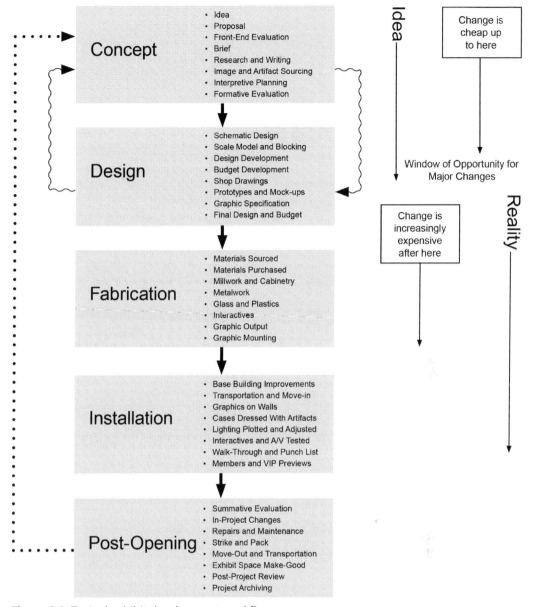

**Concept**
- Idea
- Proposal
- Front-End Evaluation
- Brief
- Research and Writing
- Image and Artifact Sourcing
- Interpretive Planning
- Formative Evaluation

**Design**
- Schematic Design
- Scale Model and Blocking
- Design Development
- Budget Development
- Shop Drawings
- Prototypes and Mock-ups
- Graphic Specification
- Final Design and Budget

**Fabrication**
- Materials Sourced
- Materials Purchased
- Millwork and Cabinetry
- Metalwork
- Glass and Plastics
- Interactives
- Graphic Output
- Graphic Mounting

**Installation**
- Base Building Improvements
- Transportation and Move-in
- Graphics on Walls
- Cases Dressed With Artifacts
- Lighting Plotted and Adjusted
- Interactives and A/V Tested
- Walk-Through and Punch List
- Members and VIP Previews

**Post-Opening**
- Summative Evaluation
- In-Project Changes
- Repairs and Maintenance
- Strike and Pack
- Move-Out and Transportation
- Exhibit Space Make-Good
- Post-Project Review
- Project Archiving

Idea

Change is cheap up to here

Window of Opportunity for Major Changes

Change is increasingly expensive after here

Reality

**Figure 3.1** Typical exhibit development workflow.

changes after that, but they will have an impact on your schedule and budget, particularly if you are working with an outside contractor.

As you move into fabrication, you are passing out of the idea phase and into reality. Now you are buying, cutting, and assembling materials, and changing your mind will have a direct impact on the project cost and the schedule. What if you build the first exhibit case and realize that it looks much bigger in real life than it did in the drawing? It would have been better to find that out by testing a mock-up first. What if your graphic substrate turns out to be too floppy to stand up on its own? That too would have been better to find out earlier on before the truck delivered a big load of it and you had to negotiate with the supplier about returns. You are not able to find paint to match the colors that the designer has built the exhibit around? The redesign will cost you.

The same is true for installation. In the gallery a few days before opening is not the time to find out that pieces do not fit together as intended, but of course that will not happen because you assembled the whole thing months ago in the workshop, right? Surprises are good during the concept and design stages. Surprises are not good at all during fabrication, installation, and postopening.

## Concept

In the concept stage you will create an initial proposal, possibly carry out front-end evaluation to refine the proposal, develop the proposal into a formal exhibit brief, write a general exhibit storyline, identify possible images and artifacts to be used in the exhibit, develop an interpretive plan to outline the audience experience, and possibly carry out formative evaluation. You will also need to undertake research. This could be subject-area research to learn more about a topic such as whales or locomotives or the Great Depression, or it could mean exploring what artifacts are available to be used or borrowed for the exhibit. As this research progresses, you may go back and modify the concept one or more times. There should be a formal approval at the end of the concept stage, though what is approved and by whom will depend on your particular situation. At the conclusion of the concept stage, you will begin turning your general storyline into final exhibit text. You should have the text finalized before the approval of the final design.

## Design

In the design stage you will carry out schematic design to determine the general form and scope of the exhibit; build a scale model of the exhibit gallery and use it to block the schematic design elements; refine the schematic design through design development; prepare a project budget; create shop drawings for fabrication; make prototypes and mock-ups of exhibit elements, particularly for interactives; prepare a graphic specification for style, formatting, typography, colors, and other elements; and create the final design and budget for approval. If you are working with an outside designer, there will also be approvals for the schematic design and during the design development phase. These will have been specified in the Request for Proposals and in the contract you signed with the designer.

## Fabrication

Fabrication can be done in-house or by a contracted service provider, or a combination of both. It begins with sourcing and purchasing the necessary materials, followed by some or all of the following: millwork and woodwork, metalwork, glass, plastics, interactives, and graphic substrates. Exhibit furniture such as cases, portable walls, plinths, and bases will be built or purchased. Graphic substrates will be cut to size and prepared for graphics to be mounted. Graphics will be printed and mounted on their substrates.

## Installation

The installation phase begins with base building improvements such as making good the gallery from the previous installation and repainting if necessary. If the gallery is off-site, exhibit elements will need to be packed and transported. Graphics are mounted on walls, on panels, and in cases, and cases are dressed with artifacts. Gallery and casework lighting is plotted and adjusted, interactive and A/V elements are installed and tested, and the entire exhibit receives a walk-through to make sure it is ready for opening.

### Postopening

After the exhibit has opened, there may be in-project repairs and ongoing maintenance. Summative evaluation can be carried out to identify lessons learned for the next project or changes that should be made during the current run. When it closes, the exhibit will have to be struck and packed up, especially if it is to travel to a new location. The gallery will have to be made good to prepare it for the next installation. The exhibit team should meet for a postproject evaluation and prepare a report summarizing the lessons learned. Project components, particularly design and digital files, should be backed up and archived so that they can be easily accessed later. Loaned artifacts will need to be returned, and owned artifacts will need to be dispersed to storage.

The next four sections of the book will walk you through these stages in detail. In part II we will cover the big idea, evaluation, the exhibit brief, interpretive planning, exhibit text, and the budget. Part III will address design and curatorship. Part IV covers fabrication, installation, and closing out an exhibit project.

## Critical Success Factors

Before we begin working through the exhibit development process, I want to draw your attention to some critical success factors. There are many aspects to an exhibit project that need careful attention, and we will explore them further when we look at project management. These six aspects of your exhibit require particular attention because they can become real impediments to success if they are not handled properly.

### Concept and Audience

Your team loves the topic of the exhibit. After all, you thought of it, and it is going to be the best exhibit ever. This enthusiasm is a good thing, and it will carry you through the inevitable times when you want to walk away from it and never look back. This same enthusiasm, however, can lead you astray and cause you to create an exhibit that, while perhaps not bad in and of itself, has lost the link with the audience that you intended. As we discussed in chapter 2, the characteristics of your intended audience need to be considered at the beginning of the project. They also need to be reconsidered at intervals, especially when you make changes. Suppose you are working with a contract designer and they have proposed some interactives. Everyone on the project team likes them, and they are unquestionably clever, but are they too clever for the audience? The best way to find out is to do some formative evaluation, which we will address in chapter 6.

### Schedule

Think of the schedule as fire. We need it, and we can manage it and use it to our advantage, but if we don't manage it well it will turn on us and the consequences can be disastrous. The project schedule is a time budget. Once you start the project and set the opening date of the exhibit, the hours, days, weeks, and months between the two dates is all the time you have. You choose where to spend the time in your budget. Like the financial budget, the time budget should be on the table at every project team meeting.

For example, perhaps the research phase has taken longer than you thought. That is not necessarily a problem, but at the next project meeting you will need to figure out how much longer the research has taken and remove that "overspent" time from some other part of the schedule. If you do not stay on top of this, the overages will accumulate and you can end up being squeezed in later stages of the project. This is particularly true of fabrication, where you are dependent on external variables like materials being in stock and suppliers being able to deliver them on time before you can move to the next stage. The fabrication portion of your schedule also depends on some unalterable facts such as how fast paint and glue will dry. Like a financial budget, your time budget should have a healthy contingency built into it at the beginning of the project so that the inevitable changes and delays do not throw the whole project off track.

### Costs

Speaking of the financial budget, costs are a place where you can get into real trouble. Accurately estimating and tracking your costs is an essential part of the exhibit project. If you keep careful track of your costs, you will end up with a wealth of useful information for the next exhibit, ranging from prices for raw materials, including shipping, to the cost of finished elements such as a portable wall section or an entire exhibit case. Your initial budget should contain a contingency line of anywhere from 10 percent to 25 percent of the overall project cost.

If your team has done exhibits before, it can be closer to 10 percent. If this is the first time you have undertaken a major project, or if it is particularly ambitious or complex, then opt for the higher number. As the project progresses, the contingency can gradually be reduced and released back into the overall project budget. Whether you are responsible to a museum board, a granting agency, or a municipal finance department, you will only have one chance to tell them how much the project will cost, so your first budget should be detailed and realistic and carry a contingency to leave you enough room to carry out the project successfully.

### Scope

You would not be getting involved in an exhibit project if you were not really enthusiastic about the work that you were doing. In the concept and design stages, this enthusiasm, and the resulting creativity and flow of ideas, is a wonderful thing. There comes a point, however, where brilliant new ideas should be discussed, documented, and then set aside for the next project rather than being incorporated into the current one. If you do not exercise strict discipline on this point, your project can fall prey to scope creep. The later in a project that new ideas are introduced the larger the consequences for schedule, budget, and scope. Problems with creeping schedule, cost, and scope can all be avoided by careful project management.

### Integrity

A well-executed exhibit is one that has strong design integrity. Whether consciously or subconsciously, visitors take their cues from a project's design. The first time they encounter a title panel that introduces a new section of the exhibit, they will form an impression of the characteristics that make that a title panel and not some other exhibit element. In educational and psychological terms, the combination of those characteristics is called a schema.[1] The next time they encounter a panel that could be a title panel, they will subconsciously match what they are seeing against the schema derived from last panel they saw.

If there is a match, and it looks sufficiently like the last title panel, they will know what that element is and how to approach it. If there is not a match, they will not perceive it as a title panel. If it is not a title panel, no problem. If it is a title panel, however, and doesn't look like one, they will have been led astray by a lack of design integrity. In chapter 10 I will show you how to use design elements to reinforce the content and message of the exhibit.

If a graphic specification was prepared during the design stage, this should not happen, because the typography, color, and layout elements that make up a particular level of the exhibit such as a title panel will have been defined. Layout programs such as Adobe InDesign make this easy by enabling the user to define styles for characters, objects, paragraphs, tables, and other elements that can be applied consistently throughout the project.

If you did not create a complete graphic specification at the outset, or even if you did, you may find that you prefer a different style for an element such as an image caption. When the element is defined, or redefined, it is essential to make sure that the specifications are applied throughout the exhibit. When the visitor encounters the second, third, fourth, and following image captions, the first thing it should say to them, before they perceive the content, is "I am an image caption."

Design integrity is also fostered by looking ahead to fabrication and production as the exhibit is being designed. This means specifying the sizes of elements such as graphic panels so that they can be most efficiently gotten out of stock materials. The visitors will not notice a small change in dimensions, but failing to align the graphic panels with raw material sizes can result in significant wastage. A change as simple as creating elements in whole measurement units will also speed production. Designing exhibit elements in grids and repeatable modules based on a limited number of sizes not only makes production more efficient but also contributes to the visual rhythm of the exhibit.

### Quality

Along with design integrity, consistent quality of execution will produce a strong, coherent experience for visitors. For example, if your exhibit has bases for exhibit cases, plinths for artifacts not in cases, and bases for interactive devices, they should be made from the same materials with the same surface finishes and the same detailing and be finished to the same level. Doing so will not only greatly simplify production of these elements but will also cause them to recede into the background of the visitor's experience, where they should be. Quality of execution can be put at risk by schedule issues that impinge on the time required to achieve standards. For example, losing time earlier in the project can shorten the time available for fabrication, resulting in some pieces of exhibit furniture not receiving the same quality of finish as those that were built earlier.

### The Exhibit Team

In the not-too-distant past, the creation of exhibits was almost exclusively the prerogative of the curator. Exhibits were knowledge based, and the curator was the institutional knowledge keeper, so exhibitions served mainly as expositions of this knowledge. This approach could produce a good exhibit, but it depended almost entirely on the skills and approach of the individual curator. If they were aware of their audience, creative in their means of presentation, and friends with the education department, the result could be informative and engaging. If they came from a more academic tradition and were used to writing books and teaching, the result could be the dreaded "book-on-the-wall." Such an exhibit might be factually correct and packed full of information but unsuccessful as an engaging public experience. This is changing, however, and not a moment too soon.[2]

There is now a general recognition of the benefits, and even the necessity, of creating exhibits in a collaborative environment. The first efforts to create exhibits with teams took place in the late 1970s, and since then the process has expanded to include other members of the museum staff, external communities of interest, museum members and visitors, and the public at large. As notions of exhibit making have expanded, other professions have become involved. Interpretive planners, who once worked almost exclusively in parks with natural history interpretation, have now assumed a key role in exhibit development. I will explore this further in chapter 7.

One recent model identifies five key roles in exhibit making: client; content specialist; designer; content interpreter; and (of course) project manager.[3] By focusing on the roles rather than institutional job descriptions, it recognizes that the content interpreter, for example, could be one or more of an exhibit developer, an interpretive planner, and/or an educator. Interestingly, however, the client is still identified as the director of the institution. While it is true that the director, on behalf of the institution, writes the check that pays for the exhibit, the real client for whom the project is being carried out is the visitor. I will look more into the composition of the exhibit team in Appendix 1: Developing an Institutional Exhibit Plan.

## Project Management

Projects need to be managed in order to be successful. The authority of the project management role will vary with the size of the institution and the nature of the project, but key elements such as budget and schedule need to be driven for the project to succeed. On a smaller team, the project management hat might have to be worn by a member of staff along with another role. Larger teams and projects will typically have a dedicated project manager who works exclusively in that role.

The project manager is a generalist. It is their job to keep the team to the original vision, which presupposes that they are familiar with it and can see when the group is drifting off course. Because exhibits are creative projects, the project manager will also need to be, by turns, the referee, the coach, and the conscience of the project. As the keeper of the schedule, they will need to be mindful of what progress has been made and what is left to be done. If you are working with outside contractors, the project manager will typically also be responsible for communicating with them and managing sign-offs, drafts, revisions, and change orders.

## Partnership Exhibits

Exhibits are sometimes undertaken in conjunction with another institution or organization. These are referred to as partnership projects, but it might be more accurate to call them "relationship projects," with all that implies about both the rewards and the potential pitfalls of such an undertaking. In a partnership exhibit project, all of the critical success factors become even more important. Not only does each organization have to stay on top of schedule, costs, scope, integrity, and quality, but also the two organizations' processes and organizational cultures must be brought together to produce a successful project. If good project management is important with one institution involved, it is absolutely critical when working with partners and/or contractors and consultants.

Each institution can appoint a project manager to manage their own side, and the two project managers will then be the chief points of contact between the participants. The participants can also agree on a single project manager. In either case, the arrangement itself is not nearly as important as defining it early on and agreeing to abide by it. When the inevitable budget, schedule, or creative issues arise, you will be able to deal with them much more effectively if lines of authority and communication are clearly drawn and adhered to by all the participants.

**Chapter Checklist**

1.  Exhibit development is an iterative process, and you will sometimes need to go through a stage more than once before moving on to the next, particularly in the early part of the project, or return to earlier stages in order to take account of changes made in later stages.
2.  The early stages of an exhibit project are creative, as the project is proposed. The next stages are editorial, as the proposed content is refined and finalized. The final stages are constructive, as the content is made real.
3.  There are six critical success factors for an exhibit project: (1) relationship of concept to audience; (2) schedule; (3) costs; (4) scope; (5) integrity; and (6) quality.
4.  Exhibits should be created by teams working in a highly collaborative environment.
5.  Good project management is fundamental to creating exhibits that achieve their goals.
6.  Project management is even more important when exhibit development is undertaken in a partnership between two or more institutions or organizations.

**Notes**

1.  See for example Mac Duis, "Using Schema Theory to Teach American History," https://www.learner .org/workshops/socialstudies/pdf/session2/2.UsingSchemaTheory.pdf. Accessed September 2016.
2.  "The Making of Exhibitions: Purpose, Structure, Roles and Process," Smithsonian Institution Office of Policy and Analysis, October 2002, 12–13. Accessed October 2016 at http://www.si.edu/content/ opanda/docs/rpts2002/02.10.makingexhibitions.final.pdf.
3.  "The Making of Exhibitions: Purpose, Structure, Roles and Process," 17.

*Part II*

# Concept Development

# Chapter 4

*The Big Idea*

## One Simple Question

As you begin to shape your exhibit, ask yourself one simple question: Is my proposed exhibit telling a story or simply explaining the artifacts that comprise it? Most exhibits do both but tend more toward one approach or the other. The focus of this book is on developing exhibits that move beyond the presentation of factual information to tell a story.

## Where Do Exhibits Come From?

Here's another question: Where do exhibits come from—do they start with ideas or artifacts? Once again, these are two ends of a scale, and your exhibit will likely fall somewhere in between. During the early years of museums in North America in the late nineteenth and early twentieth centuries, most exhibits focused on collections of artifacts and the presentation of curatorial knowledge. In the last two decades, however, exhibits have become increasingly idea driven, and museums have begun to move beyond the basic facts of visitors such as numbers and demographics toward a broader and more inclusive understanding of the whole visitor experience.[1] Considering your institution in light of both of these questions will be useful in helping you develop a big idea for your exhibit.

## What's the Big Idea?

Imagine for a moment that your exhibit project is a school bus full of kids. (If you have a large project team who are not shy about expressing their opinions during meetings, that might not be so hard to do!) The bus is the project, and the kids are the exhibit content. They are all in the bus together, and they are headed toward the same destination, but they will not get where they are going without one essential thing: a driver. The big idea drives the exhibit bus. It guides the whole project to a destination, and along the way it keeps order, follows the route, makes all the right stops, and stays on schedule. It also controls who gets on the bus so you don't pick up children who are not going to your school.

The big idea will inform almost every aspect of your project, from the intended audience to the evaluation strategy to the visitor experience to the physical and graphic design. Some or all of the wording of the big idea may or may not feature in the actual text of the exhibit, but it is nonetheless embodied in all of the decisions made during the exhibit development process. The big idea should be on the table at every meeting of your exhibit design team, and it is not a bad idea to put it up on the office wall either.

According to Beverly Serrell, "A big idea is a sentence—a statement—of what the exhibition is about. It is a statement in one sentence, with a subject, an action, and a consequence. It is one big idea, not four. It also implies what the exhibit is not about."[2] The big idea should be phrased as a testable hypothesis. When you are drafting the exhibit brief (see chapter 5), the big idea will guide you in shaping your learning outcomes and evaluation strategies. As you are working on your big idea, it may help to think about what visitors would say if you asked them after seeing the exhibit, "So, what was the exhibit about?" If you have done your work well, their answer should be pretty much the same as your big idea.

Authors from Cicero to Pascal to Woodrow Wilson have observed that it is much harder to write a short piece than a long piece, and that is true of a big idea as well.[3] You will probably spend a lot of time working on this one short sentence, but it will be worth it in the end.

**A Big Idea in Action**

Here is an example of how a big idea might be developed. Imagine that your museum has a Model T Ford in the collection. Figure 4.1 illustrates a typical Model T. Donated by the founder, it was on display for many years in the entrance area of the museum, the local history equivalent of the classic dinosaur skeleton in the lobby of the natural history museum. For a time it was even incorporated into the museum's logo. It sat on a raised platform and was interpreted only by a label that read:

★ ★ ★ ★ ★

1918 Ford Model T Three-Door Touring car
    Engine: 4 cylinder, 176.7 cubic inch displacement, 20 horsepower
    Transmission: 3-speed planetary gear
    Wheelbase: 100 inches
    Length: 134.5 inches
    Weight: 1,480 pounds
    Top Speed: 45 miles per hour
    Donor: Mr. Arthur Smith

Several years ago, the car was removed from display during building renovations. Since that time, there has been a steady stream of requests to "bring back the car!" The building renovations are now complete, and it could be placed on display again. This time, however, rather than just having it in the lobby, you would like to make it the focus of an exhibit. You assemble an exhibit committee, tell them to start with a big idea for the exhibit, and put them to work. Here is what they came up with.

★ ★ ★ ★ ★

Big Idea draft #1: This Model T Ford was the first car ever owned by museum founder Mr. Arthur Smith. He kept it in running order for more than fifty years before donating it to the museum in 1979. A frequent sight around town, it transported generations of the Smith family and their friends and was driven by Mr. Smith in more than twenty consecutive Santa Claus parades.

★ ★ ★ ★ ★

**Figure 4.1** 1918 Ford Model T Three-Door Touring car.

Is this a big idea you could hang an exhibit on? Does it meet Beverly Serrell's criteria? Is it a statement in one sentence? No, it has three sentences. With a subject? Yes, the Model T Ford. An action? Well, Mr. Smith drove the car, but that is not the kind of action we are looking for. A consequence? No. This text is all useful, and it could be the background to a big idea, but it is not itself a big idea because it is simply a factual statement of the artifact's history and offers no direction about where the exhibit should or should not go. It belongs in the catalogue record for the artifact. So, you meet with the committee and break the news to them that they are not quite there yet with a big idea. They meet again and give you a new version.

★ ★ ★ ★ ★

Big Idea draft #2: This exhibit tells the story of Henry Ford and his iconic Model T, America's favorite car.

★ ★ ★ ★ ★

Is this version a true big idea? Is it a statement in one sentence? Yes. With a subject? Yes, but no, because it does not have only one subject. It includes both Henry Ford and the Model T Ford. An action? No. A consequence? No. Generally speaking, a sentence that includes the phrase *tells the story of* will not be a true big idea for an exhibit. It describes what the exhibit does, but the big idea also needs to lay out what the story is. This statement is more of an exhibit topic, and it still needs more work to refine it into a big idea. You go back to the committee again and tell them that they are closer but are still not quite there. Here is their third draft.

⋆ ⋆ ⋆ ⋆ ⋆

Big Idea draft #3: The automobile was a disruptive technology that transformed the country's economy, industry, landscape, and social structures.

⋆ ⋆ ⋆ ⋆ ⋆

Is this version a true big idea? Is it a statement in one sentence? Yes. With a subject? Yes. An action? Yes. A consequence? Yes. *The automobile* [subject] *was a disruptive technology* [action] *that transformed the country's economy, industry, landscape, and social structures* [consequence]. With this as a starting point, the job of the exhibit is to demonstrate that the automobile was indeed a disruptive technology by exploring how it transformed the country's economy, industry, landscape, and social structures. This big idea is truly big, and it is larger than the artifact(s) on display, which means that it reaches out from them to establish a wider context.

Very rarely, if ever, will you arrive at a finished big idea on the first try. I would almost be suspicious if you did, because it is an iterative process, and because we know that it is harder to write a short piece than a long piece. Taking the example above, you can see that the three drafts move from a bare statement of facts, through an intention, to a focused thesis statement. By spending time crafting a big idea, this institution has advanced from simply displaying an artifact with a "tombstone" label giving the bare facts to presenting an interpretive exhibit that will explore cause and effect and relate the artifact on display to the visitors' own lives.

Focusing on a single big idea does not diminish the exhibit. The much-loved Model T will still be a center of attention. Mr. Smith will still be acknowledged as the donor of this signature artifact. The charming stories of what the car meant to Mr. Smith and his family will still be included. The exhibit can still introduce Henry Ford and tell the story of how the Model T became America's favorite car. The difference is that all of these elements will be presented within a broader context that offers a much richer visitor experience.

The car on the platform with the tombstone label might have pleased antique automobile enthusiasts, but the majority of visitors might have seen it, thought to themselves, "Oh, that is an old car," and moved on. With the concepts of disruption and transformation introduced by the big idea, visitors can now come away understanding how the automobile has changed the country. They can also come to understand the artifact's impacts on aspects of their daily lives, such as roads, architecture, and signage, that they do not really see because they are so commonplace.

Does every exhibit need to have a big idea? Not necessarily, but it is not a bad goal to strive for, because even the smallest-scale projects will be enriched if they are developed this way. There will probably always be a place for catch-all exhibits such as the old favorites *Treasures from the Collection*, *Curator's Corner*, or *New Acquisitions*, but if your museum is to be more than a cabinet of curiosities, those should not make up the bulk of your exhibit programming. As Serrell notes, "Exhibitions that lack a big idea are very common. And they show it because they are overwhelming, confusing, intimidating and too complex. There are too many labels, and the texts do not relate to the objects. The labels contain too many different ideas that do not clearly relate to each other. They are hard to grasp. They are typically underutilized—the majority of visitors move through them quickly, stopping at only one-third of the elements."[4]

A well-written big idea is a very useful exhibit development tool. It is your elevator pitch when you are talking to funders or writing a grant application. It is your defense against scope creep. It is a clear statement of what you are trying to accomplish with the exhibit, which will set up your evaluation strategies. It can be the hook for marketing the exhibit. It is a touchstone for your team and for the contract professionals you bring in to the project.

If you develop a clear big idea and stick with it, chances are your exhibit will tell a story rather than just explain the artifacts it contains. Whether the exhibit began with an artifact such as the Model T Ford, or an idea such as "What are the forces that shaped our modern world?," working with a big idea can help you to create a compelling visitor experience, and it will amply repay all of the time you put into developing it. It can sometimes seem like the hardest part of the project, but that is only because it is one of the most important.[5]

## Chapter Checklist

1. Good exhibits tell stories as well as just presenting factual information.
2. Good exhibits are driven by a single big idea.
3. The big idea informs and guides every aspect of the exhibit project, from preliminary design to final evaluation.
4. A good big idea requires time and effort to develop.
5. Having a strong big idea ensures that your exhibit tells a story.

## Notes

1. "The Making of Exhibitions: Purpose, Structure, Roles and Process," Smithsonian Institution Office of Policy and Analysis, October 2002, 4. At http://www.si.edu/content/opanda/docs/rpts2002/02.10 .makingexhibitions.final.pdf. Accessed October 2016.
2. Beverly Serrell, *Exhibit Labels: An Interpretive Approach* (Walnut Creek, CA: AltaMira Press, 1996), 1.
3. http://quoteinvestigator.com/2012/04/28/shorter-letter/. Accessed November 2016.
4. Serrell, *Exhibit Labels: An Interpretive Approach*, 7.
5. Exhibit designer Paul Orselli reinforces this point in a 2014 post on his blog "Exhibitricks: A Museum/ Exhibit/Design Blog," when he says, "Crafting strong Big Ideas, and testing your concepts out with visitors, is hard! It takes time to get the foundational ideas for an exhibition in place, and it takes institutional commitment to keep working at it, and trying things out to get honest responses from visitors and advisors." http://blog.orselli.net/2014/10/whats-big-idea.html. Accessed November 2016.

# Chapter 5

*The Brief and Request for Proposals*

**Developing the Exhibit Brief**

The exhibit brief is one of the most important documents in the exhibit development process. Some are briefer than others, but the purpose is always to deliver a concise overview of the whole project. The brief summarizes only the essential details of the exhibit because each of the aspects that it presents will be outlined in more detail later. The brief will be a touchstone throughout the project, and a copy of it should be brought to every meeting.

The brief is also a sales tool and pitch book that can be used to introduce the project to staff, board, volunteers, and funders. Often the language from the brief can be used in a grant application, and it will also form the basis for the request for proposals if any components of the project are being put out to bid. The exhibit brief should address six key aspects of the project: (1) The Big Idea; (2) Audience(s); (3) Means of Expression; (4) Visitor Experience; (5) Learning Outcomes; (6) Budget. The template is framed as a series of questions.

We will return to the Model T Ford we introduced in chapter 4 to develop our big idea and walk through the template to develop an exhibit based on it. I have found it useful to keep the brief very schematic in its format so that the reader can see both the questions and the answers. In this example, the answers to the questions in this hypothetical exhibit brief are shown in italics, and my comments on the answers are in square brackets following the italicized text.

## *The Big Idea*

- What is the title of the exhibit?
    - *Wheels of Change: How the Automobile Shaped Our World* [Writing the title with two parts separated by a colon allows the first part to be evocative and the second part to be more factual.]
- What is the big idea of the exhibit?
    - *The automobile was a disruptive technology that transformed the country's economy, industry, landscape, and social structures.* [As noted in chapter 4, this meets all of Beverly Serrell's criteria for a true big idea. The exhibit will be devoted to exploring how the disruption and transformation occurred.]
- What is the exhibit all about?
    - *Inspired by John Heitman's book* The Automobile and American Life, *this exhibit is about revealing the extent to which the advent of the automobile initiated significant change in many*

## The Exhibit Brief

The Big Idea

- What is the title of the exhibit?
- What is the big idea of the exhibit?
- What is the exhibit all about?
- Why is it being created?
- What will it achieve?
- Why should a visitor come to see the exhibit?

Audience(s)

- What is the primary audience for which the exhibit is intended?
- What are the characteristics of that audience, and how will the exhibit address them?
- Are there secondary audiences?
- If so, what are the characteristics of those audiences?

Means of Expression

- What is the range and nature of the artifacts that will be used?
- Will the exhibit include interactives?
- Will the exhibit include audio?
- Will the exhibit include video?
- Will the exhibit include other elements?

Visitor Experience

- What are the inspirations for the design of the exhibit?
- What will the exhibit feel like to visit?
- What are the mood, theme, and structure of the exhibit experience?
- What will audience(s) see and do in the exhibit?
- What kinds of programming will be offered in conjunction with the exhibit?
- What is the expectation for the average length of stay?

Learning Outcomes

- What is the expectation for the knowledge and understanding visitors will bring to the exhibit?
- What is the expectation for the knowledge and understanding visitors will take away from the exhibit?
- How will these be measured?

Budget

- What is the overall budget for the exhibit as a cost per square foot?
- How is that divided among all of the exhibit components, including any required capital improvements to the gallery?
- What are the funding sources for the exhibit?

*important aspects of our lives and the way those changes have continued to the present day.*[1] [This is further clarification of the big idea.]

- Why is it being created?

    ◦ *This exhibit is occasioned by the return of a much-loved museum artifact that was removed from the building to make way for renovations. The renovations are now complete, and we are able to respond to considerable audience demand to have the car on exhibit again. Following the creation of the new interpretive plan for the museum last year, we are now committed to presenting our artifacts through exhibits that create meaningful visitor experiences by exploring the causes, effects, and context of the objects on display.* [The answer to this question should link the exhibit to larger organizational initiatives such as a strategic plan—in this case, they are the opportunity presented by the completion of work on the building and exhibit redevelopment initiated by a new interpretive plan.]

- What will it achieve?

    ◦ *We hope that this exhibit will help our visitors to understand the far-reaching implications of technologies, such as the automobile, that are so pervasive and commonplace in our daily lives that they are often taken for granted. Though cars are highly visible as objects, the extent to which they have shaped the world we know today can be almost invisible because it is such an integral part of our lives.* [This question articulates broad goals for the exhibit that may be refined further in the Learning Outcomes section below.]

- Why should a visitor come to see the exhibit?

    ◦ *Museum members, volunteers, and others in our immediate community will come because they remember the Model T being on display and are eager to see it again. Others will come to see the exhibit because the advertising material for it will emphasize that it explores the way in which cars have shaped our world. Teachers will bring their classes because the exhibit connects with the "Transformations" theme in the new grade 5 curriculum document.* [This is always a fair question and a good one to pose to the exhibit team from time to time to remind them of their audience. It is possible to get so caught up in one's own enthusiasm for or interest in the topic as to lose sight of the larger purpose of the exhibit. This is also a very typical question for a local news reporter to ask museum staff at the end of an interview about their new exhibit, so it is good to have a short and snappy answer ready.]

## Audience(s)

- What is the primary audience for which the exhibit is intended?

    ◦ *Members of our community, those who Falk and Dierking would call "affinity seekers" who are "motivated to visit a particular museum or more likely a particular exhibition because it speaks to their sense of heritage and/or Big 'I' identity or personhood."* [An exhibit can and should have more than one audience, but you should try to identify the primary one for which it is being created.]

- What are the characteristics of that audience, and how will the exhibit address them?

    ◦ *They are likely to remember the car being on display.*
    ◦ *They may know the donor or members of his family.*
    ◦ *They may have ridden in the car themselves.*
    ◦ *The exhibit will address this audience by placing the car on display and telling the story of its acquisition and display.*

- ○ *The exhibit will expand on this story by going beyond the immediate facts to explore the wider implications of the automobile, of which this is a well-known example.* [Answering this question might make your exhibit team want to go out and conduct some front-end evaluation, as outlined in chapter 6, before proceeding further.]

- Are there secondary audiences?

  - ○ *School-age children, particularly those in fifth grade because of the curriculum link*
  - ○ *Visitors to our community, whose motivation for visiting is as "Explorers"*
  - ○ *Vintage automobile enthusiasts, whose motivation for visiting is as "Professionals/Hobbyists"* [As noted by Falk and Dierking in chapter 2, good exhibits offer multiple points of access that align with a variety of visitor motivations.]

- If so, what are the characteristics of those audiences?

  - ○ *Fifth-grade children are very verbal and solve problems by talking about them. They are focused on peer relationships and are able to think about abstract concepts. They enjoy classifying and organizing and are good at solving problems.*
  - ○ *Visitors are interested in sense of place and the stories of our community and what makes it unique.*
  - ○ *Vintage automobile enthusiasts are interested in the artifacts themselves and will be knowledgeable about the details of the car, curious about how much of it is original, and want to know how much is new or restored. They will be quick to spot items that are anachronistic or not "correct" for the particular year and model.* [There is a great deal of research about the characteristics of different audience segments, particularly with regard to the developmental stages through which children pass as they grow up.]

### Means of Expression

- What is the range and nature of the artifacts that will be used?

  - ○ *The following artifacts are either from the museum's own collections or will be loaned by local collectors with whom the museum has already been in contact: the Model T; the donor's original documentation for the car, including service records and operator's manual; signage and sales literature from an original local Ford dealership; vintage maps of the surrounding area; a vintage gasoline pump from the same era as the car; and aerial photographs of the surrounding area and other parts of the county.* [At this stage it is not necessary to provide an exhaustive list, but it should give the reader of the brief a sense of the scale and scope of the exhibit and indicate whether the items are owned or loaned.]

- Will the exhibit include interactives?

  - ○ *Yes. The principal interactive will be a reproduced body section from a 1920s Ford Model T equipped with a rear-projection screen so that visitors can be captured by cell phone video "riding" in a vintage car. A wall-mounted interactive will allow visitors to manipulate map layers to illustrate the growth of the interstate highway system.* [You may not know at this stage how these interactives are to be fabricated or operated, but it is important to include a description of them as a prelude to the Visitor Experience section below.]

- Will the exhibit include audio?

  - ○ *A section of the vintage automobile dashboard will be equipped with a radio through which visitors can "tune in" music from each decade from the 1920s to the present by moving the dial. When the dial is turned, a one-minute medley of popular songs from the selected era will* be played, after which the radio will go silent until the dial is turned again. The sound will be audible at a low volume throughout the exhibit. [Again, as with the interactives, this can be an aspirational section that outlines the role that audio will play in the exhibit without specifying exactly how it will be produced.]

- Will the exhibit include video?

  ◦ *Yes. A small theater area equipped with car seats mounted on the floor will show a continuous program of historic newsreels about highway construction, traffic congestion, and other elements of automotive history.* [Again, as with the interactives, this can be an aspirational section that outlines the role that video will play in the exhibit without specifying exactly what footage will be used, although the general availability of the desired kind of material should be investigated and confirmed as early as possible in the project.]

- Will the exhibit include other elements?

  ◦ *Possibly. Negotiations are underway with the head office of the AAA to borrow items, particularly vintage highway maps, from their archival collections.* [Other potential elements should be included here even if they have not yet been confirmed.]

### Visitor Experience

- What are the inspirations for the design of the exhibit?

  ◦ *Images of roadside sights and architecture, including motels, restaurants, service stations, attractions, and billboards. Aerial photographs of highway interchanges. Images of traffic jams. Images of automobile dealerships from various eras. Images of automobile factories and scrapyards. Images of Model T Fords, images of cars from different eras, automobile advertising materials.* [This section can be a collage of images, words, quotations, colors, and other elements—it is a scrapbook of ideas, not all of which, or any, will necessarily make their way into the finished exhibit.]

- What will the exhibit feel like to visit?

  ◦ *Visitors should be drawn in by the familiar (the vintage car) but exposed to new and thought-provoking connections and consequences (the effects of the car). The tone should be respectful but forthright—the exhibit will neither celebrate automobiles nor condemn them, but will rather explore their implications. Detailing can be picked up from automobile-related environments, such as automobile showrooms, service stations, and roadside experiences.* [Describing this in writing will let the non-design-oriented members of the project team get involved. If you are working with a contract designer, they will appreciate the additional insight this section will provide into your team's goals and vision for the exhibit.]

- What are the mood, theme, and structure of the exhibit experience?

  ◦ *The exhibit may be structured around the life cycle of an individual automobile to illustrate the theme of "from promise to problem," from the initial excitement of a new car to the issues of disposing of it at the end of its life. On this narrative spine, the exhibit will feature additional information from particular eras illustrating the interdependence of the themes surrounding the car. For example, one progression might be: cars need roads to drive on and service stations to refuel, and their occupants need food and rest and signage to direct them.* [Here again, even if the in-house team is not designing the exhibit itself, the contract designer will appreciate these insights.]

- What will audience(s) see and do in the exhibit?

  - *See artifacts; sit in the rear-projection interactive and be filmed "riding" in the car; watch video clips; listen to audio evoking different historical periods; explore map layers; reflect on the role the automobile plays in their own lives and in the lives of earlier generations of their family.* [This section recapitulates and summarizes earlier elements about interactivity and media.]

- What kinds of programming will be offered in conjunction with the exhibit?

  - *Regular docent tours for casual visitors and booked groups; curriculum-based school-age field trips; weekend car-themed birthday parties; a midsummer weekend antique car show.* [Outlining the programming to be developed ensures that public programming and the museum's educators will be intrinsically involved in the development of the exhibit, together with docents and volunteer tour guides.]

- What is the expectation for the average length of stay?

  - *Twenty to twenty-five minutes for a typical visitor group.* [This estimate will provide a benchmark for evaluation during the exhibit.]

### *Learning Outcomes*

- What is the expectation for the knowledge and understanding visitors will bring to the exhibit?

  - *Members of the primary audience will likely be familiar with the car and/or the donor and may have seen it displayed previously.*
  - *Members of the secondary audiences will have varying degrees of subject matter knowledge, ranging from almost none to a considerable amount.*

- What is the expectation for the knowledge and understanding visitors will take away from the exhibit?

  - *Visitors should leave with insight into the complex web of technological, physical, geographical, and social implications of the automobile. Based on their previsit opinions, they may find their own views confirmed, questioned, or confounded. None of these is necessarily a goal of the exhibit, the purpose of which is rather to encourage understanding and reflection and mindfulness about the consequences of a technology that is so much a part of our everyday lives.*

- How will these be measured?

  - *Through front-end and summative evaluations, including discussion groups, administered questionnaires, and "visitor-badge" voting at the end of the exhibit.* [Articulating these outcomes and evaluation approaches in the brief ensures that they flow directly from the big idea for the exhibit.]

### *Budget*

- What is the overall budget for the exhibit as a cost per square foot?

  - *The preliminary budget for the exhibit, utilizing some contracted services but doing the majority of the work in-house, is $40 per square foot.*

- How is that divided among all of the exhibit components, including any required capital improvements to the gallery?
  - *The capital improvements to the base building have been addressed through the recently completed renovations and are not funded by this project. Major portions of the funding will be allocated for the interactive experiences and for the framing, matting, and presentation of the vintage AAA highway maps.*
- What are the funding sources for the exhibit?
  - *Museum operating budget; sponsorship from local Ford dealership.* [It may be challenging at first to arrive at per-square-foot costs for exhibits, but that information can sometimes be recovered from previous projects if sufficient records were kept. This will become easier as the team carries out more projects. Such an order-of-magnitude cost estimate can help show the relative size and complexity of the exhibit and illustrate which elements (graphics, artifacts, interactives, programming) have the greatest effect on costs.]

## From the Brief to the Request for Proposals

If any significant portion of the exhibit, such as research, writing, design, fabrication, installation, or evaluation, is being put out to bid, you will need to create a request for proposals, usually referred to as an RFP.

Developed from the exhibit brief, this document details not only the overall project but also the scope of work required of the contractor. The more detailed your RFP, the higher the quality of the bids you will receive in response.

For some projects, particularly those carried out by a level of government, the requirements for an RFP can be quite stringent, and there may be templates you are required to use. In the same way that the exhibit brief informs the RFP, the RFP forms the basis for the contract, letter of agreement, or memorandum of understanding you will sign with the successful bidder.

There are many ways to write an RFP, but this list summarizes the main components that should be included for an exhibit project in which you are hiring a consultant to design, fabricate, and install the exhibit. The list can be amended as necessary to match the scope of the project. A sample RFP for this exhibit is provided in Appendix 3.

1. INSTITUTIONAL BACKGROUND: Outline the organization's vision, mission, and any other details that bear on this particular project.
2. EXHIBIT PURPOSE: Include the big idea from the brief to tell the proponents what you're trying to accomplish with the exhibit.
3. EXHIBIT OBJECTIVES: Include the desired visitor experience and the learning objectives in the brief.
4. EXHIBIT COMPONENTS AND SCOPE OF WORK: Include the means of expression in the brief and outline exactly what work needs to be carried out by the consultant during the contract.
5. APPROVALS: Specify at what stages, and by whom, work done for the project will be approved. Typical approval milestones include concept, schematic design, design development, and final design.

6. CONTRACTOR WILL PROVIDE: Outline what parts of the exhibit the museum will not do because the contractor will be responsible for them.

7. MUSEUM WILL PROVIDE: Outline what parts of the exhibit the consultant will not do because the museum will be responsible for them. Unless there are other parts of the project being put out to bid separately, items six and seven should cover the whole project scope outlined in item four.

8. BUDGET: Specify the total budget for the contract and whether the total is with or without taxes.

9. PROJECT SCHEDULE: Either create a detailed schedule including milestones, meetings, presentations, activities, and deliverables for the consultants to adhere to or create an outline schedule with start, finish, and milestone dates and make the creation of a detailed schedule part of the consultant's work.

10. PAYMENT SCHEDULE: Break the total into payments tied to the deliverables and/or project milestones, beginning with a deposit invoice and ending with a percentage of the overall budget held back as retainage, with payment dependent on final approval of the work.

11. DELIVERABLES: Outline exactly what work the consultant will produce and when and in what form it will come to you.

12. OWNERSHIP OF WORK PRODUCT(S): Specify that all of the work product(s), including designs and creative work, will be the property of the institution at the conclusion of the project. Consultants may request the right to use work carried out during the project for their own firm's portfolio and promotional purposes.

13. SUBMISSIONS TO INCLUDE: Firm experience, budget, methodology, schedule, resumes for participants, break down between principal and junior staff time, and references for, and examples of, previous relevant work.

14. PROPOSAL COSTS: Specify that the institution will not be responsible for any costs incurred in preparation of the proposals nor will any payment be made for proposals.

15. PROPOSAL EVALUATION CRITERIA: Specify how the proposals will be evaluated and emphasize that they will all be evaluated on the same criteria.

16. PROPOSAL SUBMISSION: Specify how many hard and soft copies of proposal documents are to be provided and when and where they are to be delivered.

17. PROPOSAL ACCEPTANCE: Specify that the institution is not necessarily obligated to accept either the lowest cost nor any proposal submitted. Specify how and when the winning proponent will be notified, and how and when unsuccessful proponents will be notified.

18. FAILURE TO PERFORM: Specify the consequences and remedies if the contractor fails to deliver on the work outlined in the RFP.

19. CHANGES: Specify the procedure for submitting and approving change orders to modify the original scope of work.

20. INSURANCE: Specify what liability and other insurance the contractor will be required to provide, and to what dollar value.

21. INSTITUTIONAL CONTACT TO WHOM QUESTIONS SHOULD BE ADDRESSED: Specify one individual as the official institutional representative and how they should be contacted.

## Retaining and Working with Contract Professionals

A relationship between your institution and a contract exhibit professional such as a designer, fabricator, or interpretive planner is like most other relationships—it requires finding a good match to start with and working to maintain the relationship. In the end you will get out of it as much as have you put into it. The exhibit brief and the RFP provide details about exactly what each partner in the relationship will provide and how it complements the work of the other partner.

Before drafting the RFP, it is worth discussing where your institution is in terms of its knowledge, skills, ability, and comfort level for exhibit development. If it is your first major project, you may want the consultant to do proportionately more of the work. If your team has created a number of exhibits, you may have a very clear idea of what you need and only require assistance with very specific parts of the project. Being aware of where you are on this scale, from a complete turnkey project where the contractor runs the whole exhibit development process to hiring out only selected parts, will help you choose the most suitable contractor for the job.

Clarity about expectations, good communication throughout the project, and prompt action to resolve conflicts are key to a successful contract. These qualities will also be much appreciated by the firm that you hire. You should also aim to select a contractor whose vision, approach, and working style are compatible with your own institution. For the duration of the contract, they will almost become a member of your staff, so they should be chosen with as much care as would a new hire. Exhibits are creative projects, done to deadlines, with a lot at stake, and it is important to start with as high a degree of comfort as possible that you are working with the right people.

The larger the firm you are contracting with, the more important it is for their proposal to specify how much time will be devoted to your project by the firm's principals and senior and junior staff. If the firm is chosen because of its previous work, you need to ensure that you will be getting an appropriate amount of time devoted to your project by the principals who did that work. If the principal comes to the first meeting but the majority of the work is done by junior staff, you may not be getting what you thought you were when you hired them.

### Chapter Checklist

1. The exhibit brief is one of the most important documents in your exhibit project. Not only does it lay out the vision for the exhibit and the means by which that vision will be realized, but parts of the brief can also be used for seeking grants and other funding. It sets up the criteria on which the exhibit will be evaluated. Leave enough time in the early stages of the project to get the brief right.
2. Share the brief with everyone on the project team and bring it to all of the meetings.
3. A well-written exhibit brief contains most of the information you will need to create an RFP if parts of the project are being put out to bid.
4. Select and hire contract exhibit professionals with the same care and attention to detail that you would use to hire new staff.

### Note

1. "The automobile and its related infrastructure transformed everyday life as well as our basic values. . . . It influenced, among other things, the nature and structure of the communities we live in, how we define and value community, and the design of our homes and other living spaces." John Heitman, *The Automobile and American Life* (Jefferson, NC, and London: McFarland & Company, Inc., 2009), 1.

# Chapter 6

## *Evaluation*

How well do you know the people who visit your museum? What are their motivations for visiting? What was the main influence on their decision to visit? Who did they come with? Where did they come from? How long did they stay in your exhibit? What parts of the exhibit did they engage with? Was their experience meaningful to them? What did they take away from it? Will they tell others about their experience? If so, what will they say? Will they return for another visit? How many visitors have you had this week, this month, this season, or this year? What were the peak days? What were the slow days?

If you have ever tried to answer these questions, you have carried out an evaluation. If you have ever wondered about these questions, or been asked for this information, then you should undertake an evaluation. Exhibit evaluation explores the distance between what creativity and education researcher Dr. Ronald A. Beghetto calls "the exhibit as planned versus the exhibit as experienced."[1]

There is no such thing as a perfect exhibit, but by carrying out an evaluation of your project, you can make progress toward that ideal. As Beverley Serrell says in *Exhibit Labels: An Interpretive Approach*, "Exhibit evaluation is about making improvements."[2] An evaluation of your exhibit is not a pass/fail test, or an admission of failure if you find aspects of it that could be improved, but rather an acknowledgment of the complexity of human communication and therefore also of exhibit making. This chapter offers a general introduction to the subject of exhibit evaluation. Before undertaking an evaluation project, though, you should familiarize yourself with the significant body of literature and case studies available on the topic in order to design an evaluation that is suited to your institution and will produce meaningful results. A good starting point is the *Practical Evaluation Guide: Tools for Museums and Other Informal Educational Institutions* by Judy Diamond, Jessica Luke, and David Uttal, which has an extensive list of references.[3]

When you ask questions during an evaluation project, you should be prepared for all of the answers you get, even the negative results. Museum audience researcher and evaluation consultant Ben Gammon points out that undertaking an evaluation project presupposes that you are willing to act on the results and make improvements: "Ultimately the outcome of an evaluation study must be to cause change—whether the change is in the activities of the project sponsor, the museum, the exhibit designer or all three of them; and whether that means repeating and expanding successful projects or modifying unsuccessful practices. . . . If at the end of an evaluation process nothing is changed there was no point in conducting the evaluation. This needs to be the guiding principle in the planning and execution of all evaluation projects."[4]

A commitment to making evaluation part of your exhibit projects is really a commitment to understanding your visitors' experience of your exhibits. If you ask someone after their visit, "Well, did you enjoy it?," they are likely to answer only "yes," "no," or "yes, but . . ." It is better to ask those questions than none at all, but a well-designed evaluation project will reveal what lies behind those short answers and what led a visitor to arrive at their assessment of the experience. An evaluation can offer insights that you can incorporate into your current exhibit and/or future projects. As figure 3.1 shows, the exhibit workflow takes feedback from the evaluation of an exhibit and incorporates it into the concept for the next one. According to the *Evaluation Toolkit for Museum Practitioners*, exhibit evaluation can:

- Enable us to understand our visitors/users or nonvisitors/nonusers better . . . and improve the services we offer them;
- Identify strengths and weaknesses and where resources should be directed in the future;
- Ensure that learning is shared and acted upon within the organization;
- Define the quality of what we do;
- Anticipate problems that can be resolved early on;
- Strengthen accountability and motivate staff and users; and
- Demonstrate to funders the impact of the organization.[5]

Evaluation can take place before, during, and after an exhibit project. There are four kinds that are usually carried out: front-end, formative, remedial, and summative. Front-end evaluation assesses the current state of the potential audience, what visitors know, and what their expectations are. "The primary goal of front-end evaluation is to learn about the audience before a program or exhibit has been designed to better understand how visitors will eventually respond once the project has been developed."[6] Front-end evaluation can identify misconceptions among audience members about a topic, or differences in perception between the institution and its audience. It can clarify what an audience is and is not interested in. Surveying or interviewing visitors during front-end evaluation can engage them in the exhibit development process and generate excitement among key influencers.

Formative evaluation ensures that exhibit elements such as directions, instructions, information, graphics, vocabulary, and text are expressed appropriately for the intended audiences. "Formative evaluation provides information about how well a program or exhibit functions or how well it communicates its intended messages. . . . The evaluator measures visitor responses to models, plans, or prototypes of the program or exhibit." It often makes use of mock-ups or prototypes of interactives and rough edits of videos and computer games.

Remedial evaluation takes place as soon as the exhibit is open and the real world has met your carefully designed visitor experience. There will be things that you need to fix and parts of the experience that looked good on paper but just do not work in the gallery. "It is useful for troubleshooting problems and informs museum staff and designers about simple improvements that can be made to maximize the visitor experience . . . such as lighting, crowd flow or signage issues."

Summative evaluation takes place at the conclusion of a project. This can be either at the close of a short-term exhibit or once the exhibit has been open for at least a year for a longer-term project. "It can be as simple as documenting who visits an exhibit or participates in a program, or it can be as complex as a study of what visitors learned."

If you have created your exhibit brief using the outline in chapter 5, you have already set some of the parameters on which you can evaluate your exhibit's success. In order to understand "what is the expectation for the knowledge and understanding visitors will bring to the exhibit?," you will need to establish a pre-visit baseline through front-end evaluation. In order to understand "what is the expectation for the knowledge and understanding visitors will take away from the exhibit?," you will need to carry out a summative evaluation by means of a questionnaire, interview, or focus group. To answer the question "what is the expectation for the average length of stay?," you will need to carry out an observational study once the exhibit is open. To explore "what will the exhibit feel like to visit?," you will need to conduct some interviews or set up a graffiti wall during the remedial or summative evaluation phase.

No matter what kind of project you are undertaking, you should be familiar with the vocabulary of evaluation:[7]

- QUANTITATIVE, QUALITATIVE, DEMOGRAPHIC DATA: Quantitative data is numerical information that can readily be measured, such as how many people attended the exhibit, or how many provided a particular answer on a questionnaire. In order to be valid, quantitative data must be gathered using a standardized approach and predetermined response categories. Qualitative data is more abstract and narrative, such as a visitor's description during an interview of how they felt about their experience. Behaviors, feelings, and preferences are examples of qualitative data. Demographic data is quantitative information about visitors such as their income, employment, education levels, and place of residence.
- INPUTS, OUTPUTS, OUTCOMES: Inputs such as staff time, materials, and supplies and funding are required to produce outputs. Outputs, such as a new exhibit or a program, are the result of the inputs. Outcomes are the consequences of the outputs, such as an increase in attendance figures as the result of an exhibit or program.
- GOALS, AIMS, OBJECTIVES: Goals and aims are large: "The goal/aim of this project is to increase our level of visitor engagement." Objectives are smaller: "To increase our level of visitor engagement, we will make a presentation to all four of the high schools in the community in the next twelve months." Objectives are set in order to reach a goal.
- BASELINE: If you do not know the situation before you start an evaluation project, you will not have a basis for comparison in the future. A baseline is a measurement of the current state of affairs: "The results of the assessment undertaken before launching the exhibit renewal project indicate that 45 percent of visitors surveyed say that they are likely to make a return visit to the museum within the next twelve months."
- KEY PERFORMANCE INDICATORS: The means by which you will measure how well you have done. "There are three key performance indicators for this project: repeat visitation, satisfaction rating, and length of stay."
- OPEN-ENDED QUESTION, CLOSED-ENDED QUESTION: An open-ended question has no set response: "Tell us what you learned from the exhibit." A closed-ended question has a definite answer: "yes, no, (a), (b), (c), (d), all of the above, none of the above." Open-ended questions produce qualitative data. Closed-ended questions produce quantitative data.
- LEADING QUESTIONS: Leading questions direct respondents toward a particular answer and produce biased data: "When will you visit the museum again?" suggests that it is wrong to not visit the museum again and does not offer a way to say that is not the participant's intention to do so. To avoid asking leading questions, break them down into steps, each with options for the answer: "Do you intend to visit the museum again? Yes or no. If so, is it likely to be within the next: Three months? Six months? Nine months? Twelve months? More than twelve months?"

## Should You Hire a Consultant?

Should you carry out your own evaluation, or is it better to work with a consultant for all or part of the project? Assuming that you have resources to retain a consultant in the first place, the answer depends on several factors. Is this the first evaluation project for your institution? You may want to bring in a consultant to build your in-house capacity to carry out subsequent projects and use the first project for staff training. What is the scope of the proposed evaluation? You may want to bring in a consultant for a larger study so that the inevitable day-to-day changes in priorities that come with running an institution do not throw the project off schedule. Is the evaluation for a contentious project, or could the results be disruptive? You may want to bring in a consultant to introduce an arms-length relationship between staff and the findings of the study. Having the consultant report the findings to the museum's board or governing authority can make it easier for staff to implement the results.

Museum evaluation researcher Barbara J. Soren describes an evaluation project where she served as a consultant to four small- to medium-sized institutions who jointly retained her to work with them:

> We embarked on a project to implement a system of audience-based performance measures, or ways to measure outcomes for visitors. . . . Key components of the project were to be collaboration, learning from one another, and professional training. At the end of the audience-based performance measures project, the group concluded that it is probably fair to assume that most museums, large and small, know that evaluation is a good thing. However, since most museum workers have little experience with evaluation, it becomes one more task to find time for among cataloguing projects, preparing tours, event planning, and writing media releases. If they have not been involved in anything more than counting bodies through the turnstiles, contemplating formal evaluation of exhibitions, programs, events, or general operation can be very intimidating. The group found that the audience-based performance evaluation was an effective planning tool, and was also a crucial communication tool. It enabled the entire team to know what is going on in other people's heads as museum staff prepare for events or programs.[8]

If you do decide to work with a consultant, you should develop a detailed Request for Proposals (see chapter 5 and Appendix 3) so that both they and the institution have a clear idea of who is responsible for what.

If your institution does not have the financial resources to retain a consultant, it is still worth carrying out an evaluation project, but you should match the nature and scope of the project with the available resources. A large-scale project that depends on extensive statistical analysis may be taking on too much. Fortunately, there are other means available. Barbara Soren recommends three achievable and cost-effective ways to understand your visitors' experience:[9]

1.  PARTICIPANT OBSERVATION: As participants, evaluators use their presence as an advantage in collecting information, fully integrating into the experience observed, and not attempting to be inconspicuous. Evaluators can sit on a bench in the gallery and write notes as they observe visitors, or stand in the gallery with a clipboard noting behaviors on a checklist. If visitors ask evaluators what they are doing, it is an opportunity to ask for an interview after the visit to the gallery. Observations can indicate how many visitors are going to an exhibition, how they are interacting with particular components, what group members talk about, and how visitors respond to objects and interpretive materials. Counting the number of people in an area is the most basic kind of observational study. A checklist is useful for

noting behaviors observed. It also is helpful to track visitors' movements using a tracking form or gallery map with displays or objects people can choose to experience.

2. CONVERSATIONAL INTERVIEWS: Interviews help to assess visitors' thoughts and experiences. Interviews can be informal as if you are having a conversation with a visitor or group, semistructured in which the interviewer has specific topics and issues to cover during the interview but leaves open exactly how to ask the questions, or structured with predetermined questions and response categories. The structured interview is simplest to analyze. Most important for meaningful responses is the wording of the questions the interviewer asks . . . to help interviewees feel comfortable and safe. Interviews need an introductory script explaining what museum staff is evaluating, and an indication of how long it will take individuals to complete. Questions can be open-ended in a qualitative approach, probing for deeper responses. Or questions can be closed-ended using a quantitative approach, as in multiple-choice questions, ranking scales, or rating questions. Negative feelings should be on the left side of a scale or rating, and positive responses on the right side in order not to bias responses. Interviews can be engaging and fun with pictures or images to indicate, for example, what the visitor is ranking or rating.

3. ON-SITE OR ONLINE WRITTEN QUESTIONNAIRES: Questionnaires are useful with limited staff or volunteers because an evaluator does not have to be present when visitors complete them at the museum or online. A disadvantage to using questionnaires is that there is no way to clarify visitors' responses or to validate the accuracy of responses. It is very important to pilot-test questionnaires with a small sample of visitors beforehand to ensure that individuals clearly understand questions, that the order of questions is appropriate, and that responses do not appear to be ambiguous. Generally, the longer it takes to complete questions on the questionnaire, the fewer the number of people who will respond to all of the questions. Completing a questionnaire should be as enjoyable an experience as possible. If individuals are completing the questionnaire in the museum, they should be able to sit down at a table comfortably and know where to return the form after they have completed it. One of the most common types of questionnaires is to collect demographic information about visitors, or gather a participant profile after an interview. These types of questionnaires should not include personal information such as income, where people live, or [their] ethno-cultural, religious, or political background.

## Setting Up an Evaluation Project

To get started, ask yourself:

- What staff, time, and funding resources are available for the project? Will it use staff, volunteers, interns, summer students?
- Why are you undertaking the evaluation?
- What is the question or questions you are trying to answer? Limit the scope of the study to answer a few key questions. If you want to know more, consider carrying out a second study.
- What type of evaluation will you carry out?
- Will there be more than one type of evaluation used for this exhibit?
- Who will carry out the analysis of the data you gather?
- How will the results of the study be presented, and who will write the report?
- Who will use the results of the study?
- What methods will be used to carry out the evaluation, and are they appropriate to the intended participants?
- Who are the intended participants?
- What sample size do you need to produce meaningful results?

After answering these questions, draft a plan for your evaluation. Like your exhibit brief, the evaluation plan can be used as a pitch document to get decision makers on board with the project, particularly with regard to the staff and financial resources that will be required. An evaluation plan should contain the following sections:[10]

- PROJECT DESCRIPTION: A one-to-two-page description of the exhibit, including photographs, as well as the timeline and overall purpose of the evaluation.
- EVALUATION OBJECTIVES: Your objectives are crucial for every evaluation study you do. They will guide what methodologies you use, your evaluation strategies, and how you analyze and present your data. What are the key questions or issues that will frame the evaluation? What do you want to know? This section should also clarify the purpose of the evaluation by indicating what will not be studied.
- EVALUATION DESIGN: What is the overall approach of the study? Is it comparative, exploring how different groups of visitors view the same exhibit? Is it descriptive, seeking a better understanding of one segment of the museum's visitors?
- METHODS: How will the data be collected, and by which methods? What will the sample size or sizes be? Will the study use both quantitative and qualitative methods?
- PROPOSED TIMELINE: When will the study begin? How long will data collection, data analysis, and report writing take?
- PRODUCTS: Will there be a formal presentation of the results? A summary report? An in-depth report?

There are a wide range of research methods that can be used in each type of evaluation, and some can be used for more than one type. Table 6.1 shows the strengths, weaknesses, audiences, and uses of a variety of methods.[11] The most common tools used for the four types of evaluation under discussion are:

- Front-end evaluation: interviews, focus groups, facilitated surveys/questionnaires, self-completed surveys/questionnaires, visual methods, graffiti walls
- Formative evaluation: mock-ups, prototypes, trial runs of programs
- Remedial evaluation: tracking, observation, interviews, surveys/questionnaires
- Summative: tracking, observation, timing, exit interviews, facilitated surveys/questionnaires, self-completed surveys/questionnaires, structured comment books, diaries, graffiti walls

## Data Collection

The size of sample you will work with depends in part on the context of your evaluation. A larger institution might have hundreds or thousands of people passing through its turnstiles each day, whereas at a smaller museum, it might take you a month or more to hit the thousand-visitor mark. Having said that, even at museums with a smaller visitor flow, you will need to capture enough responses to make your results meaningful. It might sound impressive to say that you have surveyed 10 percent of your total audience, but if that is only ten of the one hundred visitors that you received during that time, you may need to look for other ways to increase the sample size.

As a general rule, the larger the conclusion you wish to draw from the study, the larger the sample size should be. A decision about a proposed major long-term exhibit should not be made with data from only a few visitors because the results would not be quantitatively significant. A meaningful focus group, however, could be carried with as few as five people because the in-depth

**Table 6.1** Evaluation Methodologies

| Method | Strengths | Weaknesses | Groups | Uses |
|---|---|---|---|---|
| Comment Books | • Simple and cheap<br>• Quick and easy to complete<br>• User free to express opinion | • Only some people can complete<br>• Limited information obtained | • People who are motivated to give opinions<br>• Literate people | • Gives a general feel for how exhibit is perceived<br>• Identifies specific issues |
| Interviews | • Can obtain in-depth views<br>• Can get a better sample than when people self-select | • Time consuming<br>• Interviewer needs skills and training<br>• Yields a great deal of data | • Difficult with children<br>• Can be threatening to some people | • Getting in-depth views from a good cross-section of people |
| Focus Groups | • Obtains in-depth views<br>• Group interaction stimulates discussion | • Difficult to recruit participants<br>• Facilitator needed<br>• Time-consuming analysis | • Difficult with children<br>• Group situations are difficult for some people | • Getting in-depth views from a specific group |
| Questionnaires | • Simple and cheap<br>• Obtains answers to specific questions<br>• Data easy to analyze | • Only some people complete<br>• Limited range of responses | • People who are motivated to give opinions<br>• Literate people | • Obtaining responses to particular questions rather than consultation |
| Visitor Observation | • Records what actually happens<br>• Can get a good sample | • Requires skill and planning<br>• Intrusive<br>• Yields a great deal of data | • Most people | • Formative, remedial, and summative evaluation |
| Diaries | • In-depth and longitudinal data<br>• Understanding processes | • Intrusive<br>• Confidentiality issues<br>• Difficult to recruit participants | • Literate, reflective, motivated people | • Understanding behavioral changes<br>• Sharing experiences |
| Visual Methods | • Used where literacy is an issue<br>• Likely to engage certain groups such as children | • Hard to analyze<br>• Generally does not give specific answers to questions | • Those who are averse to other forms of data collection | • Working with groups that will not engage with other methods or learning styles |
| Graffiti Walls | • Simple and cheap<br>• Displayed comments engage subsequent participants | • Only some people complete<br>• Limited information obtained | • People who are motivated to participate | • Gives a general feeling for how exhibit is perceived<br>• Identifies specific issues |

personal discussions will yield a great deal of qualitative information. As well as the size of the sample, you should decide how it will be obtained. Four typical ways of selecting the sample are:[12]

1.  SYSTEMATIC SAMPLING where there is an equal sample size in each demographic group of interest (e.g., age, gender);
2.  REPRESENTATIVE SAMPLING in which there are sample sizes in each category (e.g., age, gender) that is in proportion to the number of visitors in that category who visit the museum (e.g., males and females);
3.  PURPOSEFUL SAMPLING that fills in gaps in data the evaluator is collecting (e.g., specific age groups);
4.  OPPORTUNISTIC OR CONVENIENCE SAMPLING, which gives the evaluator the opportunity to select visitors who are available at the time of data collection.

## Analysis and Report Writing

Completing the data collection for your exhibit evaluation is a milestone, but do not be fooled into thinking that because you have carried out the last interview in the gallery that you are nearing the end of the project. Analyzing the data and writing the final report will take a significant amount of time, at least as long as it took to collect the data in the first place. According to Ben Gammon, "An effective evaluation report should:

*   [be] as short as possible, providing a concise overview of the results and the conclusions. [The] methodology, background theory, references should be included in appendices at the end of the report;
*   provide a clear assessment, based upon the theoretical model, of the evidence for success and failure of the exhibit;
*   make good use of graphics to convey data concisely;
*   make good use of high-quality images of the exhibit so that the reader can understand the exhibit design, e.g., the positioning of the controls, the information provided for visitors;
*   be persuasive, presenting logical arguments, supported by valid data; and
*   be delivered on time. Particularly for formative evaluation it is vital that designers get the information in time to make the necessary changes."[13]

## Chapter Checklist

1.  Evaluation is an essential part of making exhibits. The information you obtain from an evaluation should be used to inform your next exhibit project.
2.  Evaluation is labor intensive and time consuming but worthwhile nonetheless. Choose achievable objectives for your first project. Carrying out several smaller-scale studies will gradually build up a picture of your visitors.
3.  In order to make it worth doing, an institution should commit itself to acting on the findings of the evaluation.
4.  Evaluation should be carried out before, during, and after an exhibit is developed.
5.  There are many research methods that can be used to carry out an evaluation, from the simple (a passive questionnaire) to the complex (a tracking and timing study of visitors moving through the gallery). Each has its uses, and a single project may use several methods.

**Notes**

1. Ronald A. Beghetto, "The Exhibit as Planned Versus the Exhibit as Experienced," *Curator* 57, no. 1 (2014): 1–4.
2. Beverly Serrell, *Exhibit Labels: An Interpretive Approach*, second edition (Lanham, MD: Rowman & Littlefield, 2015), 133.
3. Judy Diamond, Jessica L. Luke, and David H. Uttal, *Practical Evaluation Guide: Tools for Museums and Other Informal Educational Institutions*, second edition (Lanham, MD: AltaMira Press, 2009).
4. Ben Gammon, "Planning Perfect Evaluation of Museum Exhibits," at http://bengammon.com/advice .html. Accessed May 2017.
5. Renaissance East of England, *Evaluation Toolkit for Museum Practitioners*, 15–16, at http://visitors.org.uk/ wp-content/uploads/2014/08/ShareSE_Evaltoolkit.pdf. Accessed May 2017.
6. The quoted definitions for front-end, formative, remedial, and summative evaluation are from Diamond et al., *Practical Evaluation Guide*, 4.
7. Definitions adapted from *Evaluation Toolkit for Museum Practitioners*, 18–20.
8. Barbara J. Soren, personal interview, June 2017.
9. Barbara J. Soren, personal interview, June 2017.
10. Diamond et al., *Practical Evaluation Guide*, 5–6.
11. Adapted from *Evaluation Toolkit for Museum Practitioners*, 52.
12. Barbara J. Soren, personal interview, June 2017.
13. Gammon, "Planning Perfect Evaluation of Museum Exhibits."

# Chapter 7

*Interpretive Planning*

## What Is Interpretation?

In his 1957 book, *Interpreting Our Heritage*, Freeman Tilden defined interpretation as: "An educational activity which aims to reveal meanings and relationships through the use of original objects, by firsthand experience, and by illustrative media, rather than simply to communicate factual information."[1] If this sounds like the definition of a museum exhibit, it is no accident, for although they are often described as "educational," exhibits are primarily interpretive experiences.[2] If you think back to the two studies referenced in chapter 1, which asked visitors what they thought contributed to the ideal museum exhibit, you will see that most of their answers were about everything but the simple communication of factual information.

Tilden's book offers six principles of interpretation that we should keep in mind when developing exhibits.[3] As you read these, try substituting *exhibit* or *exhibit development* for *interpretation* to see how well these principles match up with what we have been discussing for exhibits.

1. Any interpretation that does not somehow relate what is being displayed or described to something within the personality or experience of the visitor will be sterile.
2. Information, as such, is not interpretation. Interpretation is revelation based on information.
3. Interpretation is an art, which combines many arts, whether the materials presented are scientific, historical, or architectural.
4. The chief aim of interpretation is not instruction, but provocation.
5. Interpretation should aim to present a whole rather than a part.
6. Interpretation addressed to children (say, up to the age of twelve) should not be a dilution of the presentations to adults but should follow a fundamentally different approach.

## What Is Interpretive Planning?

Interpretive planning is what you do to create the kind of visitor experience that Tilden describes above, whether you work in a museum or a national park. Within museums, however, the term can be understood in several ways. At a strategic level, the entire institution can (and should) have an interpretive plan. In the same way that a collections plan guides the development of the artifact collection, an interpretive plan is a core policy document that shapes the institution's public programming. An interpretive plan does not exist on its own. Like other institutional documents such as the mission statement and the collections plan, it should be informed by and respond to the institution's overall goals and objectives.

The institution's interpretive plan and its collections plan function as two related frames of reference. The collections plan guides the movement of artifacts into (and out of) the collection because ideally acquisition and deaccession decisions should be made to enable the museum to tell stories that will fulfill its mission. The interpretive plan causes the (temporary) departure of objects from storage and sends them out to the public as they are incorporated into exhibits and programs.

At a project level, you can create an interpretive plan for a single exhibit or program that will be a distillation of the institution's overall interpretive plan. For some exhibit developers, an interpretive plan is synonymous with an "exhibition plan or exhibition brief." As we have defined in this book, however, the exhibit brief is more general, and the interpretive plan is more detailed.[4] In either case, the interpretive plan is an important document that takes the general objectives in the exhibit brief and shows exactly how they will be accomplished. It will also inform later stages such as the writing of exhibit text. An interpretive plan should also embrace program elements beyond the labels, panels, and experiences of the exhibit itself to include curriculum-based experiences for school-age audiences and related public programming for general audiences.

### What Role Do Interpretive Planners Play?

In recent years, interpretive planning has also emerged as a distinct job function on the staff of museums. In larger institutions, interpretive planner can be a job title. In smaller museums, it can be a stage in the process or a perspective you introduce during the creation of an exhibit or public program by encouraging your team to step aside from their usual roles (remember the curse of knowledge in chapter 2?) and think about the exhibit from the visitor's point of view. There are also many consulting firms offering interpretive planning services that can be brought on board for a particular project.

What do interpretive planners do? One way to think about it is to say that they are advocates for the visitors' experience because interpretive planning is all about the audience.[5] Not every visitor to an exhibit can have a knowledgeable guide or interpreter to take them through like the visitors in figure 7.1, so interpretive planning aims to replicate their quality of experience through other means such as text, images, videos, audio segments, and interactives. Experienced interpreters have the skill to size up their audiences and get a sense of their needs and expectations very early in the tour. Without an interpreter there in person, there is a greater demand placed on the interpretive media in the exhibit.

One interpretive planner describes their role in exhibit development as "the bridge between the information inherent in an object or topic and what the visitors bring to the table—their knowledge base, references, experiences, learning styles, attitudes, and more. Really, interpretation is about communication. In a museum context, communication manifests as a variety of interpretive vehicles—labels, text, installations, interactives, images, and more—that act as tools for visitors to access the meaning in our objects."[6] To do this, interpretive planners work on both details, such as editing text to make content from subject matter experts suitable for a general audience, and larger aspects of the project, such as coordinating all of the content streams in the exhibit to ensure that they are coherent and consistent. If, by Tilden's definition, all exhibits are interpretive, then all exhibit development is an act of interpretive planning, and the interpretive planner should be considered a resource for the entire team and every aspect of exhibit development.

**Figure 7.1** Visitors in museum gallery with interpreter.

### Creating an Interpretive Plan for Your Exhibit

In the exhibit brief you wrote short descriptions of the big idea, audiences, means of expression, visitor experience, and learning outcomes for your exhibit. In the interpretive plan these aspects will be discussed and planned in more detail. Having agreed in the brief what you want to share with your visitors, the interpretive plan will go into detail about exactly how you will create their experience.

One interesting way to start this process off is by creating a word cloud. Bring your exhibit team together and give them a set period of time, perhaps five or ten minutes, to write down words that they feel describe what they want the exhibit to feel like for visitors. Run the resulting lists through an online word cloud generator and then bring the team back together to review the results.[7]

This process has many advantages over a traditional brainstorming session. It is a secret ballot that frees up participants to anonymously express ideas that they might otherwise be reluctant to publicly share. It is also an easy way to solicit contributions from a large group of people. It automatically weights the words based on frequency of use and presents the results graphically instead of statistically, and the finished word cloud can be enhanced with colors and graphics to help the visual thinkers.

As well as contributions from individual team members, you can feed in the entire exhibit brief and any background research that has been done for the project. If the results are inconclusive, the process can also be repeated to further refine them. Out of the word cloud will emerge a single word describing the visitor experience. This is the interpretive goal of the exhibit that will inform every stage of its development.

Once you have identified this interpretive goal, the next step is to use an interpretive planning lens to see your exhibit project from the visitor's point of view. Here is how an interpretive planner at Toronto's Royal Ontario Museum describes that process:

> The lens through which to do interpretation is the lens of the visitor. An interpretive planner shouldn't choose what is cool or what they personally think is interesting, they should always focus on them (the visitors) and should always ask why they are making every decision. The interpretive perspective is from the point of view of the visitor—what will they think, consider, take from an experience, and understand. With that object installed in that way, or that label written in that way, what perception will a visitor have? What barriers will there be between them and the information? What misconceptions might someone take from it? In interactives, by doing that action, what will visitors think about the message it delivers? What's a sensible order for the information to be delivered to a layperson? Will they remember that concept six sections later? Do they know what a term means the first time they encounter it? It's easy to take for granted the knowledge base that we have within a museum. Interpretive planners have the responsibility to take themselves out of that context and know that someone visiting won't have the same knowledge base. And they have to identify the gaps and fill them in.[8]

By focusing on the audience experience, an interpretive plan bridges the distance between visitor and exhibit.

## Writing the Interpretive Plan

To write the interpretive plan for your exhibit, return to the brief and expand the sections highlighted in italics below to describe exactly what the exhibit will contain:

### The Big Idea

- What is the title of the exhibit?
- What is the big idea of the exhibit?
- What is the exhibit all about?
- Why is it being created?
- What will it achieve?
- Why should a visitor come to see the exhibit?

### Audience(s)

- What is the primary audience for which the exhibit is intended?
- What are the characteristics of that audience, and how will the exhibit address them?
- Are there secondary audiences?
- If so, what are the characteristics of those audiences?

**Figure 7.2** Visitor viewing museum exhibit on her own.

### Means of Expression

- *What is the range and nature of the artifacts that will be used?*
- *Will the exhibit include interactives?*
- *Will the exhibit include audio?*
- *Will the exhibit include video?*
- *Will the exhibit include other elements?*

### Visitor Experience

- What are the inspirations for the design of the exhibit?
- What will the exhibit feel like to visit?
- What are the mood, theme, and structure of the exhibit experience?
- *What will audience(s) see and do in the exhibit?*
- *What kinds of programming will be offered in conjunction with the exhibit?*
- What is the expectation for average length of stay?

### Learning Outcomes

- *What is the expectation for the knowledge and understanding visitors will bring to the exhibit?*
- *What is the expectation for the knowledge and understanding visitors will take away from the exhibit?*
- *How will these be measured?*

### Budget

- What is the overall budget for the exhibit as a cost per square foot?
- How is that divided among all of the exhibit components, including any required capital improvements to the gallery?
- By continuing to use the brief to organize the interpretive plan, you will ensure that you are still working on the same big idea and within the same concept that you outlined at the beginning of the project. Developing your general ideas more fully may also cause you to modify another part of the project, and this will be easier to do if you have the whole brief in front of you. For example, as you list the specific artifacts that will be in the exhibit, you may find that either an artifact is not available for loan, or that there is a better example than the one you originally envisioned, or that an entirely new item has come to your attention. In order to be fully integrated into the exhibit, this change should be reviewed against the rest of the brief.

### Integrating Program Planning into Exhibit Planning

Exhibits are experienced by both casual visitors and those participating in organized educational and public programs. The interpretive planning you do to develop your exhibit should apply to all of its audiences, and planning for educational and public programming to accompany the exhibit should begin as soon as work on the project begins and not be tacked on as an afterthought. Good public programming advances the museum's mission and offers additional ways to engage with the content of an exhibit, so it is much more than just an activity or a craft that is created after the exhibit is designed. The learning outcomes articulated in the interpretive plan should specifically mention the audiences for organized programs.

The exhibit's physical design should take account of how groups will move through and make use of the spaces in the exhibit. Will there be spaces that are large enough to contain a typical group, and do you know how large a typical organized group is at your institution? Does the lay-out of the exhibit allow all members of the group good sightlines to see the docent or teacher? If a group is using a particular section of the exhibit, is it designed in such a way as to still permit casual visitors to move through while the program is underway? Do the interactives permit more than one person at a time to participate, or are they likely to cause a traffic jam when used by a group? Is there sufficient space around them for others to observe while the activity is going on?

The design of the text and graphics should also support their use by groups. A text panel could work very well for one or two visitors to read it from close up, but what if the content on the panel is going to be used by a docent working with a group? Could it be designed to work with both audiences? If not, is it possible to develop an alternative means of interpretation for the larger audience? There may be activities that work equally well for both kinds of audiences. You may find that the puppet theater that was created specifically to support the grade 4 program also works very well for casual visitors with children if you just leave the puppets out after the program finishes. You may also find that it works just as well for the adult audience that you attract in the evening.

In chapter 4 we wrote this big idea for an exhibit featuring a Model T Ford: "The automobile was a disruptive technology that transformed the country's economy, industry, architecture, landscape, and social organization." In chapter 5, we developed a brief for this exhibit, which we decided to call *Wheels of Change: How the Automobile Shaped Our World*.

Here are three ideas for educational and public programs derived from the brief that explore the big idea.

- Program Idea #1: Road Trip!
    - Intended for elementary school groups in grades 4 to 7, this activity explores how people get from here to there. As part of the overall exhibit design, the floor of the gallery has been turned into a series of roads and communities made from applied heavy-duty vinyl. Different sections of the gallery represent different time periods, ranging from country lanes and dirt roads to the first paved roads to interstates and superhighways. These are sufficiently general that they appear to be part of the decorative scheme to casual visitors, a kind of visual background music. For this program, however, the vinyl graphics on the floor are the base map on which the activities are built. Similar to a large-format board game, students are divided into groups, one per historical period, and must make their way from their start to their destination. They are assigned resources to make the trip, including money, food, and fuel. They are also told their car's average speed, how likely it is to break down, and how far it can go on a tank of gas. They work in groups to make their trip and keep a trip journal, and then they come back together to report on their experiences. Museum staff help them to compare the different journeys and develop an understanding of the infrastructure that has arisen to facilitate automobile use and how it has affected the landscape.

- Program Idea #2: From Our Car to Your Car

    ○ Intended for high school and junior high school groups, this program explores the automobile as artifact. Students are divided into two groups. One works together to remember, describe, and record all of the features that were in the last automobile they traveled in. They take turns describing what they remember while one student acts as the recorder. The other group explores the Model T. Because of the way it has been put on display, they are able to crawl under, around, in, and on the car, which they do after a reminder about how to treat museum artifacts. They also document details of the car, with one student recording their observations. Both groups are asked to document the details of "their" car in order to describe it to someone who has never seen one before. The groups then get back together and share their observations. A museum staff member helps by grouping them in categories to facilitate comparison, and then engages the group in a discussion of form and function from a material culture perspective that helps to understand the technology and development of the automobile.

- Program Idea #3: Paved with Good Intentions

    ○ Intended for college students and adults, this program takes place over two half-days. The first half-day features a curator's tour of the exhibit followed by a guided discussion. The second half-day includes a bus/walking tour and a wrap-up lunch. The focus is on understanding the transformations that have been wrought by the automobile. The gallery session and following discussion initiate a consideration of the economic, industrial, architectural, landscape, and social impacts of the automobile. The walking/bus tour takes participants out into the community to observe these effects firsthand.

## Chapter Checklist

1. Exhibits are interpretive experiences.
2. Interpretation goes beyond the presentation of facts to reveal meanings.
3. Plan your interpretation from the visitor's point of view.
4. Use the exhibit brief as the basis for interpretive planning.
5. Integrate public programming into your exhibit development process.

## Notes

1. Freeman Tilden, *Interpreting Our Heritage*, fourth edition, revised and expanded (Chapel Hill, NC: The University of North Carolina Press, 2007), 33.
2. As for example in M. B. Alt, D. C. Gosling, and R. S. Miles, *The Design of Educational Exhibits* (London: Routledge, 1998).
3. Tilden, *Interpreting Our Heritage*, 34–35.
4. Hugh Spencer, "Interpretive Planning," in *The Manual of Museum Exhibitions*, ed. Barry Lord and Gail Dexter Lord (Walnut Creek, CA: AltaMira Press, 2001), 378.
5. Courtney Murfin, "Interpretive Planning: All About the Audience," webinar delivered for the Ontario Museum Association, September 10, 2015. Archived at https://members.museumsontario.ca/sites/default/files/members/InterpretivePlanningWebinar_10Sept2015.pdf. Accessed December 2016.
6. Courtney Murfin, personal interview, November 2016.
7. There are a number of free web-based word cloud generators, including WordClouds (wordclouds.com) and Wordle (wordle.net).
8. Courtney Murfin, personal interview, November 2016.

# Chapter 8

*Text*

## The Role of Text in Exhibits

No matter what their subject or intended audience, almost all exhibits involve some text, from the most minimal "tombstone" labels containing just the bare facts to large interpretive panels.[1] Text is an essential aid to helping visitors appreciate artifacts and use insights to "read" the exhibit story that you have "written" with your artifacts. At an earlier time, some curators and exhibit designers maintained that artifacts spoke for themselves, and that exhibit text was a distraction from a "pure" experience of the material on display.[2] While this may be true in a few instances and for very particular segments of the audience, it is not the case for exhibits that are intended to engage a range of audiences and work with a variety of visit motivations. Artifacts cannot speak, but they can be "read." In order to read them, however, visitors need access to the appropriate vocabulary, grammar, and syntax. Exhibit text provides this information. Just like literacy itself, "reading" artifacts is a skill that can be learned, and well-written exhibit text can help visitors acquire it.

In her provocative book about interpretation in art galleries and museum, *The Interpretation Matters Handbook: Artspeak Revisited*, UK arts and culture writer Dany Louise asks, "Why does interpretation matter?" Whether you prefer more or less text in exhibits, she says "if there are going to be wall panels and labels, wouldn't it be great if they were all brilliantly written?" How often, she says, "have you walked into a gallery . . . read the written panels next to the artworks, and felt none the wiser? Have you felt that they haven't told you what you wanted to know, left you with more questions than answers, or that you just haven't understood?"[3]

What is the role of the text in the visitor's experience? Is it to neutrally convey information? Is it to create a storyline that is parallel to, and sometimes intersects with, the artifacts and images on display? Is it to drive the exhibit experience and lead the visitor's experience of the artifacts? Or is it to follow the artifacts by simply providing additional information to supplement the visitor's visual experience of the pieces on display?

All of these approaches make sense in different contexts, and none is necessarily right or wrong, but it is important to be clear from the beginning of the project what role the text will play in the visitors' overall experience of your particular exhibit. In the context of an art museum or an exhibit that is intended to create a contemplative mood, the visitors' direct and unmediated experience of the artifacts themselves may be the primary purpose, and so you may find a minimalist presentation of the work and its label, as in figure 8.1. In this case text will play only a supporting role. In an exhibit illustrating a complex topic such as a geological process, individual artifacts may be less visually compelling than in the art museum (think metamorphic rocks versus an impressionist painting). Here the text may be used to create the main exhibit flow within which the artifacts are experienced and made meaningful, as in the archaeological exhibit in figure 8.2.

**Figure 8.1** Simple presentation of art work and label.

**Figure 8.2** Archaeological artifacts embedded in text and graphic panel.

It is hard to consider the role of exhibit text fully without also discussing design. We will take this up in detail in chapter 10, but a brief consideration here will help to illustrate the differing roles text can play in an exhibit. If the text is laid out in a traditional label format, in discrete chunks of fairly small type, it would be difficult to use it to create an exhibit flow and guide the visitors' experience even if that was your stated intention. The size and placement of the words alone would set them in a subordinate role to the artifacts. On the other hand, if the same artifacts were included in an exhibit where the text was boldly presented in large graphic panels, such as in figures 8.3 and 8.4, it would set up a different expectation of its relative importance.

**Figure 8.3** Small artifact embedded in large-text panel.

**Figure 8.4** Detail of small artifact embedded in large-text panel.

## Why Language Matters in Museums[4]

Language matters in museums for the same reason it matters in the world at large. Words have meanings, and people use language to share and understand those meanings. You may hear the view that the language used in museum exhibits should be as neutral as possible so as not to intrude into the visitors' experience of the artifacts. This sounds admirable, but in practice it represents a missed opportunity to use a powerful interpretive tool. You would not make an exhibit without using color, so why deprive yourself of the advantages of well-written and engaging text? It is also difficult to create truly neutral language, and even if you did succeed, it is quite possible that no one would want to read it. Remember, you are making an exhibit to offer a visitor experience, not writing an income tax form. Museum exhibits are curated through choices about what to include and what to exclude, so they are by their very nature neither neutral nor encyclopedic. Effectiveness and inclusiveness are more important goals for exhibit text than neutrality.

When considering the point of view of your project, it is important to refer to the intended audiences that you outlined when you drafted the exhibit brief. This is particularly true when addressing controversial topics, or those on which there are deeply held and differing views. For example, the Smithsonian Institution's 2003 exhibit of the B-29 bomber *Enola Gay* engendered fierce controversy, and led Roger Launius, the associate director of Collections and Curatorial Affairs at the National Air and Space Museum, to say, regarding how the intended audience determined the form and content of the exhibit, "Do you want to do an exhibition intended to make veterans feel good, or do you want an exhibition that will lead our visitors to talk about the consequences of the atomic bombing of Japan? Frankly, I don't think we can do both."[5]

Rather than chasing a probably unobtainable neutrality by draining your exhibit text of style and character, it is more important to watch for unintended biases or implicit points of view. For example, gendered language is still in common usage, intentionally and otherwise. It is not sufficient, as it was in earlier days, to say that one gender is meant to include all, particularly since the default gender is usually male. Unless a historic piece of writing is being quoted directly, you can easily avoid such words as *manned* and *mankind* by substituting the gender-neutral alternatives *staffed* and *humanity*. *Man-made* can become *artificial*, *synthetic*, *processed*, *manufactured*, or *constructed*. It can be harder to find a word-for-word replacement for some gendered expressions, so proportionately more of the text may need to be rewritten to avoid having to use that expression at all.[6]

Bias can also manifest itself in less obvious ways. One study of the language used to describe fish and animals in zoos and aquaria found that some species, such as sharks, were most often described in fear-based language, using words such as *menacing* and *mysterious* and emphasizing physical features such as their teeth. Lions, by comparison, were more often described in admiring terms using words like *magnificent* and *noble*. Tropical fish were often characterized as *exotic*. In all of these cases, such language foregrounds one view of the species and excludes others. If the description of a shark begins with fear-based language, it is much harder to get past the emotional reaction and discuss its role as one of many species in an ecosystem. If the tropical fish are described as *exotic*, they seem removed from us and from the very real consequences of our ecological choices.[7]

Similar language is used in history museums, such as when describing the *Titanic*, which is often referred to as *doomed*. The shipwreck was indeed a tragedy, but reaching first for the most obvious and commonplace words to describe it can undermine efforts to bring a new understanding to the subject and reduce the exhibit to sensationalism instead of analysis and inquiry.

The curatorial voice can present value judgments as foregone and indisputable conclusions, closing the door on visitors' own views. Watch out for judgmental adjectives such as *magnificent*, *beautiful*, or *spectacular*. The role of the exhibit text should be to explore the meaning(s) of the artifact while also acknowledging that multiple interpretations are possible and thus still leaving some room for the visitors' own thoughts. The artifact may indeed be magnificent in the opinion of some, but the exhibit needs to show visitors how and why that judgment was arrived at rather than presenting it as a fact.

When writing exhibit text you also need to consider who is speaking and whether your institution does or should have a point of view. Exhibit text is most often written by an omniscient narrator, a literary style in which the narrator is outside the story being told and is aware of everything up to and including characters' innermost thoughts and feelings. Such a style may seem neutral, but it can also be bland and overwhelming. You may wish to consider introducing a more personal voice.

This can be the collective voice of everyone working at the museum, as for instance when you say, "When we began to explore the history of this artifact, we found something we did not expect." You could also go further and feature the work of an individual member of staff, providing biographical information and letting them speak in their own words to narrate the exhibit. This approach can help bridge the gap between a personal tour with a guide and a self-guided experience based on reading text. The conversational tone developed by this personal text can make even difficult subjects more approachable.

If your institution is to have a distinctive voice in your exhibits, you will need to be mindful that it does not overpower the visitors' own perspectives by keeping it distinctive but not dominant or overly authoritative. Creating a personable institutional voice rather than using an impersonal and omniscient narrator can help visitors feel as if they are on a shared voyage of discovery with the narrator. You may also want to create an institutional style guide. As well as stating preferred usages, such as whether canoes are described as *birchbark* or *birch-bark*, this can give examples of how and how not to write in the institution's voice. Once your institution has defined a point of view, a style guide can ensure that it is used consistently and effectively.

**The Place of Text in Exhibit Development**

You could create an exhibit by selecting some artifacts, arranging them in a room, and then writing a label for each of them. I hope by this point in the book that it is clear that while you could do this, you do not want to develop an exhibit this way, because doing so would sell both your visitors and your artifacts short. The text and the artifacts should be treated as equally important parts of the story you are presenting to your visitors. One or the other may be more prominent in a particular section of the exhibit, but like the song says, "You can't have one without the other."

All of the elements that you outlined in the Means of Expression section of your exhibit brief (artifacts, interactives, video, audio) need to be developed concurrently with the exhibit text. It is inadvisable to write more than the most basic exhibit text in a separate word-processed document without reference to what the visitor will encounter in the gallery. Such an exhibit script can very quickly become an essay in itself rather than an integrated part of the visitors' experience.

The best way to mitigate this risk is to write the text in the graphic panel layouts, with the artifacts themselves (or at least good images of them) in front of you as you do so. Using the guidelines for the length of different kinds of exhibit text elements discussed below, placeholders can be created in the layout program you are using to design the graphic panels. These placeholders can be set up in the chosen typeface and point size of the finished text using dummy text of the appropriate number of words for that element, as shown in the exhibit panel layout in figure 8.5 Because Latin closely resembles English in its average word length, it is often used to produce this text, known as "greeking." An online search will turn up any number of websites where you can specify how many paragraphs of greeked text you require, and they will be generated in Latin (typically beginning "Lorem ipsum dolor . . ." or any number of humorous alternatives). As the development of the exhibit progresses, you can replace the greeked words with the actual text.

# MAIN Title

Subtitle subtitle subtitle

## Nibh Exerci Quadrum

Nibh exerci quadrum nullus quibus nisl modo meus nostrud paulatim praesent. Luptatum singularis ut interdico quae luptatum ullamcorper in quod eum esse. Tation abdo in comis commoveo augue nullus blandit abigo te.

Bis neque mara ymo secundum amet ut nullus molior dolus vero luptatum. Populus luctus iusto sed nisl virtus immitto accumsan opes. Aptent vel sed et. Exputo occuro suscipere esse et lobortis. Macto transverbero diam enim consequat autem qui vero occuro vel quod ingenium.

Iriure acsi duis opes incassum loquor damnum eligo ullamcorper vicis duis suscipere. Illum nibh abdo typicus. Refoveo et vulputate nulla qui iusto. Imputo molior tation os. Esca persto

Nibh exerci quadrum nullus quibus nisl modo meus. Nibh exerci quadrum nullus quibus nisl modo meus nostrud.

Nibh exerci quadrum nullus quibus nisl modo meus. Nibh exerci quadrum nullus quibus nisl modo meus nostrud.

Nibh exerci quadrum nullus quibus nisl modo meus. Nibh exerci quadrum nullus quibus nisl modo meus nostrud.

**Figure 8.5** Exhibit panel mock-up with greeked text.

Writing your exhibit text in the layout program in this way will let you see exactly how much space and how many words you have available to get your message across. This method is much better than taking word-processed text that was written out of context and trying to fit it (usually by editing down) into the layout.[8]

## Who Is Exhibit Text For?

Exhibit text is for the visitors. This may seem obvious, but it needs to be said here because it has not always been the case. If you draft an exhibit brief that identifies the primary audience as other curators or historians working in your field, then you have embarked on a very different project than an exhibit for general visitors. You may wish to consider using other means, such as the exhibit catalogue, that are better suited to communicating with your professional peers than a public exhibit.

There was a time not too many years ago when visitors were blamed for exhibits that did not "work" as they were supposed to. Even as noted an authority as the pioneering museum visitor studies researcher Chandler Screven wrote, in a book about the use of text in exhibits that was published in 1995, "Visitors often do not (or cannot) follow instructions, they ignore important relationships, and attention appears more or less random and unfocused."[9] Given what we now know about learning styles and motivations, the visitors he refers to sound as though they are having a pretty typical unstructured, socially motivated, informal museum learning experience, and if there is blame to be laid for that exhibit not meeting its goals, it should not be laid on them.

Similarly, a 1986 Visual Literacy Survey administered by the Museum of Modern Art's Department of Education concluded that "they [visitors] have little awareness that chronology, stylistic or media groupings lie behind many installation and exhibition choices. They exhibit little ability to identify themes or to recognize their function as categories of organization."[10] In other words, museum visitors do not think like art historians.

There is a substantial difference in approach between an exhibit that is organized the way art historians think and an exhibit that acknowledges that the way art historians think about art is but one possible approach to what is on display. The discourse of art historians about art is of interest to their professional peers, but does what they say correspond to what visitors want to know? As education researcher Philip Yenawine notes, discussing the work of cognitive scientist Abigail Housen, "Most of her subjects, it turns out, are beginning viewers, including most interviewed in museum galleries and some who work in museums. . . . Their stream of consciousness comments about art contain no evidence that they either think or talk like art historians, the people who write most [art] museum labels and catalogues." Substitute "historians" or "curators" for "art historians" and the same can be said of other kinds of museums.[11]

The last word in this discussion belongs to the audience. In the words of interpretive planner Courtney Murfin, "The number one thing to keep in mind with exhibit text is that visitors don't know what's in our heads. . . . The other assumption we make is that visitors naturally want to know what we have to tell them. That's not true. Just because we think something is important to communicate doesn't mean a visitor will think it's important for them to know."[12]

## What Kinds of Text?

The different levels of text used in exhibits can be described according to their purpose. Your exhibit may include some or all of these types, listed here in descending order based on their visual and graphic prominence in the exhibit:

- Title: The title not only names the exhibit but also advertises it. In an institution with several exhibits on display at the same time, the title can be a key element in a visitor's choice about which exhibit to see. It needs to be engaging to catch their attention but also descriptive to signal what it is about. *Mighty Mammals* is a descriptive and alliterative phrase, but *Mighty Mammals: When Mastodons Walked the Earth* is a better exhibit title because it provides more specific information.
- Introduction: Introductory text is the first thing most visitors will read as they enter the exhibit. It is often given a strong graphic treatment through large lettering and dramatic lighting. If the title draws visitors in, the introduction helps to confirm their decision to see the exhibit. Like the title, some or all of the introduction is often used as advertising copy. The classic movie trailer beginnings "In a world where . . ." and "A long time ago . . ." are examples of strong introductory text.
- Main Text Panels: As the name suggests, main text panels are the workhorses of your exhibit text. They are the principal carriers of the written message, and act as signposts to different sections and key topics. They should be given a size and graphic treatment that reinforces their importance. Between them, the title, introduction, and main text panels should contain all of the important concepts in the exhibit and correspond to the learning outcomes in the brief.
- Secondary Text Panels: Secondary text panels expand upon topics introduced by main text panels. They should not be used to introduce new ideas or important information related to the learning outcomes, which belong at the main text panel level.
- Artifact Labels: Labels are directly related to individual artifacts. They are the most traditional and expected form of exhibit text. They should be concrete and specific, referring directly to what visitors can see while they are reading the labels. They are a third level of information and should be less visually prominent than main and secondary text panels, while still being large and clear enough to be easily read.
- Image Captions: Image captions can be used to interpret the content of an image, or they can simply identify it. For instance, an image of a painting reproduced in a graphic panel (as opposed to the actual painting, which would receive an artifact label) might be identified with a caption containing the artist, title, medium, and date, but it could also discuss the subject of the work and relate it to other artifacts on display.
- Image Credits: Credits acknowledge the source of an image that is reproduced in the exhibit. Often the provider of the image will have a credit line they require you to use.

Once you have determined what kind of text your exhibit will use, make a chart that maps what you will say onto how you will say it by identifying each of the text elements in the exhibit. You do not need to write the actual text yet, but indicating what content will be covered in the introduction, main text panels, secondary text panels, labels, and captions ensures that the right content is in the right place and that you are presenting what you promised in the exhibit brief.

## How Much Text?

As you write exhibit text, it is helpful to put yourself in the visitors' shoes. To really get the feel of this, try writing standing up, when you're a little tired, thinking about having to go to the bathroom soon and have a small child tugging on your hand. This will remind you of just how many things are competing for the visitors' attention when they read your writing.

I have spent several thousand words in this chapter discussing how to create effective exhibit text, but the text you write for your exhibit should be much shorter. Like the big idea, the exhibit text that finally goes on display will be a product of many rounds of revising and editing. Brevity is just as important for the words in the exhibit as for the idea behind the exhibit. The visitors' time in your exhibit can be shorter than you think, as little as ten minutes or less, even for a substantial show, and the text is but one part of their experience.

Research has shown that an average visitor reads at about 250 words per minute in an exhibit setting. An average two-thousand-square-foot exhibit has a length of stay of six to ten minutes. If the visitor spent the whole ten minutes reading, they could read up to 2,500 words. Deduct 50 percent of the time for looking instead of reading and the total goes down to 1,250 words. Deduct 75 percent of that for talking, walking, and resting and it goes down to 625 words, or about twenty-one text blocks of thirty words each, which is not a lot of words at all.[13]

Rather than "how many words should there be in a label?" a more relevant question to ask is "how few words can the label have and still be effective?" It is a much better idea to write down to the need than up to a length. Large, dense blocks of text are not visually appealing in the informal learning environment of an exhibit, so writing too much text can mean that visitors will read little if any of it.

We will discuss it further in chapter 10 when we talk about design, but here are some general guidelines for text length that I have found work well in the type sizes typically used for exhibit panels:

- Title: four to fifteen words.
- Introduction: five to twenty-five words.
- Main Text Panels: 25 to 150 words in blocks of no more than 50 words each.
- Secondary Text Panels: twenty-five to one hundred words in blocks of no more than fifty words each.
- Artifact Labels: twenty-five to seventy-five words.
- Image Captions: twenty-five to seventy-five words.

**Editing and Proofreading**

As you start to write exhibit text, it is important to remember that good writers have good editors. Having your text edited is not an admission of failure on your part, nor does it mean that there is something wrong with your writing. As the author of the text, you are working on individual trees. The editor's job is to manage the forest. This can range from simple copyediting for grammar, style, and consistency to substantive or structural editing that focuses on content, organization, and presentation. You will be involved in editing your own work as you revise it, but before it is ready to go on the wall in the exhibit, it needs to be reviewed by another pair of eyes.

It is exhilarating to see your exhibit copy up on the wall after the exhibit opens. It is mortifying to spot a typographical error on one of your brand-new panels. The only thing worse than finding a typo yourself is having someone else find it for you.

Proofreading is an essential part of writing for exhibits. What is the worst mistake you can make? Trying to proofread your own writing. What is the second-worst mistake you can make? Trying to proofread on-screen without printing a hard copy. And the third-worst mistake? Trying to proof-read on-screen in a computer layout program like InDesign without exporting to .pdf first. The on-screen guidelines, menus, and other features of the program distract your eye from the text and lead you to overlook typos or gaps in meaning. Exporting from your layout program to a .pdf copy strips these supports away and refreshes your ability to see the text clearly, as does proofing only from a hard copy. Proof thoroughly, proof often, and develop a circle of trusted proofreaders with whom you can share your text and layouts at every opportunity.

Printing exhibit panels on 11" × 17" sheets like the example in figure 8.6 allows enough room for mark-up. After you've made each suggested change or correction, mark it off on the hard copy and save each round of hard-copy proofs until the panels are produced so you can keep checking for errors and make sure that errors you corrected in the first round of edits do not creep back in later. I have found it best to set up a regular routine for proofing. I mark up hard copy with a red pencil, and after the changes have been entered on the computer, I stroke the mark-up's through with a yellow highlighter. This way, you can see at a glance if they have been completed.

## Tips for Writing Text

So you are ready to write. Well, almost ready, because there is one more thing to do. Print out these words from an experienced interpretive planner and put them where you can see them from your desk: "For everything you write, ask 'so what?' For everything you put in an exhibition, ask 'so what?' We have to fill in that meaning for visitors. That's what interpretation is. The goal is to never leave the 'so what?' question open. And that doesn't mean more text. It means clear text that follows an arc and makes a point so that visitors will know why we showed them this object, why this period of history is important, why this artwork is such a masterpiece, or why this specimen can change our understanding of the world."[14]

One useful piece of advice about writing exhibit text is also the title of a publication: *If You Can't See It Don't Say It*.[15] Exhibit text is there to move the exhibit forward by establishing connections between the artifacts on display and the ideas behind the exhibit. It is not an essay in itself—that is the role of the exhibit catalogue. Writing your text in the exhibit layouts will help you follow this rule.

Another good work to have on your desk is *Gallery Text at the V&A: A Ten Point Guide*, written by Lucy Trench, the Victoria & Albert Museum's educator and interpretation editor.[16] She says:

1.  Write for Your Audience [and remember that it is not fellow curators and historians]
2.  Stick to the Text Hierarchy and Word Count [and because you are going to use greeked text blocks in your graphic panel layouts, this will be easy to do]
3.  Organize Your Information [and because you have mapped out the proposed content onto the available text elements you are already on top of this]
4.  Engage with the Object [in other words, if you can't see it, don't say it]
5.  Admit Uncertainty [by writing as a person, not an omniscient narrator]
6.  Bring in the Human Element [by providing biographical information about who wrote the text and allowing them to write in their own voice]
7.  Sketch in the Background [by moving beyond scholarly information and linking the artifacts with people's lives]

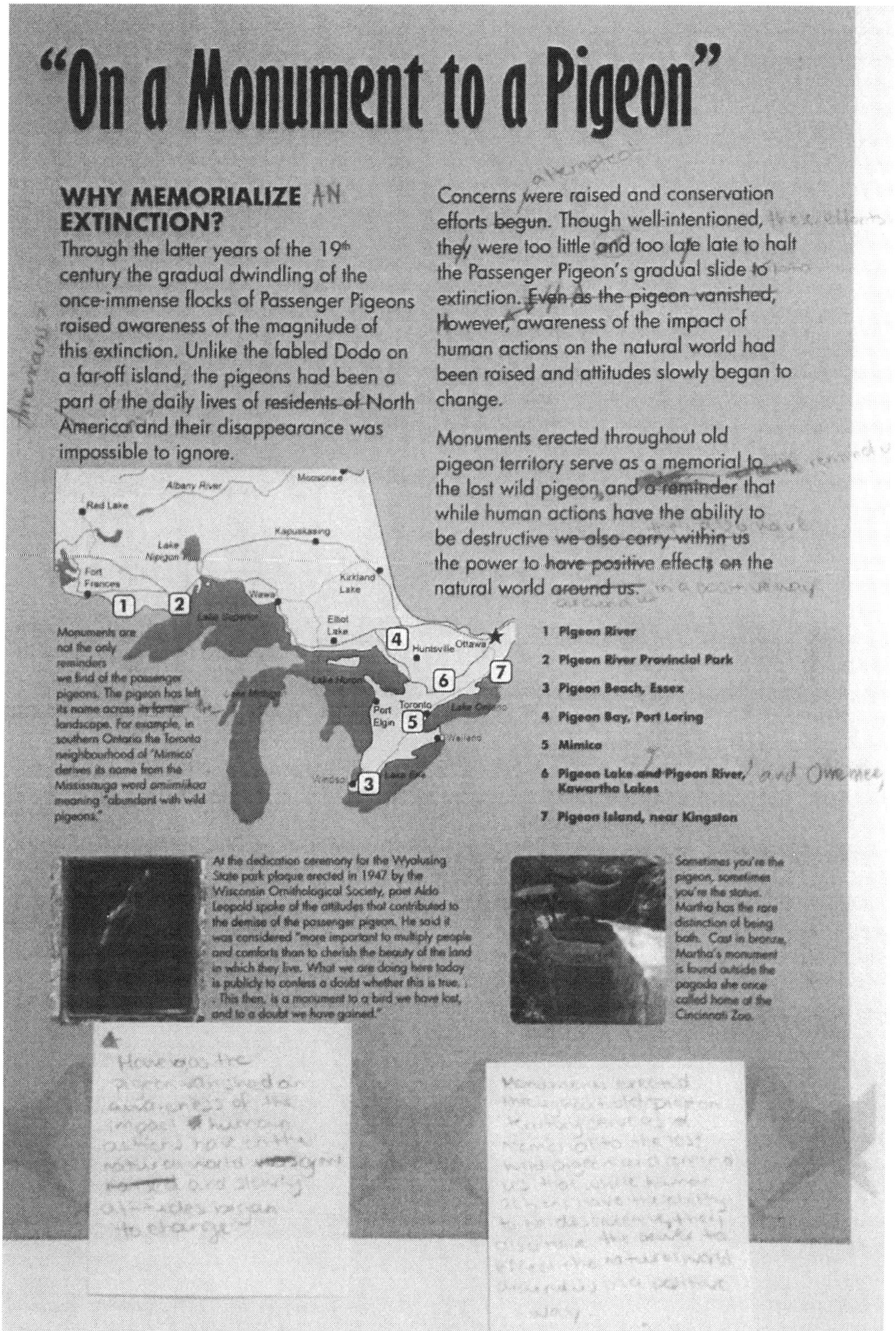
"On a Monument to a Pigeon"
WHY MEMORIALIZE EXTINCTION?
Through the latter years of the 19th century the gradual dwindling of the once-immense flocks of Passenger Pigeons raised awareness of the magnitude of this extinction. Unlike the fabled Dodo on a far-off island, the pigeons had been a part of the daily lives of residents of North America and their disappearance was impossible to ignore.
Concerns were raised and conservation efforts begun. Though well-intentioned, they were too little and too late late to halt the Passenger Pigeon's gradual slide to extinction. Even as the pigeon vanished, However, awareness of the impact of human actions on the natural world had been raised and attitudes slowly began to change.
Monuments erected throughout old pigeon territory serve as a memorial to the lost wild pigeon and a reminder that while human actions have the ability to be destructive we also carry within us the power to have positive effects on the natural world around us.
Monuments are not the only reminders we find of the passenger pigeons. The pigeon has left its name across its former landscape. For example, in southern Ontario the Toronto neighbourhood of 'Mimico' derives its name from the Mississauga word omiimikaa meaning "abundant with wild pigeons."
Red Lake
Fort Frances
Lake Nipigon
Kapuskasing
Kirkland Lake
Wawa
Elliot Lake
Huntsville
Ottawa
Toronto
Port Elgin
1 Pigeon River
2 Pigeon River Provincial Park
3 Pigeon Beach, Essex
4 Pigeon Bay, Port Loring
5 Mimico
6 Pigeon Lake and Pigeon River, Kawartha Lakes
7 Pigeon Island, near Kingston
At the dedication ceremony for the Wyalusing State park plaque erected in 1947 by the Wisconsin Ornithological Society, poet Aldo Leopold spoke of the attitudes that contributed to the demise of the passenger pigeon. He said it was considered "more important to multiply people and comforts than to cherish the beauty of the land in which they live. What we are doing here today is publicly to confess a doubt whether this is true. . . This then, is a monument to a bird we have lost, and to a doubt we have gained."
Sometimes you're the pigeon, sometimes you're the statue. Martha has the rare distinction of being both. Cast in bronze, Martha's monument is found outside the pagoda she once called home at the Cincinnati Zoo.

**Figure 8.6** Exhibit panel draft marked up for editing. Photo by author, courtesy of the Regional Municipality of Halton.

8. Write as You Would Speak [by using a conversational tone to soften the potentially domineering institutional voice]
9. Construct Your Text with Care [and have it reviewed by a good editor]
10. Remember Orwell's Six Rules [as laid out in his 1946 essay "Politics and the English Language"]:

   ○ Never use a metaphor, simile, or other figure of speech which you are used to seeing in print
   ○ Never use a long word where a short word will do
   ○ If it is possible to cut a word, always cut it out
   ○ Never use a foreign phrase, a scientific word, or a jargon word if you can think of an everyday equivalent
   ○ Break any of these rules sooner than say anything outright barbarous

I find it helpful to have some images and objects available for inspiration as I start to draft exhibit text. Sometimes these are just general images, but in other cases you will have images already that you will use in the exhibit itself. For our exhibit to reinterpret the Model T Ford, I did some research in the extensive collections of The Henry Ford Museum in Dearborn, Michigan, and selected the image in figure 8.7, which I thought could be turned into the title panel for the exhibit.

**Figure 8.7** Young boy viewing General Motors model highway, 1959. From the collections of The Henry Ford Museum, P1774.X.141.

**Sample Exhibit Text**

Here is some text for the exhibit we wrote for the brief in chapter 6, which has been written with these guidelines in mind.

- The Title:
  - *Wheels of Change: How the Automobile Shaped Our World* [ten words]
- The Introduction:
  - Whether you know it or not, almost everything you do and see in a typical day of your life has been affected by the automobile. Let's go for a drive and find out how. [thirty-five words]
- A Main Text Panel:
  - Changing the Landscape. There is no point in having an automobile if there is nowhere to drive it, so the new machines caused new roads to be built. To travel on these new roads, both vehicles and drivers needed support services, so the service station was born. Journeys might extend over several days, so drivers and passengers needed a motel (a short form of "motor hotel") in which to spend the night. Cars traveled much faster than horses and carriages, so roadside advertising changed by becoming bigger and more noticeable. You might want to eat in your car during a trip, so the drive-in was created. [107 words]
- A Secondary Text Panel:
  - The Architecture of the Automobile. The new technology required new forms of buildings. Early service stations were often designed in picturesque styles featuring turrets and country cottage detailing. By the 1930s, architects were turning away from these historical forms and beginning to design in the streamlined Art Moderne style. The smooth lines and swooping curves of this late version of Art Deco matched the new speed and progress of the automobile better than a rustic little cottage. [seventy-eight words]
- An Artifact Label:
  - The style of this 1920s gas pump reflected both technology and consumer demand. The glass reservoir on top held the gasoline before it was transferred to the automobile. As well as allowing the fuel to flow by gravity feed, it proved to the motorist that fuel was really being fed into the tank. [fifty-five words]
- An Image Caption:
  - The picturesque style of this early 1930s gas station, with its steeply pitched roof, tall chimney, and welcoming front door, would be supplanted within a few years by the streamlined machine-age look of the newer Art Moderne style, which matched the cars that were serviced there. [forty-six words]

**Inspiration**

Each year the American Alliance of Museums holds a contest to recognize excellence in exhibition label writing. Judged by a jury of museum industry peers, the winners offer both insight into what makes a label good and inspiration for your own work. The current and past years' winners can be seen at http://aam-us.org/about-us/grants-awards-and-competitions/excellence-in-label-writing.

## Chapter Checklist

1. Exhibit text is more than just labels for artifacts.
2. The language you use to write exhibit text should be engaging, suited to your intended audience, and free of bias and assumptions.
3. Exhibit text is important, but less is often more, so choose your words carefully.
4. The most important rule for exhibit text is "if you can't see it, don't say it."
5. Have your text reviewed and edited by someone other than the writer.
6. Have your text proofread by someone other than the writer.

## Notes

1. A note about terminology: some of the references cited and quoted here refer to *exhibit labels*, but I have used the broader term *exhibit text* to include all of the words in the exhibit, from titles to interpretive panels to artifact labels and image captions.
2. "Historically, the use of exhibit text in public exhibitions has been resisted by curators and designers under the guise of arguments like 'the objects can speak for themselves,' 'exhibits are for those whose interests and backgrounds allow them to benefit,' 'museums are not for lay audiences,' 'too much text in and around exhibits distracts from the visual properties of the objects,' 'labels are here for those who can benefit from them, not for the lay visitor,' and 'people don't read labels anyway.'" Chandler Screven, "Preface," in *Text in the Exhibition Medium*, ed. Andrée Blais (Hull, QC: Société des musées du Québec, Musée de la Civilisation, 1995).
3. Dany Louise, *The Interpretation Matters Handbook: Artspeak Revisited* (London, UK: Black Dog Publishing, 2016), 7.
4. I am grateful for some of the insights expressed in this chapter and particularly this section to Mary Kate Whibbs and Lindsay Marlies Small and their presentation "In a Manner of Speaking: Why Language Matters in Museums," delivered at the 2016 Ontario Museum Association conference.
5. Roger D. Launius, "American Memory, Culture Wars, and the Challenge of Presenting Science and Technology in a National Museum," *The Public Historian* 29, no. 1 (2007): 7.
6. There are many online resources that offer gender-neutral alternatives. See for example The National Council of Teachers of English "Guidelines for Gender-Fair Use of Language" at http://www.ncte.org/positions/statements/genderfairuseoflang. Accessed December 2016.
7. Mary Kate Whibbs, unpublished research paper summarized in "In a Manner of Speaking: Why Language Matters in Museums."
8. "In many institutions, label planning and preparation seldom are properly integrated with other exhibit planning. Examples abound, including the practice of preparing exhibits and then turning them over to a third party to prepare interpretive text, or requiring label writers to prepare labels before other exhibit content and organization have been decided. The educational-motivational-informational aspects of exhibits operate as a total system. Creating an effective whole is impossible unless scientist-scholars, designers-fabricators, and labels-graphics specialists work together at every stage of planning." Screven, "Motivating Visitors to Read Labels," in *Text in the Exhibition Medium*, 125.
9. Screven, "Preface," in *Text in the Exhibition Medium*, 21.
10. MoMA study cited in Philip Yenawine, "Writing for Adult Museum Visitors," www.museum-ed.org/writingforadultmuseumvisitors/. Accessed November 2016.
11. Philip Yenawine, "Thoughts on Writing in Museums," www.vue.org. Accessed November 2016.
12. Courtney Murfin, personal interview, November 2016.
13. Beverly Serrell, *Exhibit Labels: An Interpretive Approach* (Walnut Creek, CA: AltaMira Press, 1996).
14. Courtney Murfin, personal interview, November 2016.
15. Kris Wetterlund, *If You Can't See It Don't Say It: A New Approach to Interpretive Writing* (Minneapolis, MN: Museum-Ed, 2013). Available as a download from http://www.museum-ed.org/wp-content/uploads/2013/09/If-You-Cant-See-It.pdf.
16. Lucy Trench, *Gallery Text at the V&A: A Ten Point Guide* (London: Victoria & Albert Museum). Available as a download from http://www.vam.ac.uk/__data/assets/pdf_file/0009/238077/Gallery-Text-at-the-V-and-A-Ten-Point-Guide-Aug-2013.pdf.

# Chapter 9

*Budget*

## Money and Time

In chapter 3 we talked about the importance of keeping on schedule, and how a schedule was really a time budget. Now we come to the other of those two perennial human concerns: money. Whether your exhibit budget is small, medium, or large, it needs to be carefully managed. Nowhere is this more important than at the start of an exhibit project. Consider these two scenarios.

\* \* \* \* \*

Exhibit Budget Development Method #1: You are developing an exhibit proposal for your museum's upcoming annual budget. The exhibit budget has to go to a board meeting for approval late in your museum's fiscal year. You have not had as much time as you would wish to develop the specifics of the exhibit, so you do a quick calculation and come up with a figure by adding up all of the costs you can think of and knowing what you can likely sell to the board. The board thinks this figure is reasonable and approves the exhibit budget. By April of the following year, as you are deep into work on the exhibit, it has become evident that your initial calculation was not as accurate as it should have been, and so you go back to the board to ask for more money.

Exhibit Budget Development Method #2: You are developing an exhibit proposal for your museum's upcoming annual budget. You pull up the budget template that you developed and get the binder you have been using to track the costs of the last three exhibits you have created. You only have a general brief for the exhibit at this point, but you know the size of the gallery and have decided that the exhibit will be moderately dense and contain some multimedia and interactive devices and a lot of graphics. Using the information collected from past exhibits, you estimate these costs. Because your brief is not detailed yet, you also add a 20 percent contingency. By April of the following year, as you are deep into work on the exhibit, it has become evident that your initial calculation was not as accurate as it should have been and so you use some funding from the contingency you have been carrying. Even with this, the finished exhibit comes in below the figure you initially quoted to the board.

\* \* \* \* \*

I will let you tell me which of these scenarios you would most like to be involved in and discuss at your annual performance review(!). The dollar amount spent on the exhibit is the same in both cases, but the way it was arrived at was very different. The moral of the story is that you will get one chance and one chance only to provide a cost for your project, so it had better be a good number. How do you develop such a number?

## Elements of a Budget

In the exhibit brief you laid out the vision for your exhibit. In the interpretive plan you went into more detail about what you want to say, and to whom, and by what means. In the budget you will determine what financial resources you need to accomplish this.

The exhibit budget should capture enough detail to let you accurately monitor the costs of the project but not so much that you spend more time on accounting than exhibit development. If this is your first exhibit project, begin with some broad categories to develop your budget, and keep a spreadsheet for each category that details the actual expenses. At the end of the project, you can review the detailed costs in each category and use this information to create an exhibit budget template for subsequent projects.

Start with broad categories for exhibit expenses. The answers to the following questions will help you develop your project budget.

The overall approach you take to designing your exhibit will also affect the cost. Per-square-foot costs will be different for an exhibit of large technology artifacts such as boats or automobiles than for an exhibit with a large number of smaller artifacts in glass cases. Your design vision will also change the cost. If the exhibit has a "loose" layout, with more than the code-required circulation space between elements, it may cost less than a "tight" layout with more content in the same space. Adding an open program or assembly space to the exhibit will also reduce the cost per square foot.

## Estimating Costs

As shown in our two exhibit budget development scenarios above, it is easy to back yourself into a corner with estimates of exhibit costs. The safest way to protect your project (and your own reputation as someone who brings projects in on time and on budget) is to begin by creating a worst-case scenario for the maximum that the exhibit could cost. If you take this route, you can work to reduce or minimize costs and lower the total if needed. This is a better approach than underestimating costs and having to cut certain parts of the project later on. At this stage in the project, the budget is only an estimate, but that is no excuse for not making it the best possible estimate.

In order to accurately estimate your costs, you will have to do some research. If you have produced exhibits before, you can turn to the information you kept about expenses during previous projects. Contractors can be asked to quote on defined items such as electrical installations or renovations to the gallery. Media equipment such as monitors and digital players can be priced online. Raw materials such as plywood, paint, and graphic substrates can be priced online or in-store. Standard service provider items such as mounted graphic output from a print or signage shop can be priced per square foot. Rental equipment costs can be easily obtained. You will very quickly compile a large amount of information, and if you organize it properly, it can become a valuable resource.

Items that cannot be priced exactly can be accounted for in the budget with a general allowance amount, such as "allow $1,000 for contracted artifact preparation." In other situations, contract service providers will sometimes be willing to give you an "upset limit," which is a price they guarantee will not be exceeded. If the work comes in at a lower cost, you will only pay that amount,

**Exhibit Budget Questions**

- Gallery

  - Does the gallery need repairs or maintenance following the deinstallation of the previous exhibit?
  - Does the gallery need upgrades for the new exhibit?
  - Will the work be done by staff?
  - Will the work be done by contractors?
  - Does it require materials and supplies?

- Design

  - Will the work be done by staff?
  - Will the work be done by contractors?
  - Does it require materials and supplies?
  - Is the exhibit densely laid out, or is there a lot of circulation space?
  - Is there a lot of media or interactivity?
  - Is there a lot of high-technology equipment?

- Research

  - Will the work be done by staff?
  - Will the work be done on contract?
  - Will it require travel and/or accommodations?
  - Does it require materials and supplies?

- Rights and Permissions

  - Will the exhibit require the use of images or other material for which rights must be purchased?
  - Graphics
  - Will the work be done by staff?
  - Will the work be done by contractors?
  - What are the per-square-foot costs?
  - How many square feet of graphic panels will be required?
  - Are there specialized graphics such as maps?
  - What are the costs for materials and supplies?

- Artifacts

  - Do the artifacts selected for the exhibit require cleaning, conservation, restoration, or other work to prepare them for exhibit?
  - What are the per-square-foot costs?
  - Do they require mounts, stands, bases, mannequins, or other equipment?

- Fabrication

  - What items will have to be fabricated for the exhibit?
  - Are elements of the exhibit being constructed in-house?
  - What are the costs for materials and supplies?
  - Are elements of the exhibit being constructed on contract?

- Furniture

  - Will the exhibit use existing cases, plinths, vitrines, benches, and other furniture?
  - Do they need to be refurbished for the exhibit?
  - Will the exhibit use purchased cases, plinths, vitrines, benches, and other furniture?

*(continued)*

- Media
  - Will the exhibit use existing computers, monitors, digital hardware, and software?
  - Will new equipment have to be purchased for the exhibit?
  - Will the A/V elements require scripting, shooting, editing, and production?
  - Will the A/V elements be produced in-house?
  - Will the A/V elements be produced by a service provider?
  - Will the exhibit have an accompanying website or page?
  - Will this be created in-house?
  - Will this be created on contract?

- Signage
  - Will the exhibit need interior signage?
  - Will the exhibit need exterior signage?

- Loans
  - Will the exhibit use loans from other institutions?
  - Are there costs for packing, transportation, and permissions?

- Security
  - Will the exhibit require additional security?

- Installation
  - Will the installation require contract labor?
  - Will the installation require materials and supplies?
  - Will the installation require rental equipment?

- Preview and Opening
  - Will there be a members or VIP preview?
  - Will there be a formal opening?
  - Will there be costs for bar, catering, and for serving staff?

- Insurance
  - Will the exhibit require additional insurance coverage?

- Marketing
  - Will you purchase print or online advertising?
  - Will you create brochures, rack cards, or other print materials?

- Program Development
  - Will the programming be developed by staff?
  - Will the programming be developed on contract?
  - Does it require materials and supplies?
  - Does it require equipment?

- Evaluation
  - Will the work be done by staff?
  - Will the work be done on contract?

- Traveling
  - Will the exhibit be traveling to other venues?
  - Will it require cases and packing materials to travel?

or they may offer to split the difference with you. This kind of pricing is also known as "time and materials," in which the contractor specifies the cost for materials, labor, and a fixed overhead percentage. The alternative is a "fixed price" contract that quotes a firm cost for the work.

Depending on your experience and comfort level with this process, you may want to leave yourself some room to maneuver when it comes to pricing. You also need to allow for wastage when pricing raw materials such as plywood, fabric, or paint. If the project is of longer duration, you may need to account for price fluctuations in some of your items. These may work to your advantage, however, when equipment such as electronic or A/V components goes on sale. If materials are being shipped, especially cross-border, do not forget to account for shipping, customs, and brokerage fees as well as currency exchange rates. Remember to allow for sales taxes too.

It is best to round up the quantities of individual items required for the exhibit. In estimating sheet goods such as plywood, flooring, or fabric, calculate how much you think you need and then round up to the nearest whole sheet, whole yard, or case, box, or lot. If you have not worked with that material before, you might want to add an extra 10 to 15 percent to the quantity and then round up again. When the budget is complete, you will also need to add a contingency amount. The simplest way of doing this is to take the final budget figure, including all applicable fees and taxes, and add an additional percentage. This is a lump sum that is not yet allocated to any particular part of the budget. It is there as an insurance policy against unforeseen costs, changes in material costs, additional work required, or other factors not accounted for in the original budget.

If you have carried out an exhibit project before and are confident in your team and know your contractors and have obtained accurate estimates, the contingency can be on the low end of the scale, around 10 percent. If it is your first major project, if your budget has more allowances than precise quotations, or if you anticipate change orders in contracted work, the contingency should be higher, up to 20 percent. As you work through the project, funds from the contingency can be applied as needed to keep the project on track. The closer you get to the end of the project, the lower your exposure to potential cost changes, and the more confident you can be in the final cost estimate. At this stage it is sometimes possible to release some of the contingency to use for upgrades or items that were not included in the original scope of work, particularly if you have been at or below budget up to that point.

As individual budget items are completed, return to your original budget and make another column for actual as opposed to estimated costs. As the budget is replaced with actual costs, you can track the positive or negative variance from the budget to get a sense of how accurate your budgeting was. This budget reporting should be discussed at every meeting of the exhibit project team so that issues can be identified and addressed as early as possible.

When creating your budget, do not be tempted to reduce or even eliminate the contingency amount to lower the project cost. By doing so you leave yourself vulnerable to cost overruns. If the budget plus the contingency is more than you have to spend, it is a signal that you may need to revisit the project scope and scale back certain elements. Even well-planned budgets can be thrown off track by unforeseen circumstances, and you will need the contingency to deal with those. For instance, I was involved in a museum capital project to construct a new exhibit building. The project was well planned and carefully managed, but after design and cost estimating, and prior to the start of construction, the southeastern United States was hit with a major hurricane. Although the museum itself was well to the north of the zone affected by the hurricane, the damage from the storm and the resulting repairs to buildings caused the price of construction materials, and in particular plywood, to double and then triple, which in turn increased the cost of our project significantly.

## Budget Reality Check

When you have gathered all of the cost information you can and made allowances or best estimates when you do not have hard numbers, it is time to prepare a cost estimate. In large capital construction projects, this is a formal process performed by a professional cost estimator. You may not need to go that far, but this is the stage for complete honesty. Use accurate figures. Don't forget to include taxes and shipping fees. Make worst-case estimates. Your goal is to create a realistic and achievable budget for your project.

But what if, despite your best efforts, you end up with too much exhibit and not enough budget? Do you plunge ahead and hope for the best? Not if you want to have the chance to do another exhibit. Instead, you spend some time on value engineering your project. Value engineering, also known as value management, is a formal process used in engineering and manufacturing to ensure the products deliver the most value and performance at the lowest possible cost. Because the method takes into account both cost and value, it does not simply mean doing the same thing for less money.

As we understand it in the context of exhibit making, value engineering means going through your project and budget, before any money is spent, and making sure that the project is internally consistent. A value-engineering perspective involves looking for alternative ways to deliver functions that cannot be accommodated within the budget. If a custom-built interactive is too expensive, is there a simpler alternative to deliver the same experience? If you were going to pay a service provider, could you do it yourself instead? Could you deliver the same exhibit content with one less display case? Could exhibit furniture from the previous exhibit be refurbished and reused?

Your point of reference for making these decisions, as always, should be your vision for the visitor experience. Make sure you always review the scope of the project before you try to do it more cheaply. A smaller high-quality exhibit is generally preferable to one that is larger and more cheaply executed.

## Controlling Costs

The best way to control costs is through a detailed and well-researched budget that limits or eliminates the possibility of unpleasant surprises. Once the budget is set and the project begins, costs should be accurately tracked and reported so that trends and issues can be dealt with as soon as possible. When purchasing materials for work that you will do yourself, buy them in the largest possible size and largest feasible quantity. For example, you can buy graphic substrates such as Sintra, Fome-Cor, and Gatorfoam from retail stationery or arts and crafts stores, but they are typically only available in smaller sizes and at a premium price. If you have the space and equipment to store and work with standard 4' × 8' sheets, the per-square-foot cost of these materials can be substantially reduced. The same is true for standard-size sheets of plywood. Purchasing commonly used exhibit hardware, such as picture wire, picture hangers, and fasteners, in bulk quantities reduces the initial cost and protects you from having to stop work while you purchase more of an item.

As you work with these bulk materials, you will quickly accumulate scraps and off-cuts that can be kept in inventory and used to reduce the cost of future projects, offering further savings. You can often save substantially on delivery charges by making a single larger order. Having additional materials on hand also lets you recover quickly from errors in measuring or cutting that would otherwise require an additional order and delivery of more material or the use of staff time to go and purchase it.

If your institution has developed a multiyear institutional exhibit plan, you can plan ahead to build up your stock of exhibit materials, furniture, and equipment. If the capital costs of acquiring bases, vitrines, display cases, and A/V equipment are planned in advance, you can amortize the cost over several projects as each one in turn will add to your stock of equipment. You will want to purchase multiples of the same item so that everything has a consistent look and size, so look for open-stock products from established manufacturers and suppliers.

Table 9.1 shows a preliminary budget for the *Wheels of Change* exhibit that was outlined in the exhibit brief in chapter 5. The size of the gallery is 1,500 square feet, so according to the exhibit size typology in Appendix 1 (table A1.1), this is an "Extra Large" exhibit. The preliminary budget was drafted by staff and will be refined with the consultant as the exhibit progresses. It assumes that the design work and graphic production will be contracted out but that the museum also has access to a group of skilled volunteers who will be able to fabricate elements that the designer has created. The budget also assumes that internal staff costs will not be charged back to the project.

The budget is divided into stages that correspond to the exhibit development workflow shown in table 9.1. The only costs in the Concept stage are for the acquisition of rights to reproduce images and use recorded music for one of the interactives. At this early stage, these are allowances only. The design work will be contracted out, with the designer's scope of work specified in the Request for Proposals in Appendix 3.

The Fabrication section of the budget includes allowances for the material and equipment that will be used to fabricate components of the exhibit. Some of the estimates, such as those for plywood, lumber, laminates, acrylic sheet, and graphics, have been developed by estimating quantities and applying typical local pricing. In other cases, as with the A/V and audio components, the budget includes general allowances that the consultant will use to specify particular items. As noted in the Request for Proposals, museum volunteers will fabricate the interactive elements, so the budget amounts for the car body, wall map, dashboard, and theater interactives do not include labor costs.

Installation costs include renting a van to transport the interactives to the museum and the rental of a scissor lift to install overhead elements, along with estimated costs for opening events. A 20 percent contingency has been applied to the overall cost, and the exhibit comes in at $76 per square foot. The interactives would normally drive the per-square-foot cost up, but in this case the cost is lower because they are being fabricated by volunteers. The fact that the feature artifact is an automobile on a plinth also helps to lower the overall costs because it takes up a relatively large amount of the exhibit gallery.

**Table 9.1** Preliminary Budget: *Wheels of Change*

| | Cost | Notes |
|---|---|---|
| Concept | | |
| Brief | $0 | Staff time |
| Research and writing | $0 | Staff time |
| Image and artifact sourcing | $0 | Staff time |
| Image rights | $1,000 | Estimate 20 images at $50 each |
| Music rights | $1,000 | Allowance |
| Design | | |
| Gallery model | $0 | Staff, made from materials on hand |
| Design | $35,000 | Contract design |
| Interactive prototypes | $1,000 | Contract design, built by staff |
| Interactive testing and evaluation | $0 | Staff time |
| Fabrication | | |
| Plywood | $2,000 | Estimate 20 sheets at $100/sheet |
| Lumber | $500 | Allowance |
| Laminates | $1,000 | Estimate 10 sheets at $100/sheet |
| Acrylic sheet | $625 | Estimate 5 sheets at $125/sheet |
| Fasteners | $150 | Allowance |
| Paint | $1,000 | Allowance, for gallery and exhibit furniture |
| A/V | $5,000 | Allowance, to be specified by designer |
| Audio | $5,000 | Allowance, to be specified by designer |
| Graphics | $3,000 | From sign company, 2,000 sf at $15/sf |
| Display Cases | $10,000 | Allowance |
| Additional track lighting heads for gallery | $1,250 | 10 at $125 each |
| Car body interactive | $10,000 | Contract design, built by staff |
| Wall map interactive | $5,000 | Contract design, built by staff |
| Dashboard music interactive | $2,000 | Contract design, built by staff |
| Newsreel theater interactive | $5,000 | Contract design, built by staff |
| Matting and framing | $2,500 | 10 at $250 each |
| Installation | | |
| Equipment rental | $500 | Van, scissor lift |
| Members preview night reception | $750 | Food and beverage |
| Public opening reception | $1,500 | Food and beverage |
| Honorarium | $250 | Guest speaker |
| Postopening | | |
| Summative evaluation | $0 | Staff |
| Project archiving | $0 | Staff |
| Maintenance and repair | $0 | From existing maintenance budget |
| Subtotal | $95,025 | |
| 20% Contingency | $19,005 | |
| Total | $114,030 | |
| Cost/square foot | $76 | 1,500-square-foot gallery |

**Chapter Checklist**

1.  Careful budgeting and cost control are essential to the success of an exhibit project.
2.  Always include a contingency amount in your exhibit budget. The greater the amount of risk and uncertainty, the higher the contingency should be.
3.  Track your expenses to build up a database of information to use in estimating future projects.
4.  Purchase materials in bulk whenever possible to lower their cost.
5.  Create a multiyear exhibit plan to gradually build up your stock of exhibit furniture and equipment.

*Part III*
# Design Development

# Chapter 10

## Design

### Who Is a Designer?

According to exhibit designer Philip Hughes, the answer is everyone: "Display is an innate element of human behavior, constantly practiced in our daily lives. Most homes have casual arrangements of treasured possessions and images, organized by personal preference and intended to reflect, and be reflected upon, by their owners and others."[1] As with cabinets of curiosities, such displays are created for a limited, "in-the-know" audience of friends and family and do not need to address larger questions of context or meaning. These "casual arrangements" might be a great way to organize your living room, but making a display that pleases you is not an effective organizing scheme for a museum exhibit where you need to communicate with others.

### The Role of the Exhibit Designer

Reflecting scientific efforts to classify and understand the world around us, early museum exhibits featured taxonomically based arrangements that emphasized order and sequence, as seen in figure 10.1. Whether they showed natural history specimens or historical artifacts, these displays typically featured large numbers of items densely arranged, with military precision, in geometric patterns. While they may have held the interest of subject-matter experts, it could be hard going for less knowledgeable or less committed visitors. You could say that such exhibits were arranged but not truly designed.

A designed exhibit is one in which the elements and their presentation have been consciously positioned to communicate meanings, creating a visitor experience that Hughes calls "a comprehensible three-dimensional journey."[2] The key word here is *consciously*. Design is a powerful means of drawing visitors' attention to your exhibit and clarifying and reinforcing its intended meaning(s). Consider the examples in figure 10.2.

In the upper image, an artifact in a case is surrounded by a text panel, framed images, and their associated labels. They vary widely in size, shape, and placement, and two of the labels are in the shadows cast by the frames. There is no clear focal point and no implicit message to the visitor about what to look at first, or even any confirmation that the various elements are, in fact, related to each other. The label for the artifact in the case is mounted vertically on the front of the plinth at a height that makes it difficult for an adult to read.

In the lower image, basic principles of design have been applied to make the exhibit panel visually coherent and more engaging. The elements from the upper image have been rearranged into

**Figure 10.1** Traditional taxonomic-style display.

one wall-mounted panel that integrates text and graphics into a single layer. The panel uses an enlarged image as a background for greater visual impact. The title has been presented in larger type to become a focal point. The two images have been enlarged to the same size, and they, together with the captions and the related text block and title, have all been aligned with at least one other element on the panel for emphasis. The label that was on the plinth for the artifact has been incorporated into the panel text, where it will be easier to read for the adult and still accessible to the children. Finally, the panel has been referenced to the figure of a visitor of typical height to check its vertical positioning for accessibility.

As you can see in figure 10.3, the same principles of design can be applied to the floor plan of the entire gallery. In the upper floor plan, all of the various pieces of exhibit furniture have been placed against the walls of the gallery, leaving the center of the space entirely open. There are occasions where this might be necessary, as for example if the space also had to be used for lectures or large tour groups, but otherwise it represents a missed opportunity to shape the visitor's experience and make it more engaging. In the lower floor plan, one entrance has been temporarily closed off by a movable wall. When visitors enter, they see a movable wall that carries introductory material and, by presenting a wider opening to the left, guides them to turn that way into the exhibit. Exhibit furniture has been moved off the walls and out into the gallery.

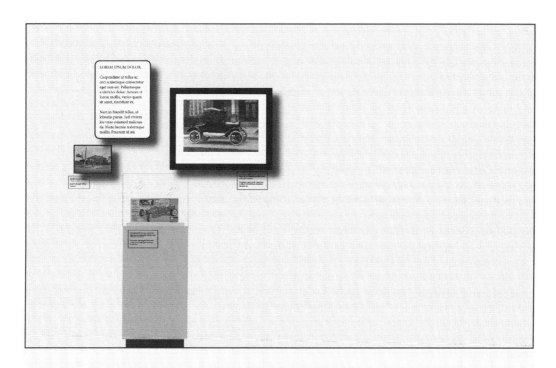

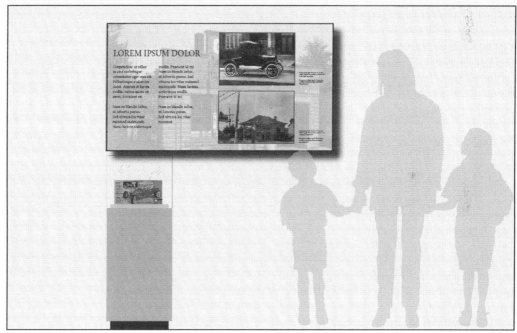

**Figure 10.2** Before-and-after views of redesigned exhibit elements.

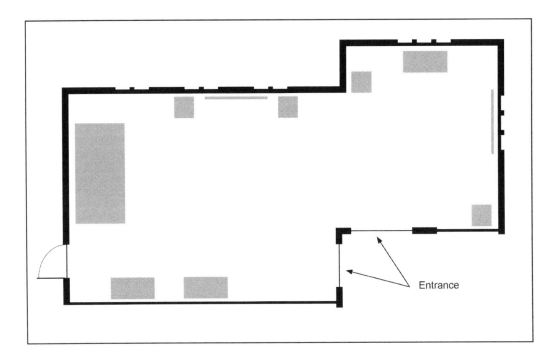

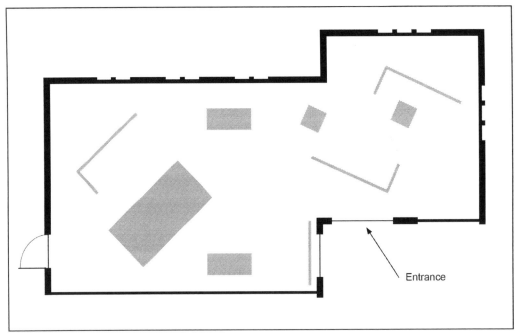

**Figure 10.3** Before-and-after views of rearranged exhibit furniture.

Some of the furniture has been placed at angles to the long axis of the room to vary the circulation options. Movable walls break up the sight lines so that the entire exhibit is not immediately visible from the entrance. This encourages circulation and a sense of discovery as different elements come into view. By moving the elements of the exhibit off the walls and making use of the three-dimensional space of the room, visitors are guided through an experience that unfolds in time and space as they encounter the exhibit, creating Hughes's "comprehensible three-dimensional journey."

## Panels

There is one design activity you can do that will help, almost more than anything else, make your exhibits engaging, effective, and professional looking. What is it? Organizing the disparate parts of your exhibit into panels of a consistent size and format with a definite focal point and a visual arrangement that reinforces the content.

As you saw in figure 10.2, even though exhibits are made from a number of discrete parts, including artifacts, artifact labels, text panels, title panels, intro panels, and credit panels, the whole thing can be brought together to make an engaging visitor experience. If there are too many little pieces on the wall, each with their own hard edges and shadows, your work can come across more like a bulletin board than an exhibit. In terms of visual impact, bigger is better. With the digital design tools now readily available, there's no excuse not to group the elements of your exhibit by theme into a series of panels on which all elements are output and mounted in one continuous layer.

If this is done well, no one should notice. Visitors are not likely to say, "My, what solid, coherent graphic panels you've created" (unless they're taking an exhibit planning and design course). But they will notice in the end, because the overall experience of the exhibit will be clear and informative. Rounding up all of those little pieces into panels will heighten the impact of your exhibit and provide clear focal points for the visitors' attention.

Integrating text, graphics, and sometimes artifacts is an opportunity but also a challenge. What is the best way to arrange the elements within the panel? Consider the two examples in figure 10.4. At the top is an old-style exhibit panel that accompanies the display of locks and keys in figure 10.1. With its facing pages and columns of text and images, it is almost literally a book on the wall. Such a formal layout might work for a book that is read sitting down in quiet circumstances over a period of time, but it will not attract visitors in a visually busy exhibit setting where many things are competing for their attention. The information on the panel is all interesting and relevant, but there is far too much of it for a single panel. The white background, black type, and grayscale images do not create much visual interest, and the title is unlikely to be noticed. The images have not been integrated with the text or used to good advantage.

The lower panel has been designed for an exhibit environment. The images are varied in size, shape, and position. Some are presented in circular vignettes, others have been enlarged and used as backgrounds, and another still has been enlarged even more and silhouetted. The size of the text varies to indicate its relative importance, and the title is the largest type on the panel. Text is presented directly adjacent to what it interprets, as for example with the block to the right of the silhouetted figure.

The upper panel is dense and visually unappealing, and many visitors would likely walk right by it. The lower panel is high impact and engaging. The difference between them lies in the application of basic principles of design.

In *The Non-Designer's Design Book: Design and Typographic Principles for the Visual Novice*, graphic designer Robin Williams recommends using four fundamental principles of design: proximity, repetition, alignment, contrast.[3] How many of these principles have been used in creating the lower example in figure 10.4?

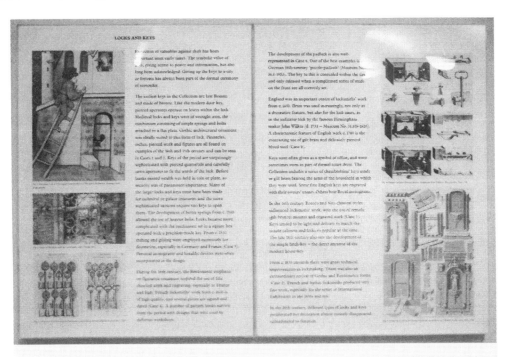

**Figure 10.4** Two examples of exhibit text panels.

What size should exhibit panels be? In an exhibit environment with many things competing for the visitor's attention, larger is definitely better. As we saw in figure 10.2, grouping smaller elements into a larger panel makes a more effective presentation. In deciding what size to work with, you will want to consider the best way to present your material but also think about various industry standards that come into play. The first of these is the standard sizes of the material that your graphic panels will be mounted on, known as the "substrate."

For anything more than one quick panel on craft store 20" × 30" Fome-Core, you will be buying big sheets and cutting them into smaller pieces. The basic unit of typical substrate sheets that you would use is four feet by eight feet. If the material is sourced from Europe, it might be 1,200 mm × 2,400 mm, which is just a little larger. To confuse things a little, some types of plywood will mix metric and imperial units, so you might be purchasing a 4' × 8' sheet of 6 mm plywood.

Even if you're not making panels yourself, but rather sending your files for output and mounting, your service provider will appreciate you working with these standard sizes when you design your panels. They are also buying their substrate in standard 4' × 8' sheets, and the reduced waste from using sizes that match the sheet may help lower the cost of your project. I would suggest making your exhibit panels at least as big as the standard poster sizes of 18" × 24" or 24" × 36". Both of these can easily be gotten out of a standard 4' × 8' sheet of substrate, along with a third, larger size of 36" × 48". Because the resulting panels can be used in either portrait or landscape orientations, this gives you six possible sizes to work with. Figure 10.5 shows some possible combinations that can be cut from a single 4' × 8' sheet. You will notice that the sizes

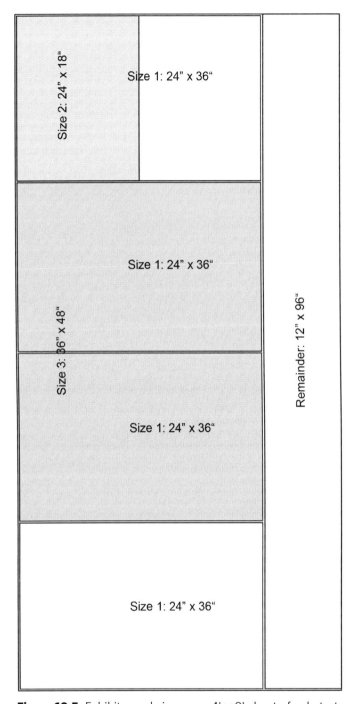

Size 2: 24" x 18"

Size 1: 24" x 36"

Size 1: 24" x 36"

Size 3: 36" x 48"

Size 1: 24" x 36"

Size 1: 24" x 36"

Remainder: 12" x 96"

One possible layout for getting standard exhibit panels out of a 4' x 8' sheet. This piece can yield two 35" x 47" panels; four 23" x 35" panels; eight 23" x 17" panels or some combination thereof.

The 12" x 96" remainder can be used for horizontal "dashboard" panels, model-making or hanging battens.

The long vertical cut should be made first, followed by each of the horizontal cuts.

**Figure 10.5** Exhibit panel sizes on a 4' × 8' sheet of substrate.

have been changed on the sheet layout: 24" × 36" is now 23" × 35"; 18" × 24" is now 17" × 23"; and 36" × 48" is now 35" × 47".

Why have they been reduced? When you cut the panels out of a larger sheet, each pass of the saw blade turns some of the material into dust, leaving a slot known as the "kerf." A typical kerf allowance is ⅛", but it can be more or less depending on your saw blade (and how steady your hand is). If you cut a 48" wide sheet evenly into two pieces, therefore, they will each be a little less than 24" wide. It's much better to deliberately cut them a little smaller and get exactly the same size each time, so we have gone down to a 23" width.

The reduced panel sizes shown also take account of the sizes of large-format print media. If you are working with a service provider to output your graphics, they may give you some size guidelines to work within to make the most efficient use of your materials. If you are printing the graphics yourself, you will need to make some calculations. For example, say we want to produce a 23" × 35" panel. The photo paper we use comes in rolls that are either 42" wide or 36" wide. We could print the panels flopped onto their sides on 42" paper, but that would waste at least 5" of paper with each print. So we should use the 36" wide paper because it matches our panel width, right? Sounds good, but unfortunately a 36" wide roll of photo paper has to have some blank margin on each side because large-format printers that use roll media typically do not print edge to edge. These margins vary from printer to printer, but 35" or 35½" might be the most width you can get on 36" paper.

Another thing to consider when planning your panel sizes is "bleed." Graphic panel layouts typically include this extra width and length to facilitate the final fitting of the print to the panel, as seen in figure 10.6. Some of this will be trimmed once it has been laminated onto the substrate, so the printed area needs to start out larger. This one might be a full 24" × 36" with the bleeds in order to produce a finished size of 23" × 35". Another reason to reduce your panel sizes is that although nominally 4' × 8', sheets of substrate can sometimes vary in size as they come from the manufacturer. I have seen 4' × 8' sheets that are ⅛" or more under or over the stated size, so reducing the finished size of your panels as suggested here will also protect you in the event that you get an undersized sheet of stock.

You can see from this example how much more wasteful of substrate and print media it would be to design exhibit panels that are an odd size, such as 49" × 38", and how even with a standard size such as 24" × 36" you need to understand your materials and the production process before you start designing. By preplanning the media sizes before beginning to design, you can give your exhibit a clear visual structure and make the best use of materials. You can also align your standard panel sizes with different levels of information so that a main subject panel is always larger than a highlight panel to offer visitors visual cues as they navigate the exhibit.

In order to speed production and reduce the potential for error, it is also a good idea to keep your panel dimensions to even sizes. There's nothing to be gained, and many potential mistakes to be made, from specifying panels that are 23.375" × 35.125" instead of 23" × 35". Innovative content makes for a good exhibit, but there's no reason that it can't be delivered on standard sizes of panel like the ones shown here. Your visitors will not notice, and whoever is fabricating your panels will appreciate it very much.

This line is on the outer edge of the bleed area, most of which will be cut away when the panel is mounted.

This line is on the crop marks to which the panel will be trimmed when it is mounted.

This line shows the safe area. All text and images should be kept inside this line to avoid being cut off during mounting and trimming.

MAIN Title

Subtitle subtitle subtitle

## Nibh Exerci Quadrum

Nibh exerci quadrum nullus quibus nisl modo meus nostrud paulatim praesent. Luptatum singularis ut interdico quae luptatum ullamcorper in quod eum esse. Tation abdo in comis commoveo augue nullus blandit abigo te.

Bis neque mara ymo secundum amet ut nullus molior dolus vero luptatum. Populus luctus iusto sed nisl virtus immitto accumsan opes. Aptent vel sed et. Exputo occuro suscipere esse et lobortis. Macto transverbero diam enim consequat autem qui vero occuro vel quod ingenium.

Iriure acsi duis opes incassum loquor damnum eligo ullamcorper vicis duis suscipere. Illum nibh abdo typicus. Refoveo et vulputate nulla qui iusto. Imputo molior tation os. Esca persto

**Figure 10.6** Bleed area, crop marks, and safe area on an exhibit panel layout.

In addition to standards for substrate size, large-format print media, and layout bleed, you will also need to consider cropping in your layouts. A layout program such as Adobe InDesign will let you specify a bleed setting when you create the document. When you export the document to a .pdf for printing, the outer edge of the bleed area will be indicated by small horizontal and vertical marks at each corner. Inside that will be another set of small horizontal and vertical lines called "crop marks," showing you the edges of the document minus the additional bleed area.

Inside the crop marks you should create a "safe zone" for your text and images. This should be set well inside the crop marks, perhaps 2" on each side for a 24" × 36" panel. Although the intention is always to trim the mounted panel exactly to the crop marks, variations in the size of the substrate and the mounting and laminating process might mean that the crops do not align exactly with the edges of the substrate and proportionately more of the graphic might have to be trimmed when it is mounted. The only graphics outside the safe zone should be background colors or images that will not affect the overall panel if they are trimmed off. Unless you are very confident in your printing, trimming, and mounting skills, it is also a good idea not to include borders at the edges of your exhibit panels for the same reason.

## Typography

The most beautiful exhibit in the world isn't much good if it frustrates visitors who try to engage with it. There is plenty of room for creativity in design and typography, but there are also some basic guidelines you can follow to ensure that your exhibit text is accessible to the widest possible audience.

There are a multitude of different typefaces out there, but you do not necessarily get a point for each additional one that you use. Your brilliant and innovative exhibit can get its message across with only a few well-chosen typefaces. Remember, the key goal of an exhibit is communication, and well-chosen typography is one of the ways to achieve that, while inappropriate typography can be a huge impediment. Just like your visitors, different typefaces have different personalities and are better at some things than others. It is important to consider not only the legibility of the typeface you are choosing but also its mood and associations. Figure 10.7 offers some examples and general rules for the use of type in exhibits.[4]

It is helpful to know some of the terminology associated with typography. A description of an exhibit panel type that you hear from your designer might sound something like this: "For the body copy, we'll use Gill Sans Condensed, set 24 on 28." This means that the typeface Gill Sans will be used for the main exhibit text, in the condensed font, laid out in the 24-point size with 28 points of vertical space between each line of type. Figure 10.8 provides some key typographical definitions that will help you when discussing type with your designer or when you are making typographical decisions yourself.

CHILDREN'S GALLERY

A formal classical serif typeface such as Trajan is probably not the best choice to indicate the entrance to the fun zone.

The *Hindenburg* disaster in 1937 marked the end of the use of rigid airships for passenger transportation.

Comic Sans might be a good choice for the children's gallery, though it is over-used, but it is definitely not suitable for discussing tragedies.

Gill Sans 18 point

**Franklin Gothic Medium 18 pt**

Futura Medium 18 point

For signage and way-finding, use a clean and broad-spaced sans-serif typeface.

Century 18 point

Times New Roman 18 point

Garamond 18 point

For artifact labels and body copy on text panels, use either a sans-serif or a simple serif typeface.

# General Rules for Exhibit Typography

Maximum number of words for individual wall, case and floor-mounted labels: **75**

Maximum number of words for text panels on dashboard stands: **125**

Maximum number of words for wall-mounted text panels: **300**

Maximum number of characters in a line of text in one column: **50**

Suggested point size of a title for a typical graphic panel: **250**

Suggested point size of a sub-title for a typical graphic panel: **100**

Suggested point size of body text for a typical graphic panel: **42**

Suggested point size of image captions for a typical graphic panel: **24**

Suggested point size of image credits for a typical graphic panel: **12**

Maximum number of lines of type in a centered layout in a single block: **4**

**Figure 10.7** Exhibit typography guidelines.

| | |
|---|---|
| Gill Sans is a typeface<br><br>Times New Roman is a typeface<br><br>**Hattenschweiler is a typeface**<br><br>Futura Book is a typeface | **Gill Sans Ultra Bold Condensed**<br><br>**Gill Sans Extra Condensed Bold**<br><br>**Gill Sans Ultrabold**<br><br>Gill Sans Condensed |
| A typeface is a family of fonts, such as Gill Sans. | A font, as the term is used in digital typography, refers to different members of the family. |

| | |
|---|---|
| This is Gill Sans Regular<br><br>*This is Gill Sans Italic*<br><br>**This is Gill Sans Bold**<br><br>***This is Gill Sans Bold Italic*** | Gill Sans 12 point<br><br>Gill Sans 18 point<br><br>Gill Sans 32 point |
| A type style such as Italic, Bold or Light, can be applied to an individual font. | Type size is measured in points, of which there are 72 per inch. |

| | |
|---|---|
| This paragraph is set in Gill Sans 11 point with 14 points of leading between the lines. This paragraph is set in Gill Sans 11 point with 14 points of leading between the lines.<br><br>This paragraph is set in Gill Sans 10 point with 17 points of leading between the lines. This paragraph is set in Gill Sans 10 point with 17 points of leading between the lines. | This line of type has 0 tracking<br><br>This line of type has tracking of -75 thousandths of an em<br><br>This line of type has tracking of +75 thousandths of an em |
| Leading (pronounced "ledding") is the vertical space between lines of type in a layout. | Tracking is an adjustment in the space equally within a group or line of letters. |

| | |
|---|---|
| AVENGE<br><br>(No kerning between A and V)<br><br>AVENGE<br><br>(Kerning adjusted between A and V) | This paragraph has full justification. This paragraph has full justification. This paragraph has full justification. This paragraph has full justification. This paragraph has full justification.<br><br>This paragraph has left justification and a ragged right margin. This paragraph has left justification and a ragged right margin. This paragraph has left justification and a ragged right margin.<br><br>This paragraph has right justification and a ragged left margin. This paragraph has right justification and a ragged left margin. This paragraph has right justification and a ragged left margin.<br><br>This paragraph has centered justification. This paragraph has centered justification. This paragraph has centered justification. |
| Kerning adjusts the space between particular pairs of letters. | Justification refers to how the beginning and ends of the lines of type are treated. |

**Figure 10.8** Typography definitions.

## Digital Imaging

The advent of desktop scanners has revolutionized exhibit design and production. Digital imaging puts capabilities into the hands of a museum that would have required an entire print and photography studio only a few years ago. In order to make the best use of a scanner, you need to know a little about the nature of the digital image. There are two ways to be a digital image: raster or vector. As with all rules, this one has exceptions, but these are the main ones.

### *Raster Images*

A digital photograph is almost always a raster image. Raster images are pixel based. Each pixel can be assigned a numerical description of the color it should be. For digital images and those printed on inkjet printers, each color will be described by a numerical value for R(ed), G(reen), and B(lue). For images to be printed on an offset press, the colors are described by numerical values for C(yan), M(agenta), Y(ellow), and K(black).

Because they are composed of pixels, raster images are resolution dependent. You may have already discovered this if you've tried to enlarge a low-resolution photo. The image can only go as big as the information that was captured when it was taken before it starts to break down into jagged-looking pixels. For scanning, that means that you need to think a bit about the final use of the image before you scan it.

For offset printing on a traditional four-color press, for high-quality digital printing, and especially for an art book or a coffee-table book on coated stock, you will generally need the image resolution to be 300 dots per inch, or dpi, at the final size. If the original size is already at the final size, it can be scanned at 300 dpi. If the original is larger than the finished size, it can be scanned at 300 dpi and adjusted after scanning. If the finished size is twice as big as the original, though, it will have to either be scanned at 600 dpi at 100 percent of the original size or 300 dpi at 200 percent of the original size to finish at the correct resolution.

For inkjet printing, including large-format printing for exhibit panels, the usual standard is 150 dpi at the finished size. You can work with higher resolutions if you wish, but the extra resolution won't produce dramatically better printing results, and the resulting files can become very large.

If you scan a 3" × 5" image at 300 dpi and then blow it up to 200 percent of its original size, then the same number of pixels must cover twice as much surface area. You will have effectively reduced the image to 150 dpi. As noted above, that's still going to produce an acceptable image quality most of the time. If you enlarge the original not twice but four times as big, however, the quality will be noticeably poorer. Depending on the quality of the original and the finished appearance you are after, you might be able to take the effective resolution down to 100 dpi. The only way to find out for sure is to enlarge it, check it, and run a test on the same printer you'll be using for the exhibit panels.

A 300 dpi scan of an original offset-printed postcard.

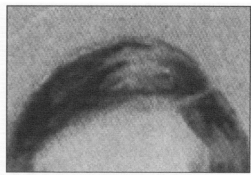

The same image enlarged 750% showing individual pixels.

A low-resolution bitmap scan of a small black and white magazine advertisement as a raster image.

The same image converted to vector art using the LiveTrace feature in Adobe Illustrator.

An image scanned from a 1960s magazine without de-screening.

The same image scanned and de-screened.

**Figure 10.9** Digital imaging examples.

## Vector Images

The vector world is a different place. Whereas the raster world is pixel based, the vector world is math based. A line in a vector graphic is made up of mathematically defined points connected by curves. In figure 10.9, the middle image in the left-hand column was scanned from an early twentieth-century magazine. The original printing in the magazine was not high quality, and the image was quite small. Even if we scanned it at a high resolution, it would not enlarge very well as there was not sufficient print quality in the original. However, there is something we can do. Using a program such as Adobe Illustrator and its LiveTrace feature, we can convert the image from a bitmap pixel-based image into a curve-based vector image.

The middle image in the right-hand column shows the image after it has been converted to vector. Notice how the appearance has changed. It is not chunky and pixelated any more, and instead looks smoothed over and simplified. The shapes formerly made of pixels have been translated to a series of curves with fills and strokes. It will still need some adjusting after conversion because the program makes judgment calls, based on parameters you set before converting it, about how much detail to include and how faithfully to replicate the original image. With a vector file, each of these individual points and their associated curves can be edited to refine the appearance of the image. More importantly, the image is no longer resolution dependent, and could be enlarged to the size of a billboard with no loss in quality.

You will also need to be aware of how your original image was printed before you scan. If the image is from a book, or a magazine, or a postcard, chances are it was printed using halftone dots on an offset printing press. The image at the top of the left-hand column in figure 10.9 is an early twentieth-century postcard that was printed this way. The halftone process translates the image into a series of overlapping dots that can be seen through a magnifying glass. When it is scanned, the spacing and alignment of these halftone dots can conflict with the alignment of the pixels in the digital image, resulting in a moiré pattern of squares or diamonds. This can be remedied with descreening. The bottom left-hand image in figure 10.9 was scanned without descreening. The right-hand image was descreened. Descreening does not need to be applied to photographic prints or original artwork, only to their printed reproductions. Better-quality scanners have a menu setting for descreening items that are being scanned.

To scan images for use in exhibits, you need to know what you want to do with the finished image. Let's say that you're creating a 24" wide × 36" high exhibit panel and you want to use a historic photo as a full-bleed background image that covers the entire panel.

Your original photo is 8" × 10", or less than half the size of the finished panel. Remember that we need to have 150 dpi at the final size. This is not an absolute rule, and the graphics police will not show up at your door if you end up at 135 dpi, but it is best to get as close to 150 as you can. As a rough estimate, scanning that original at 300 dpi at 150 percent of the original size would probably give you enough resolution to work with. If you have some time, it can be helpful to scan the image, enlarge it to the final size, place it in your layout program, export it to a press-quality .pdf to see how it will look on screen, and then send that same .pdf to the same printer on the same media you will use for the exhibit to check the quality. If you do this at several different resolution levels, you will also have a useful set of examples for the next project.

If you want to be more precise, you will need to use an online proportional scale calculator. This lets you enter the size of the original and the size of the enlarged or reduced image and determine the percent change required. When in doubt, or when ordering from an archive, museum, or library, it is best to obtain the largest and highest-resolution scan that they are able to produce. If you are shooting your own photos for a digital design project, you should set your camera to the highest possible resolution and size to make sure you're capturing the resolution you need.

### Scanning

The scanner is a very useful tool for exhibit development.[5] For example, the pamphlet at the top of figure 10.10 has a cover that has been chewed by mice, torn, water stained, and foxed by the acid in the cheap newsprint on which it was printed. It is a very strong graphic, though, so it was worth saving and using.

The first step in rescuing it was to do a high-resolution scan. In this case, knowing that it was going to be enlarged when it was used, the scan was done in color at 600 dpi at 200 percent of the original size. The scan was then opened in Photoshop. The first step was to use the Brightness and Contrast tool to punch up the visual appearance and compensate for both fading over time and the scanner's tendency to wash out images when they are captured by making the blacks more saturated and the bright areas brighter.

Using the Clone Stamp tool, the rips and tears in the middle of the black border on either side were fixed by copying and pasting color from elsewhere in the image. The missing graphic in the lower-left corner was repaired by copying an area from the right-hand side, reflecting it vertically and pasting it on the left-hand corner, using the Eraser and Clone Stamp tools to blend it with the existing design.

Finally, the whole image was worked over again with the Clone Stamp to fix smaller blemishes. The finished result doesn't look new, but it is certainly usable for an exhibit graphic next to the original document opened to an inside spread of pages that are in better shape.

Scanned images can also be used to create graphic panels. The image at the lower left in figure 10.10 is a cigarette ad from a 1930s boating magazine. Because it is out of copyright, it can be used without requesting permission. The original, roughly 8" × 10", was scanned at very high resolution so that it could be enlarged to roughly 7' feet square. After sharpening the image and adjusting the colors and saturation, the Clone Stamp tool was used to remove the writing and image of the cigarette package. In the case of the "Chesterfield" name at the bottom of the image, this required careful work to replicate the texture of the boat's wake. After the image had been cleaned up, the exhibit title was added, and it was printed full size and mounted.

By copying an existing image with a scanner, you are entering into the question of copyright, or literally whether or not you have the right to copy it. Many works are copyrighted. Some copyrighted works can lose their copyright protection and pass into the public domain. Other works are never copyrighted and are automatically in the public domain upon their creation. Copyright law is evolving rapidly to meet the new demands of the digital age, and you should consult the websites run by the US Copyright Office and/or the Canadian Intellectual Property Office for the most up-to-date information before undertaking your project.[6]

**Figure 10.10** Image retouching examples.

## Color

Exhibits are full of colors from many sources. Paint, fabrics, floor coverings, graphics, photographs, and the artifacts themselves can all bring different colors, shades, tones, and hues into the mix. A traditional designer's sample board is a good way to work with the colors in your exhibit. If you are not sure where to start to choose colors, one easy trick is to begin with the images and artifacts you will be displaying. If you have digital photographs or scanned images, you can bring them into Photoshop and use the Color Sampler tool. When you position this on a portion of the image and click, Photoshop will display the RGB and CMYK values for that color. It can also suggest the closest Pantone spot color.

The same can be done with a good photograph of an artifact. Pulling ten or so colors right from the materials that will be on display can give you a good starting point for developing the palette for the exhibit. Once you decide on the colors you will be using, you can save them as a set of swatches and share them between all of the applications in Creative Suite. There are also color formula books that offer combinations, such as *The Designer's Guide to Color Combinations: 500+ Historic and Modern Color Formulas in CMYK* and *Color Index: Over 1100 Color Combinations, CMYK and RGB Formulas, for Print and Web Media*.[7] Because they are aimed at print designers, both of these books offer their formulas in CMYK, or process, color, but Pantone offers the "Color Bridge Guide," which shows each PMS spot color and its corresponding process equivalent.[8] You can also use an online CMYK to Pantone converter. As well as putting together a board of physical samples, you will need to spend a little more time to make sure that all of your digital devices are speaking the same color language. The colors that you will use to produce your exhibit panels and graphics can be either spot colors or process colors.

### Process Color

Process colors are produced by traditional offset printing using separations. These are printing plates that break each color down into a percentage of the four process colors: cyan, magenta, yellow, and black. Images are produced by running them through the press four separate times with four separate printing plates, one for each color. This process is still used for high-quality printed materials but would only be involved in your exhibit if you were producing a printed catalogue.

Your exhibit is more likely to be produced in a digital workflow that begins on a computer and is output on an ink-jet printer that uses three or more colors of ink to create finished images. Some large-format printers use up to six colors. Unlike process printing, however, all of the colors are combined in a single pass through the inkjet printer, and no separations are required.

### Spot Color

When you are designing exhibit panels on the computer, you are working with spot colors. The easiest way to distinguish these from process colors is to think of them as cans of paint. When you paint your house, you go to the store, select a chip, have the paint mixed, and apply it. As soon as the brush or roller touches the wall, you have applied that color, and no further mixing or layering is required.

The nearly universal standard for spot color description is the Pantone Matching System. There are others as well, such as the Munsell system, but Pantone is the most widely used by designers.

When you create a graphic in a layout program such as Adobe InDesign, you select a color swatch to apply. If you are designing for a process-color print job, you would specify the CMYK values you need to create that particular color. Because your exhibit panels are going to be printed on an inkjet printer, however, you will select a spot color. Layout programs have built-in swatch books for Pantone and other color systems. Selecting one of these, such as "Pantone Solid Uncoated," opens up a menu of available swatches. Each color will have a unique number, such as "5455 U," with the U standing for "uncoated" (paper stock). This would usually be referred to as "PMS (for Pantone Matching System) 5455 U." With a color system such as this, a designer in one country can specify a color, and a printer halfway around the world will be able to understand exactly what they mean.

Your computer monitor renders color using only red, green, and blue. Because of this and the fact that the monitor is backlit, the colors you select will appear differently on screen than they will when printed. Your monitor needs to be calibrated periodically to ensure that it is representing colors accurately. In order for you to have an accurate representation of what the finished printing will look like, it also needs to share the same color specifications as your printer. This is done through the use of color profiles, which will vary with the software and hardware you are using.

### Test Prints

Once you have aligned the color profiles for all of your devices, the safest way to avoid unpleasant surprises in the finished output is to create a test document containing swatches of all of the colors you will be using. This should be printed from your computer, on your printer, on the print media you will be using for the exhibit. If you are working with an external service provider, it is worth spending a little extra money to have them print and mount this test document. Once this is printed, you can take it into the gallery to check your lighting and use it to coordinate paint, fabrics, laminates, and other colored elements of the exhibit. You should absolutely not make these decisions based on what you see on the monitor.

### Floor Plans and Models

Models are very useful for exhibit development. If you are working with a team to develop the exhibit, having the model nearby can help focus discussions, especially for those who are not used to reading floor plans or scale drawings. Even if you are used to working with plans and drawings, seeing the project in three dimensions is helpful. If you have an existing floor plan or architectural drawing for your gallery, you can enlarge it to the appropriate scale and construct the model right on top of it.

If you do not have a drawing, a dimensioned sketch such as the one in the upper left corner of figure 10.11 can be prepared on site. Models can be built from a wide variety of materials, but Gatorfoam, Sintra, and Fome-Cor are the easiest to work with. As soon as you have completed an exhibit project, you will have plenty of scraps to use for the model for your next project. I would suggest making the model at a fairly large scale, at least 1" to 1', and making the walls the true scale height. After they are cut out, the walls can be assembled with a hot-melt glue gun. In the example shown in figure 10.11, the exhibit is to be installed in two adjoining rooms, both of irregular shape. The basic structure of the model is built first, and then exhibit panels and furniture are constructed out of scraps. In this case, the walls and floor were made from black Gatorfoam, and the exhibit components were made from white Sintra so they would stand out.

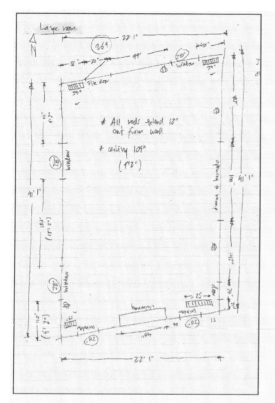

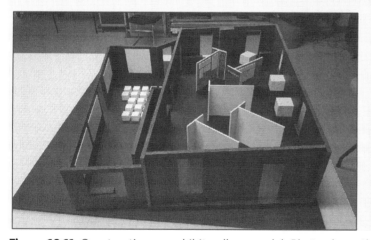

**Figure 10.11** Constructing an exhibit gallery model. Photos by author, courtesy of the Regional Municipality of Halton.

The scale walls in the bottom-left image were covered with adhesive vinyl mock-ups of the finished exhibit panels, printed from the full-sized panel layouts developed in Adobe InDesign. Other items of furniture and equipment, such as radiators and the theater-area seating, are represented by block shapes. The bottom-right photo shows a simple scale device used to check circulation width between the pieces of exhibit furniture. The short dimension is 3" (3') and the larger side is 4" (4'), representing both the minimum width for wheelchair users and a more generous clearance.

Regarding the example in figure 10.3 and the importance of getting exhibits off the walls and out into the room, this model shows a proposed exhibit for which accomplishes that. All of the display items and artifacts will be included on the six T-shaped panels in the model, leaving the walls clear and letting the room "breathe."

Physical models are useful for meetings, presentations, and fundraising, but you can also construct a digital model of your exhibit. The most commonly used software for this is SketchUp.[9] It is available in a free version, called "SketchUp Make," which is not licensed for commercial use, and also in a pro version. SketchUp is a 3-D modeling and layout tool that lets you begin with a floor plan and turn it into a three-dimensional room. There is a vast library of elements created by users, such as display cases, windows, doors, and other furniture, which can be incorporated into your design. In the example shown in figure 10.12, the upper image is a concept created in InDesign. The lower image shows the rolling boxes proposed in the upper image made 3-D and placed in a 3-D model of the exhibit space. Both elements were created in SketchUp.

## Accessibility

In previous chapters we have looked at ways to make your exhibit available to the widest possible audience. This principle of accessibility has a physical as well as an intellectual dimension. At one time, the design of public spaces was focused on making them accessible, meaning that they were designed with the needs of persons living with disabilities. This led to physical accommodations and retrofits of existing buildings, often in the form of added entrances, ramps, and handrails. While the intention was admirable, the results were often less so. In some cases, ramps were provided, but the slope was so steep that they were little better than the stairs they had replaced. In other cases, the accessible means of entrance could be used but it was separate, stigmatizing, and often inconveniently removed from the main entrance.

### *Universal Design*

In recent years, designers have moved beyond the idea of accessibility into the more inclusive realm of universal design, which begins with the idea that we all experience varying levels of ability at differing times in our lives and that it is not possible to divide the world neatly into the old dichotomy of "abled" and "disabled." According to the Centre for Inclusive Design and Environmental Access, universal design is: "an approach to design that increases the potential for developing a better quality of life for a wide range of individuals. Universal design addresses barriers faced by people with disabilities, older people, children, and other populations that are typically overlooked in the design process. UD reduces stigma and provides benefits for all users. For example, building entrances without stairs assist equally someone who moves furniture, pushes a baby stroller, or uses a wheelchair."[10] Figure 10.13 gives one simple application of universal design. The upper photo shows two standard picnic tables. The lower photo reveals that one has had the top extended at one end to allow a wheelchair to tuck in underneath it. It is not a special accessible picnic table; it is just a picnic table that everyone can use.

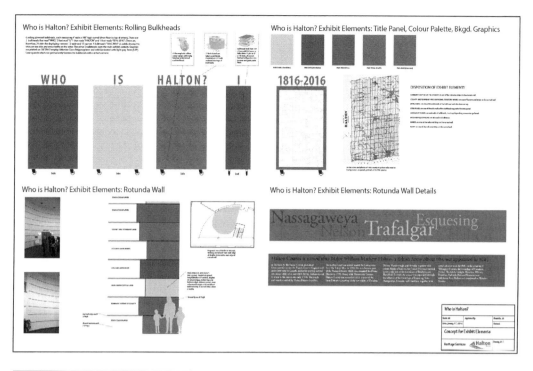

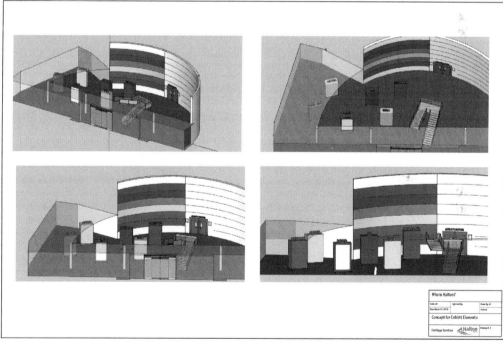

**Figure 10.12** Using SketchUp for exhibit design. Courtesy of the Regional Municipality of Halton.

**Figure 10.13** Universal design principles in action.

There are seven principles of universal design:[11]

It is interesting to note how well these principles correspond to the characteristics of good exhibits we have explored earlier in the book. After all, is there anyone who really wants illegible labels? Or glaring reflective surfaces? And who doesn't need a place to sit down from time to time? The Smithsonian Institution's *Guidelines for Accessible Exhibition Design* offers guidelines and tools for viewing exhibit development through an accessibility lens.[12]

Through its inclusive focus on tailoring design to users' needs, universal design can also avoid specific problems such as "museum fatigue," which was first identified as an issue in Benjamin Ives Gilman's pioneering 1916 journal article of the same name.[13] Gilman conducted and photographed a series of experiments in which he asked visitors to read and understand the content of exhibits. At the end of the experiments he said, "The pictures obtained indicate that an inordinate amount of physical effort is demanded of the ideal visitor by the present methods in which we offer most objects to his inspection. It is at once evident that these methods form an effective bar to the adequate fulfilment by museums of the public function they aim to support."

### Graphic Design

Accessible and universal design principles should also be applied to the graphic design and typography of your exhibit.[14] Organizing type and images on a grid system with clear alignments and repeated "building-block" units offers readers signposts to what kind of information is being presented. As discussed earlier in the chapter, clear hierarchies help readers to structure the information you present. Headlines should always be larger than subheads, for example, and image captions should be smaller than body copy.

Colors should have at least a 70 percent difference in value between the type and the background. A good test is to print the graphics in gray scale rather than color to see if they are still easily readable. If not, the contrast between them will have to be heightened. Up to a point, larger type is easier to read than smaller type, as anyone who has ever forgotten their glasses and bought the wrong item at the grocery store can tell you.

The legibility and readability of the type also matter. Some fonts are more legible than others. Fonts with unusual or highly decorative letterforms will be less legible. Readability refers to the overall effect of the chosen type and the way it is laid out on the page. There are reasons to use elaborate display fonts for one-line titles, but you would not want to read three paragraphs of the same font. If a display font is used for the headline, the content should be repeated in the body copy. Body copy should be rendered in a text font, chosen for its clear and legible letterforms. Other special kinds of type, such as all caps, underlining, and italics should also be used only when necessary. The best alignment for exhibit use is flush left and ragged right. Full justified should not be used, and centered text only sparingly.

As you begin to develop the graphic standard and typical panels for your exhibit, you should print them full size for testing. Ask a variety of staff, volunteers, and visitors for their feedback. If you are unsure what color combinations, fonts, or sizes are best, print side-by-side comparisons and find out which ones your audience prefers.

## Chapter Checklist

1. The principles of design should be used to reinforce the information and experiences offered by your exhibit. Every aspect of the exhibit should be carefully thought out.
2. Grouping the images and information in your exhibit into large and engaging graphic panels can increase their appeal and effectiveness.
3. Adhering to standard sizes makes your exhibit easier to design and build.
4. The typography used in your exhibit should also be carefully chosen to maximize its impact and accessibility.
5. Scanning and digital imaging are powerful tools for exhibit development.
6. Your exhibit should embody the principles of universal design.

## Notes

1. Philip Hughes, *Exhibition Design*, second edition (London: Laurence King Publishing Ltd., 2015), 10.
2. Hughes, *Exhibition Design*, 19.
3. Robin Williams, *The Non-Designer's Design Book: Design and Typographic Principles for the Visual Novice*, third edition (Berkeley, CA: Peachpit Press, 2008).
4. There is a welter of books out there on typography. Here are four that will help you start working with type in exhibits: *The American Alliance of Museums Standards Manual for Signs and Labels* (1995); Sean Adams, Peter Dawson, John Foster, and Tony Seddon, *Thou Shall Not Use Comic Sans. 365 Graphic Design Sins and Virtues: A Designer's Almanac of Do's and Don'ts* (Berkeley, CA: Peachpit Press, 2012); Simon Garfield, *Just My Type: A Book About Fonts* (New York: Gotham Books, 2012); and Ellen Lupton, *Thinking with Type: A Critical Guide for Designers, Editors, Writers and Students*, second edition (New York: Princeton Architectural Press, 2010).
5. A very useful reference for the many ways scanned images can be incorporated into exhibit design is Janet Ashford and John Odum, *Start with a Scan: A Guide to Transforming Scanned Photos and Objects into High-Quality Art*, second edition (Berkeley, CA: Peachpit Press, 2000).
6. US Copyright Office (https://www.copyright.gov/index.html); Canadian Intellectual Property Office (http://www.cipo.ic.gc.ca).
7. Leslie Cabarga, *The Designer's Guide to Color Combinations: 500+ Historic and Modern Color Formulas in CMYK* (Cincinnati: How Design Books, 1999); Jim Krause. *Color Index: Over 1100 Color Combinations, CMYK and RGB Formulas, for Print and Web Media* (Cincinnati: How Design Books, 2002).
8. https://www.pantone.com/color-bridge-coated-uncoated. Accessed March 2017.
9. https://www.sketchup.com/. Accessed April 2017.
10. http://www.universaldesign.com/what-is-ud/. Accessed March 2017.

11. http://universaldesign.ie/What-is-Universal-Design/The-7-Principles/. Accessed March 2017.
12. The Smithsonian Institution, *Smithsonian Guidelines for Accessible Exhibition Design.* Available as a .pdf download from https://www.si.edu/Accessibility/SGAED. Accessed March 2017.
13. Benjamin Ives Gilman, "Museum Fatigue," *The Scientific Monthly* 2, no. 1 (1916): 62–74, at https://www.jstor.org/stable/6127?seq=1#page_scan_tab_contents. Accessed March 2017.
14. The following recommendations are adapted from Registered Graphic Designers of Ontario: *Access Ability: A Practical Handbook on Accessible Graphic Design.* Available as a .pdf download from https://www.rgd.ca/database/files/library/RGD_AccessAbility_Handbook.pdf. Accessed March 2017. Their website at http://rgd-accessibledesign.com/ offers case studies, tips, and information to support accessible design in a Canadian context.

# Chapter 11

*Curatorship*

## What Does an Exhibit Curator Do?

At one time, curators played a dominant role in exhibit development, and the resulting projects were primarily expositions of curatorial knowledge. This model, which has been referred to as "curator is king," has now fallen out of favor. It has been supplanted by one in which the key role in creating an exhibit is that of the exhibit developer who may or may not necessarily be the subject matter expert or curator. The emphasis has shifted from mainly presenting knowledge to using that knowledge to create a visitor experience.[1]

In a 2015 conference presentation titled "The Museum as Digital Storyteller: Collaborative Participatory Creation of Interactive Digital Experiences," Maria Roussou and her colleagues outlined the incremental development of museum storytelling techniques, from the nineteenth century's "labeling and sequential dispositions of objects," to "more explicit spatial narratives" in the mid-twentieth century, to the current digital environment, where "the influence of digital technologies and social media puts information (the narrative) before objects." Through this development, "Museums have graduated from the mere display and presentation of collections to the creation of experiences that respond to their visitors' evolving needs and expectations."[2]

If the curator is now not necessarily in charge of exhibit projects, and if, as we have seen, exhibits are about more than just identifying and displaying objects and curatorial knowledge, what role do curators play in exhibit development today? Curators speak for the artifacts. By virtue of their training, experience, and specialized knowledge, the curators are closest to the collections that form the core of most museum exhibits. Other members of the exhibit team rely on their expertise to identify and describe the artifacts and to ensure the exhibit is historically and academically accurate and credible.

## The Meanings of Artifacts

As well as ensuring accuracy, exhibit curators use their research and understanding of the nature of the collections being exhibited to draw out meanings and frame interpretations. To borrow a phrase from literary criticism, curators explore both what and how artifacts mean.[3] The "what" of an artifact's meaning is fairly straightforward and consists of "tombstone" details about the artifact, such as what it is, what it was used for, when and where it was made, and what it is made of. The "how" is more complex, and looks beyond the object itself into the broader context of its production and use.

**Figure 11.1** Three typical museum artifacts. Photo by author, courtesy of the Regional Municipality of Halton.

To illustrate the "what" and "how" of artifact meaning, figure 11.1 shows three objects that might be found in the collection of a typical small- to medium-sized museum.

If these items were to be put on display, their basic information labels might read like this:

- MANTLE CLOCK. An ornate mantel clock such as this would have been displayed in the formal parlor of a Victorian family. Ebonized wood, faux-painted wood, ormolu bracket feet, and lion's mask details. Sessions Clock Company, Forrestville, Connecticut. Late 19th century. Collection of the Regional Municipality of Halton. 1970.226.1.
- GEOMETRIC MODEL. This sectional boxwood shape, consisting of a cone atop a cylinder, was used to teach basic geometric concepts to schoolchildren. Boxwood, leather strap, and brass nails. Date and manufacturer unknown. Collection of the Regional Municipality of Halton. 1975.702.825.
- SURVEYOR'S CHAIN. Surveyors measured distances with metal chains like this. It is 66 feet (22 yards, 100 links, 4 rods) in length. Steel with copper tally marks. Date and manufacturer unknown. Collection of the Regional Municipality of Halton. 1975.704.749.1.

The information in these labels is the denotative meaning of the artifacts. Denotative meanings are factual "dictionary definitions." Artifacts also have connotative meanings. A connotation is "the suggesting of a meaning by a word apart from the thing it explicitly names or describes."[4]

For example, a country's national flag is, at a denotative level, an assemblage of fabric pieces in a set order and arrangement of shapes and colors. Connotatively, it is a representation of a place, a people, a state of mind, and a host of other larger meanings.

Although factually correct, the exhibit text in these labels does not begin to explore what or how these artifacts might mean, nor does it reach out to engage visitors and connect the artifacts with their own lives. It therefore does not meet either the standard of interpretation defined by Freeman Tilden quoted in chapter 7 of this book: "to reveal meanings and relationships through the use of original objects . . . rather than simply to communicate factual information," or his second principle: "Information, as such, is not interpretation. Interpretation is revelation based on information." If these artifacts were displayed with these labels, it would be an example of the "the mere display and presentation of collections" referred to above.

If we inquired into what and how these artifacts mean, as opposed to what they simply are, they could be displayed together and related to each other with a larger theme. Imagine walking into an exhibit and seeing these same three pieces with the following introductory text:

- Humans are driven by the need to impose order and our will upon the world. We mark time, define space, and measure distance. Without these ordering concepts, we could not worry about being late, purchase a plot of land, or describe the structures we build. What do these three objects, and the ideas of order, space, and arrangement they represent, reveal about us as a species?

Such an exhibit would lead to a very different and potentially much richer visitor experience. It would still contain enough detail about the objects on display to do justice to them as artifacts, but those facts would be shared with visitors in an experience that also explored more of their meaning. In an exhibit such as this, these objects would have been curated and not simply displayed. Good exhibits go beyond the facts of artifacts to explore their meanings.

The Active Collections group has issued a thought-provoking manifesto that challenges museums to reexamine what and why they collect.[5] As one of seven steps they propose for museums to deal with collections more effectively, they touch upon the purpose of exhibits: "Make the Good Stuff Sing. Chances are you have artifacts that could tell incredible stories. Let them. Don't shoehorn them into an existing narrative and rob them of their power or bury them among hundreds of others. Pick a story and tell it. Be bold. All artifacts can be interpreted in many ways. Acknowledge this and choose one, the most compelling one. Don't water it down."

## Selecting Artifacts for Exhibits

In chapter 7 we saw how, even if you do not have an interpretive planner on staff or the resources to hire one on contract, someone on the exhibit team can still bring an interpretive planning perspective to the exhibit. The same is true of the curatorial perspective. If your museum or organization does not have a dedicated curator (or if you have one but they are working on other projects), someone else on the exhibit team or a guest curator can carry out the curatorial function during the development of the exhibit.[6]

One of the most important tasks of an exhibit curator is to choose which artifacts to include. The typical museum collection contains a multitude of objects, and many more are available on loan from other institutions. How do you go about selecting which artifacts to include in your exhibit

**Figure 11.2** Museum collections storage area. Photo by author, courtesy of the Regional Municipality of Halton.

from among all the possibilities offered by an artifact storage area, such as the one in figure 11.2? When you drafted the exhibit brief, you outlined your intended means of expression and the visitor experiences that would be created through them. These were further refined in the interpretive plan. With those objectives in mind you can explore which artifacts might work in the exhibit.

### Key Artifacts

The first place to look is in your institution's own collections. As long as your collections management database is in good shape, it should be fairly easy to create a list of certain kinds of artifacts that you might want to use. For example, perhaps your museum has a significant collection of dolls of various kinds, shapes, sizes, and vintages. You could put them on display as *Treasures of the Doll Collection*, but because you are reading this book you want to go further into what these artifacts mean, so you draft a big idea concerned with representations of women and how they reflect changing notions of domesticity. Just displaying the dolls will not adequately address the topic, so you do not want to stop your search for artifacts with only the dolls. You also want to look through your fine art collection, the rest of the toy collection, the textile and footwear collections, and the archives, at a minimum, for additional artifacts that speak to the big idea. It might not be quite as easy to search through these collections using the database because it will not support a query about "representations of women and changing notions of domesticity," so you will need to browse through, item by item.

At this stage you also do not know precisely what you are looking for, but there are some guidelines you can keep in mind as you search. Exhibits are a visual medium, and you should always be on the lookout for artifacts and images that will have a high visual impact. This does not necessarily mean the largest or the most colorful or the most expensive, just the ones that might provide a focal point. A single artifact could be a dramatic highlight. A particularly vivid or striking image could be enlarged to become a semitransparent scrim or major wall-mounted graphic element.

### Secondary Artifacts

Beyond these keynote pieces, you might also begin to notice material that could be introduced into the exhibit as additional themes. If you have archival collections of magazines and ephemera, for example, you might find that you have enough images of women in advertisements for household appliances that you could make them a major part of the exhibit. You might realize that using cigarette advertisements from different time periods could reinforce the points you are trying to make. Depending on the publication date of this material, it might also be out of copyright, in which case you could rework it to create large-format exhibit graphics. After searching through the collections, you will have both a core group of artifacts and a range of secondary materials and images that can be incorporated into the exhibit.

### Reviewing Choices

If you have sufficient space, it is very helpful at this point to move all of the artifacts that are being considered for the exhibit into one space so that they can be looked at together. If that is not physically possible, you can shoot new digital photos of each one and make reference scans of possible images and archival pieces. By doing this, you can eliminate the visual clutter of the storage area and begin to see what the artifacts look like in relation to each other and what additional themes or connections suggest themselves. As you move into the design phase, these artifact images and scans can also be used in layouts, mock-ups, and scale models. If you are working with contract designers, they will appreciate having the resources concentrated like this. If you are doing the exhibit in-house, staff who are working on the project but may not have the subject-area knowledge will be able to familiarize themselves with the potential artifacts, images, and archival resources.

With this pool of potential items for the exhibit, you can now revisit the exhibit brief and interpretive plan, particularly the sections concerned with the means of expression and visitor experience. Up to this point, you have been working only with artifacts from your own collections, but perhaps there is a theme you feel is crucial to the presentation and your own collection does not have a suitable example, or maybe it has no examples at all. In that case, you will have to consider borrowing an artifact from another institution. If you think this is going to be necessary, now is the time to research other collections and identify possible loans, images of which can then be added to the pool of exhibit resources.

Choosing which artifacts and images to include in an exhibit is like hiring staff. At this stage, you have posted the ad and received a bunch of resumes. Now you have to screen out the less suitable candidates and develop a short list. To do this, you will want to review each artifact for problems that could preclude its use: Under what environmental conditions can the artifact safely be displayed? Are those conditions compatible with the display environment for other artifacts, or will it need special treatment? Is the artifact currently suitable for display? Will it need cleaning, restoration, mount making, or other treatment before it can be used? If so, can those services be carried out within the available time and budget?

You may find that some of your preferred artifacts require environmental conditions that are beyond the scope and budget of the exhibit. If, after referencing your interpretive plan and confirming that there is no viable alternative artifacts to make the same point and you still want to include that artifact, there are alternatives. Reproductions, images of the artifact, and technological solutions such as a short video or a three-dimensional laser scan can be used to show the artifact to visitors. Make sure, however, that you are turning to a technological solution because it is the best means of creating your desired visitor experience and not simply because it is available.

### Making the Final Selection

After you have checked for these issues and removed any problematic artifacts from consideration, you will be left with material that could feasibly be included in the exhibit. The question now becomes: Which of the possible images, artifacts, and other materials you have assembled will best achieve the goal of the exhibit as expressed through the big idea? This stage will be exciting because it will be your first glimpse of what the exhibit might look like in three dimensions, but it is also full of temptations. Just like the exhibit text we discussed in chapter 8, less can be more when it comes to artifacts in exhibits. Just because you have it or because you think it is neat, beautiful, spectacular, fun, or otherwise interesting, or because it is worth a lot or a personal favorite, are not sufficient reasons to include an artifact or image.

When selecting images for your exhibit, be mindful of their tone and connotations. It is always preferable to use an original image instead of an artist's impression. Beware of artistic works that reinforce cultural myths and stereotypes, particularly with regard to exploration, settlement, and conquest. If you do elect to use such an image, it should be discussed and analyzed as a subjective work of art and not simply presented as a historical fact lest your exhibit appear to endorse its biases or anachronisms.

Use images to provide context for artifacts. A display of firearms might appeal to visitors' aesthetic sense, and this is certainly part of the artifact's meaning. They are, however, weapons, and an intellectually honest exhibit will also remind visitors of their destructive power and the consequences of their use.

Like the words in well-written text, every image and artifact in the exhibit must be there for a reason, and the exhibit team should be able to articulate why it is being included. There are many ways to cover the themes and provide the visitor experiences you want for your exhibit, and including an artifact is only one of them. Including all of the dolls in your collection might result in visitors thinking, "Oh, there's a bunch of dolls," and moving on to the next section of the exhibit. Selecting five or six of them that relate directly to the exhibit's theme and purpose, and giving them special display treatment, will highlight their importance and invite visitors to understand why they have been presented in that way.

Would an exhibit about coal mining better capture visitors' interest with a collection of miner's lamps and tools in a glass display case with labels, or with some of the objects used to "outfit" a life-size silhouetted photograph of a miner so they are presented in context, supported by a soundtrack of a working underground mine? Using fewer artifacts and presenting them in ways other than the traditional enclosed glass case can greatly increase the impact and interest of the exhibit. Varying the means of expression will broaden the range of visitor motivations and learning styles to which it will be appealing.

## Chapter Checklist

1. Curatorial knowledge is the foundation of exhibits, but more than just this information is required to create a compelling visitor experience.
2. Exhibits should address both what and how the artifacts on display mean.
3. Artifacts and images should be carefully chosen, and every one included in the exhibit should be there for a reason.
4. Although artifacts are at the core of exhibits, exhibit developers should vary the means of expression and look for ways beyond artifacts and descriptive labels to convey the message of the exhibit.

## Notes

1. "The Making of Exhibitions: Purpose, Structure, Roles and Process," Smithsonian Institution Office of Policy and Analysis, October 2002, 17, at http://www.si.edu/content/opanda/docs/rpts2002/02.10 .makingexhibitions.final.pdf. Accessed October 2016.
2. Maria Roussou et al., "The Museum as Digital Storyteller: Collaborative Participatory Creation of Interactive Digital Experiences," http://mw2015.museumsandtheweb.com/paper/the-museum-as-digi tal-storyteller-collaborative-participatory-creation-of-interactive-digital-experiences/. Accessed January 2017.
3. John Ciardi, *How Does a Poem Mean? (An Introduction to Literature, Part 3)* (Boston: Houghton Mifflin Company, 1959).
4. *Merriam-Webster's Collegiate Dictionary*, eleventh edition (Springfield, MA: Merriam-Webster Incorporated, 2014).
5. http://www.activecollections.org/manifesto/. Accessed March 2017.
6. "The curatorial role in exhibition development . . . may be shared with other museum professionals acting as guest curators, or may even be performed entirely by non-curators, such as artists, educators, academic scholars, consultants, collectors, students, representatives of the public for whom the exhibition is intended, or members of the community from which the collections are drawn." John Nicks, "Curatorship in the Exhibition Planning Process," in *The Manual of Museum Exhibitions*, ed. Barry Lord and Gail Dexter Lord (Walnut Creek, CA: AltaMira Press, 2001), 345.

*Part IV*

# Fabrication

# Chapter 12

*Studio*

## Why Set Up an Exhibit Studio?

Within the last decade, the evolution of computer hardware and software has made it feasible for even small- to medium-sized museums to set up their own in-house design and production facilities, particularly for the graphic panels that make up the core of most exhibits.

That is not to say that just going out and buying some equipment will make you into an exhibit designer, and this option is not suitable for every institution. But if staff are interested, observant, and willing to learn, and the institution can commit to some ongoing professional development, there are real advantages to bringing exhibit design and production in-house at your museum. Here are some of the reasons to do it:

- Creative Control: It is your museum, your collection, and your exhibit, and chances are that you have a pretty good idea what you want the finished product to look and feel like. If you bring exhibit design in-house, all of this is up to you.
- Timeliness: In a typical consultant relationship, you decide what you want, tell someone else, they tell you what they think you want, you tell them what you think of that, they go back and do another version and meet with you again, and so on and so on. Doing it all yourself can dramatically shorten project timelines. Having in-house large-format print capacity also allows for mock-ups, prototypes, and drafts to be quickly, easily, and cheaply created at each stage of the project.
- Capacity Building: By setting up an in-house exhibit design facility, your whole institution will learn about exhibit making. The hardware and software you put together to create exhibit panels can also be used to create signage, program materials, and graphics across the institution. You may also find that you have some real hidden talents among your staff and volunteers.
- Cost Effectiveness: On a typical small- to medium-sized exhibit project, up to 50 to 60 percent of the budget can be spent on contracted services. If you spend that on exhibit supplies and materials instead, you can either lower your overall cost or get a lot more exhibit for the same amount of money.
- Payback: Because of these reduced costs, an exhibit studio can pay for itself in as little as one or two years.

## Software

Design begins with software. Just a word of warning: you cannot create exhibit panels in a word-processing program. You need page layout software. Word-processing programs are based on the typewriter model of lines of text on a page. Layout programs let you create and manipulate blocks of text and images independently of single- or double-spaced lines and place them wherever you want on the page. If you have ever wrestled with putting images into a word-processed document, you will appreciate the control and flexibility of layout software. Hardware should not be an issue, as almost all current laptops, desktops, or notebooks will run these programs, though a bigger monitor makes them much easier to use, and more memory and a high-end graphics card will speed up the processing of large files.

The gold standard in design software for Mac or PC is Adobe Creative Cloud. There are many components available in Creative Cloud, but the most commonly used for exhibit design are Photoshop (for image manipulation), InDesign (for page and panel layout), Illustrator (for vector graphics), Acrobat (for .pdf creation) and Bridge (for digital asset management). Now that Adobe has switched to a cloud-based subscription model, you can start or stop the subscriptions for particular programs as you need them for projects. If Creative Cloud does not fit within your budget, there are downloadable freeware image manipulation programs such as the GNU Image Manipulation Program or Scribus, which runs on both PC and Mac platforms, and web-based programs such as Lucidpress, which is free, and Canva, available free to nonprofits or through a reasonably priced subscription.[1]

You could also use a lower-cost page layout alternative such as Microsoft Publisher, which is bundled with higher-level versions of Microsoft Office. For the Mac, there are reasonably priced layout programs such as Publisher Plus and iStudio Publisher.[2] Whatever program you use, it needs to be able to export your finished panels as high-quality .pdf files, which are the standard format for sending to service providers for printing. If you create your exhibit using digital design software, you will also be able to create an online version of your exhibit with much less effort than it would take to do it from scratch.

## Creating Exhibit Panels

Here is a typical workflow to create an exhibit panel using layout software. The specific references are to Adobe products, but the tools and processes are common to most layout programs.

- Organize your digital workspace.

  - Even a modest exhibit project can quickly generate a large number of digital files. You should decide before you begin the project what folders you will use and how you will name your files. For example, you might want to have folders for "design concepts," "panel images," "final designs," and "pdf files for production." Within each of these folders, you should develop a naming structure that you use throughout the project. For example, your image files might be named "—raw image," "—adjusted image," and "—final image." Low-resolution images, web images, and screen captures are typically noted as "FPO" (for position only) so they are not confused with high-resolution images. Once you decide on these folders and file names, you should enforce them. To keep the file size down, layout programs typically only store a low-resolution copy of the image in the layout and maintain a link to the high-resolution file. If you move your source files after the layout has been done, they will have to be relinked. An organized file structure is essential if more than one person is working on the design files, or if you are working with an outside contractor.

- Develop templates.
    - In chapter 10 we discussed the importance of organizing your exhibit around a small number of panel sizes that are consistently used for the same levels of information and of correlating these sizes with your substrate materials. At the beginning of the project, you should build a digital template for each of these sizes and ensure that it has the same settings for margins, bleed, and other document setup details as the others you will be using. It is useful to develop landscape and portrait versions for each size. These templates can be reused for other projects.
- Develop a color palette.
    - In chapter 10 we also explored resources for choosing what colors to use in an exhibit. When you have determined your color palette, you can save the Pantone, RGB, or CMYK specifications for each color as a swatch file and import it into your layout files.
- Develop a graphic standard.
    - You should develop a graphic standard for each exhibit based on the panel types presented in chapter 7: title; main text; secondary text; artifact label; image caption; image credit. For each type of panel, decide on the typeface, font, point size(s), leading, and word counts that will be used.
- Create styles.
    - InDesign lets you create "styles" to enforce these graphic standards that help keep your panels consistent throughout the exhibit. For a paragraph, for example, you can specify the character formats such as font, style, size, kerning, leading, and tracking. You can also adjust settings for indents, justification, bullets, numbering, and other attributes. Once this is done, you can give this style a name, such as "opening paragraph for secondary text panel," and apply it as needed. It is well worth your time to set these styles up at the beginning of the project, and they can be reused for other exhibits.
- Build panels.
    - Using the templates you have created, you can now begin to create your panels. You can make a separate file for each panel or a master file for one type of panel. For example, you could use the template for the main text panel and set up layers for each of the main text panels in the exhibit. By turning these layers on and off, you can export your layouts to .pdf from the same source, thus ensuring consistency of fonts, colors, and layouts. For each type of panel, you can also create a master page that specifies recurring elements, such as guidelines to keep all of the titles at the same level. In the panel layouts, you can create frames for text and images to organize the panel before placing actual content. Text frames can be filled with greeked text to which you apply the appropriate style in order to size them to the word counts you determined in the graphic standard. Image frames can either be left blank or filled with FPO images.
- Export to .pdf.
    - After the structure of the panels is built, it is a good idea to export them to .pdf to check on sizes, alignments, and consistency. During the .pdf export you can also add crop and bleed marks.

- Print mock-ups for first review.
  - If you can, it is useful to print the panels full size on bond paper and pin them up for review. If you cannot go all the way to full size, you can use 11" × 17" paper. In either case, this hard-copy review will let you spot mistakes that you are unlikely to see on screen.

- Place text and images.
  - Once you have made any required adjustments from the first review, you can begin to replace the greeked text and FPO images with final text and high-resolution files. If you decide that you need to make changes to your graphic standards, changing the required style will automatically impose that change on all instances where the style has been applied. By placing your images within frames, all required changes to the images, such as changing color balance or exposure or retouching, can be done on the master file in Photoshop. Once the adjusted image is resaved, InDesign will prompt you to update the linked file, and the panel layout will be changed to the new version. Because the frame crops the image, all scaling and cropping adjustments can be made right in the layout.

- Export to .pdf.
  - Once the final content has been added, the panels should be exported to .pdf and reviewed again.

- Print proofs.
  - After any required changes are made, final proofs should be produced for approval. These can be "soft" (viewed on screen) or "hard" (printed). These are the final check of colors, but they are also the final opportunity to proofread and spot typographical errors. For this reason, I recommend printing hard proofs and having them signed off before they are released for production.

- Create print files.
  - Once the approvals have been given and any remaining errors fixed, the files should be exported as high-quality .pdfs with all required crops, bleeds, and other marks.

## Equipment

The heart of an exhibit studio is a large-format printer. Higher-end large-format printers use UV-resistant pigment or latex inks and can accept a wide variety of print media, including photo paper, clear and opaque film, scrim and banner material, and adhesive vinyl. Aim to get a printer that can take at least 42" wide media, and go up to 60" if you can. To trim the output, you'll need a large-format rotary trimmer. A sturdy cutting table, where the whole surface is a cutting mat, is also invaluable for working with large printed output.

Your printed output will be mounted to the substrate with a cold laminator. Smaller sizes are manual; larger ones are electric. Make sure to coordinate the widths of your printer, trimmer, and laminator. You will also need a scanner with as large a platen (the surface on which images are placed to be scanned) as you can afford. Better scanners come with more sophisticated software drivers that offer more choices for descreening and other adjustments and offer the option of scanning images straight to Photoshop. Other useful features in a studio are easily accessible racks for storing rolls of print media and lots of wall space for pinning up drafts and mock-ups.

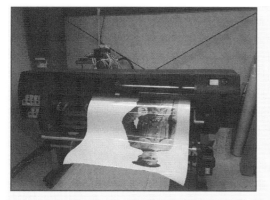

Large-format printer.

Rotary Trimmer

Cutting Table

Cold Laminator

Racks for storing print and laminating media.

Ample space for pinning up drafts and mock-ups.

**Figure 12.1** Exhibit studio equipment. Photos by author, courtesy of the Regional Municipality of Halton.

This equipment can typically be put together for around the cost of a moderately priced car, and it makes for an ideal sponsorship or grant project. The service life of the printer and related equipment is quite long, and you will quickly realize savings that repay the investment as your square-foot costs for producing exhibit panels are reduced substantially. As well as saving money on per-square-foot production costs, your design workflow will be improved through the capacity to quickly make large-format proofs, samples, and mock-ups.

## Materials

What substrates should you use for your exhibit panels? The most commonly used material is also in some ways the least appropriate for exhibit use.

### Fome-Cor

Known by the trade name Fome-Cor, it is composed of an extruded polystyrene core with clay-coated paper faces. It is available in thicknesses from ⅛" to ½" and up to 4' × 8' sheets and larger. Useful for constructing gallery models and very short-term projects, it is not suitable for exhibit panels. Why not? In the standard ³⁄₁₆" thickness, it warps, particularly if you laminate or dry-mount onto it over large areas. Even in thicker sizes, it still dents easily and the corners are particularly vulnerable to damage.

It's hard to treat the edges well, and the raw edges don't look good. If your exhibit is going to be installed for anything more than a month or two, and especially if it is going to travel to different venues, then Fome-Cor is not the best choice.

### MDF

What is a better choice? You can make exhibit panels from wood. One possibility is medium-density fiberboard, usually abbreviated to "MDF." This is an engineered product made from wood fibers that can be easily cut, shaped, sanded, and painted. It makes a nice, stable substrate for exhibit panels, albeit a little heavy. If there are conservation issues to consider because of the close proximity of artifacts, it is also available in formaldehyde-free variants known as "Medite" and "Medex." It is often used to make exhibit furniture such as plinths and case bases. It is available from most lumberyards and big-box home-improvement stores. The most commonly available thicknesses are ½", ⅝", and ¾".

MDF should not be confused with particle board, which is made from compressed wood chips, shavings, and sawdust. It does not have the smooth surface of MDF, so it is often faced with wood veneers or a melamine surface. Particle board is inexpensive but lacks strength and cannot be machined as easily as MDF, and so it is not a suitable substrate for exhibit panels.

You may also come across a product known as MDO, or medium-density overlay. This is plywood faced with resin-impregnated paper. Once used extensively by sign makers, it has been largely supplanted by synthetic materials. The paper faces give the panels a smooth and waterproof surface, so it can be used for exhibit panels, but it is not the best choice because the interior plies are still only construction grade (see below), and the surface grain shows through in raking light. This is acceptable for an outdoor sign that will most often be seen from a distance, but the surface grain will be quite noticeable in a gallery setting. As with all plywood products, the edges will need to machined or covered with molding to conceal the exposed veneers.

### Plywood

You can use other types of plywood for exhibit panels, but you need to be picky about which kinds. The surface the graphics are laminated onto needs to be perfectly smooth, because even the smallest variation in grain or surface roughness will be visible through the graphic layer. For this reason, at least the face of the plywood you will be laminating on should be "A" grade. This is sometimes combined with a lower grade on the other face, so plywood might be marked "A/B," meaning that more imperfections are permitted on one face than the other.

You should also pay attention to how many interior layers, or plies, are in the sheet. More and thinner plies mean that the sheet will be stronger and more dimensionally stable. The best choice for exhibit use is "cabinet-grade" plywood, which has more plies and smoother outer faces than "construction-grade" plywood. For example, ¾" construction-grade plywood will typically have seven or eight plies and Douglas fir outer faces. Fir has a strong grain that might show through exhibit graphics. Cabinet-grade ¾" plywood, by comparison, will have as many as fifteen plies and outer faces made of Baltic birch or maple, which have less noticeable grain. Cabinet-grade plywood is available from specialty lumber dealers and sometimes in big-box home-improvement stores.

### Gatorfoam

There are a number of synthetic products on the market that can be used for exhibit panels. One of the most widely available is sold under the trade name "Gatorfoam." Like Fome-Cor, it has a foam core sandwiched between paper faces. Unlike Fome-Cor, Gatorfoam's two outer layers of resin-bonded paper are strong and waterproof, and it doesn't warp. In the ½" thickness, it is strong enough for most sizes of exhibit panels, and it can be obtained up to 2" thick. Gatorfoam is easily cut on a tablesaw, bandsaw, or scrollsaw, and the edges can be shaped with a router. It can also be scored and snapped by hand. It is typically available in black core with black faces, white core with white faces, and white core with natural kraft paper faces.

### Expanded PVC

Another commonly used substrate for exhibit panels is an opaque, closed-cell, expanded poly-vinyl chloride board sold under the trade names "Sintra," "Komatex," and "E-PVC." It comes in a variety of thicknesses and colors and can easily be cut and machined. The most typical thick-nesses for use in exhibit panels are 3 mm (approximately ⅛"), 6 mm (approximately ¼"), and 13 mm (approximately ½").

## Techniques

### Hanging

Once you have produced your panels, how do you mount them to the wall? The easiest way is with "French cleats," also known as "split battens." These can be made from scraps of whichever panel substrate you are using. The material the cleats are made from should be at least ½" thick. For Gatorfoam cleats used with lightweight panels, they can be fasted to the panel with hot-melt glue and to the wall with screws and anchors. Wooden cleats are best affixed to panels with glue and/or airgun brad nails and to the wall with screws and anchors. Cleats should be set back at least 1" from each side of the panel so the ends will not be visible and the panel will appear to float on the wall.

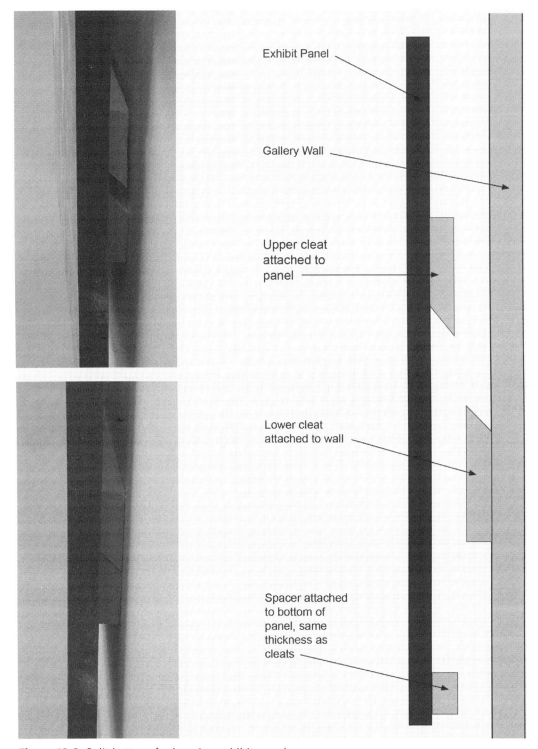

**Figure 12.2** Split battens for hanging exhibit panels.

### Panel Edge Treatments

Some types of panel substrates can be left with the cut edges exposed. The edges of MDF panels can be shaped, sanded, and then painted or varnished because the material is homogenous with no inner plies. Plywood edges can be left exposed if a "raw" edge is part of the design concept, but for most exhibits it will be better to apply a molding to cover the end grain of the plies after the graphics are complete to achieve a more finished look. Gatorfoam edges should be covered both to make the panels appear finished and also because the edge of the resin-impregnated paper face is sharp and can produce a cut if a finger is run along it. There are U-shaped plastic moldings available that can be hot-glued in place, but the corners must be mitered and they cover an additional ³⁄₁₆" to ¼" of the panel surface, so you might need to take account of this in the layout.

Place the panel face down and start applying the tape a short distance away from a corner.

Pull the tape out to the next corner, tack the corner down and then align the middle.

When you reach the starting point, overlap the tape at least one inch and cut it vertically.

Once all of the edges are taped, make a small vertical slit at each corner.

Fold the edges of the tape down onto the back of the panel, overlapping it at the corners.

The finished gaffer tape panel edging.

**Figure 12.3** Finishing the edges of exhibit panels. Photos by author, courtesy of the Regional Municipality of Halton.

A quicker alternative for edging Gatorfoam panels is to use "gaffer" tape. This is an adhesive cloth tape, not to be confused with duct or duck tape. It is used in film, television, and theater for covering cables on the floor and a multitude of other tasks. Although it has a strong adhesive, it does not leave any sticky residue when removed. It comes in a variety of widths and colors and has a matte, nonreflective surface.

To make a gaffer tape edge for a ½" thick Gatorfoam panel, 1" tape is applied continuously around the panel with one edge flush with its front face. Being careful not to pull too hard at the corners, work around each side of the panel and overlap the tape at least 1" when you reach the starting point. With a sharp knife, make a slit at each corner in the tape standing beyond the back face and then fold the excess tape down on the back of the panel one side at a time. The tape is easily renewed if it becomes damaged and can be removed if the panel is to be reused for another project.

### Cold Laminating

You will need to come to terms with your cold laminator and spend some time practicing in order to get your techniques down before you carry out a project on a schedule. The laminator applies consistent pressure over the whole width of the panel to adhere the graphic to the substrate. One way to do this is to print on adhesive media, typically a matte or gloss vinyl. After the graphic is printed, a small strip of the liner is peeled back to reveal the adhesive and the graphic is positioned at the head of the panel. The exposed adhesive is tacked in place and the panel positioned in the laminator with the graphic flopped back. As the panel travels through the laminator, the liner is pulled away from the graphic and the rollers press the adhesive down smoothly on the substrate. Another way to get the graphics to adhere is to print them on nonadhesive media and then use the laminator to lay down a thin layer of adhesive onto the substrate. After this is done, the liner is removed from the substrate and the graphic is adhered as above.

You can also purchase precut substrate boards already prepared with adhesive, though the cost is higher than preparing your own. As you work with your laminator and graphic media, you will become familiar with the quirks of the machine and the materials and learn how to deal with issues such as skew and static buildup and also to make sure that the substrates are absolutely free of dust before they are laminated.

After the panels are laminated, they are placed face down (this is where the large cutting table becomes very useful) and the bleed edges of the graphic are trimmed back flush with the edge of the substrate using a sharp blade. If you are using gaffer tape, this is applied after the edges are trimmed. If you are using plywood or MDF panels, their edges will need to be routed, sanded, and painted before the laminating is done.

With the graphic face down, peel the backing from one corner.

Peel the backing all the way across and fold it down about two inches.

Place the graphic on the substrate, align the top edge and gently rub the exposed adhesive down.

Place the panel and graphic into the laminater with the adhered end first.

Flip the graphic back and send the panel through while holding onto the backing.

Trim the excess graphic using the edge of the substrate as a guide.

**Figure 12.4** Cold-laminating exhibit panels. Photos by author, courtesy of the Regional Municipality of Halton.

## Chapter Checklist

1. Establishing an exhibit studio can lower project costs, build organizational capacity, and increase creative control of exhibit projects.
2. Organize your design project by creating folders and files, developing a color palette, setting up templates, and establishing a graphic standard.

## Notes

1. https://www.gimp.org/; https://www.scribus.net/; https://www.lucidpress.com/; https://about.canva .com/. All accessed April 2017.
2. http://www.pearlmountainsoft.com/publisherplus/; http://www.istudiopublisher.com/. Both accessed April 2017.

# Chapter 13

## *Workshop*

### Why Set Up an Exhibit Workshop?

The same advantages of creative control, timeliness, capacity building, and cost effectiveness gained by setting up an exhibit studio also apply to a workshop. The benefits you realize from establishing one or the other will increase if you establish both. The capacity to produce mock-ups of exhibit panels will be complemented by having the facilities to rapidly make prototypes of interactives, exhibit furniture, and other elements. The more you use both, the more you will accumulate offcuts and remnants. These are useful for mock-ups and samples, and if you plan your projects carefully, the material leftovers from one will save you money on materials for the next. If your team has built the exhibits in their own workshop, they also know how to fix them if they are damaged.

Building an exhibit workshop also represents an excellent opportunity to create community connections through a volunteer workforce. By carefully recruiting, screening, training, and supervising shop volunteers, you can increase your museum's engagement and realize significant cost savings. Chances are that there are skilled and retired sewers, painters, woodworkers, metalworkers, and other tradespeople and craftspeople out there in your community who might like to get involved in the museum. They can do work themselves and also teach and mentor staff and other volunteers. You will need to review the issue of volunteers working in the shop with your insurance provider to make sure you have the appropriate coverage in place.

### Tools and Equipment

As anyone who has a workshop can tell you, outfitting it with the right tools and equipment is a project that is never done, but with some careful planning you can get the shop established with some good, basic tools and then expand your capacity as needed for each project. One of the most important steps you can take in setting up your workshop is to buy good-quality tools. The premium in price you pay up front will be amply repaid in the many projects you will carry out over the service life of the equipment. Building the pieces of exhibit furniture we will discuss in the next chapter will require high-quality consumer-grade, contractor-grade, or professional-grade tools. Higher-end consumer-grade tools are sometimes also called "pro-sumer." These offer more features and are more durable than consumer-grade equipment but without the steep price of professional tools.

For the higher price, you get not only increased durability and power but also precision. For example, a portable table saw with a sheet-steel table and lightweight rip fence simply cannot be made to do work as good as a high-end model with a cast-steel table and a high-quality fence. If you have some tools already, you can also improve them by upgrading certain components.

For example, you can purchase an after-market rip fence and a zero-clearance insert that will enhance the performance of your existing table saw.

The tools you need to get started depend on what you want to produce in your shop. To make the walls, plinths, and cases discussed in the next chapter, you will be working with 4' × 8' sheets of plywood and other materials. This will require not only a shop that is big enough to handle these sheets but also tools to safely and accurately rip (cut lengthwise) and crosscut (cut crosswise) full sheets into smaller pieces.

The following tools are the foundation of a fabrication workshop that will allow you to construct your own portable walls, plinths, bases, and other items of exhibit furniture.

### Table Saw

- Used for:
  - ripping stock, long straight cuts, dadoes and rebates, beveled cuts, angled cuts, cross-cutting small stock
- Notes:
  - The workhorse tool of a woodworking shop is the table saw. You should purchase the highest-quality table saw you can afford. Look for a solid cast-steel table, sturdy fence, and large "wings" on either side of the table. These are often sold as "contractor" saws. If you can afford it, purchase a "cabinet saw." These are manufactured to higher standards with heavier-duty parts and wiring and feature an enclosed base and more powerful motor. They are heavy and typically require 220 volts instead of the normal 110 volt power, but will repay your investment with increased ease of use and accuracy of results. You will be using the table saw to cut large and heavy sheets of material, so you will need to make it safe and easy to do so. The first step is to support the material as it enters and exits the saw so that your attention as the operator can be solely focused on making the cut. In a smaller shop, portable roller stands can be set up where they are needed and put away afterward. If you have the space, it is very helpful to surround your table saw with more tables. A worktable the same height as the saw table on the outfeed side will support the material after it is cut. Similar tables on either side will support wider pieces during crosscutting. These can be made from lumber and should have laminate tops to reduce friction. For high-quality work, use a cabinet blade with sixty or more carbide-tipped teeth.
- Use and Safety Tips:
  - Lower blade below table level after use.
  - Do not stand directly in kickback path.
  - Never place hands between blade and fence when width is less than 6"; use push-stick instead.
  - Use two people when ripping stock wider than 24", one to push stock through saw and one to push it against the fence.
  - Do not use rip fence when crosscutting.
  - Always keep two hands on stock when cutting.
  - Nothing except push-stick on saw table when cutting.
  - Push stock all the way through saw and onto outfeed table before stopping.
  - Clear outfeed path before cutting.
  - Use stands for infeed support.

### Panel Saw

- Used for:
  - crosscutting and ripping large sheets of material
- Notes:
  - The panel saw's main use is crosscutting large sheets. The table saw is the best way to rip this material, but crosscutting these big pieces is easier and safer on the panel saw. A panel saw is a sizeable investment, but if you will regularly be working with large sheets of plywood, MDF, Sintra, or Gatorfoam, it is worth it. Panel saws consist of a circular saw that moves vertically on guide rails. Some saws allow you to rotate this ninety degrees and make rip cuts by pushing material through it. High-end panel saws also allow the saw to move horizontally so the material stays in one place while it is being cut. Unlike on a table saw, the large sheets are fully supported throughout the process.
- Use and Safety Tips:
  - Observe the manufacturer's recommendations for the thickness and number of sheets that can be cut at one time.
  - Clamp multiple sheets together and/or use the saw's built-in hold-downs to secure material before cutting.
  - When ripping by moving material past the saw blade, make sure the entire outfeed path is clear before cutting. You may need 8' or more beyond the saw for a full sheet of plywood.

### Miter Saw

- Used for:
  - Crosscutting material up to 8" wide, or wider if it is a sliding miter saw, at ninety degrees or other angles. On a sliding compound miter saw, both the angle of the cut and the angle of the blade can be adjusted to cut compound miters.
- Notes:
  - Mounting the miter saw on a portable stand made for the purpose allows you to make repeated cuts to the same length using the adjustable stops and supports. Because it can remove very small amounts of material from the end of a piece of stock, the miter saw is also useful for trimming pieces for close fits.
- Use and Safety Tips:
  - Keep fingers at least 2" away from blade.
  - Hold stock down and against fence when cutting.
  - Adjust stand as necessary to support whole length of stock.

### Drill Press

- Used for:
  - drilling vertical holes in wood, metal, and plastic
- Notes:
  - Like a portable drill, the drill press uses bits to make holes, but they can be made at a precise ninety degrees or other angles. A drill press is particularly useful with Forstner

bits, also known as "clockmaker's bits." Available in a variety of diameters, these bits make precise, clean-sided holes with no tear-out. Adjustable stops mean that the drill press can also make repeated holes to exactly the same depth.

- Use and Safety Tips:
  - Always use a piece of scrap wood underneath the stock being drilled.
  - Ensure that the opening in the table is centered on the drill bit.
  - Lock table in place after adjusting height.
  - Center-punch holes before drilling.
  - Clamp stock to table or hold securely.
  - Tie long hair back; no scarves, ties, or other dangling clothing.
  - Make sure chuck key is out of chuck before drilling.
  - When drilling deep holes, especially with Forstner bits, periodically raise bit out of hole to clear chips.

## Band Saw

- Used for:
  - Making curved, beveled, angled, and notched cuts in wood, plastic, and metal. Depending on what blade is used, the band saw can also be used for ripping and crosscutting.
- Notes:
  - Band saws are sized by the "throat depth," or distance between the vertical frame and the blade. Smaller band saws are usually nine or ten inches, and the most common size is fourteen inches. A variety of blades are available for band saws, ranging from ⅛" or ³⁄₁₆", which can cut tight curves, to ½" or ¾", used for ripping stock.
- Use and Safety Tips:
  - Keep fingers out of blade path.
  - Adjust height of upper bearing/guide blocks to match stock thickness +⅛".
  - Always move stock forward into the blade at the same time as curve is being cut to avoid twisting blade.
  - Use a miter gauge for crosscutting.
  - Make relief cuts before cutting sharp or tight curves.
  - Feed stock slowly and steadily.
  - Plan cuts before starting, and think about which ones to do first, especially for curves.

## Scroll Saw

- Used for:
  - making intricate cuts, such as for silhouetted cut-outs on exhibit panels
- Notes:
  - Unlike the continuous loop of a band saw blade, a scroll saw blade can be detached and inserted through a drilled hole so that it can cut in the middle of a piece of stock without making an exit path. The blades are extremely thin and can cut very tight radius curves. Like the band saw, scroll saws are measured by their throat depth.
- Use and Safety Tips:
  - Keep fingers out of blade path.

### Belt/Spindle Sander

- Used for:
  - truing edges of stock and assemblies, rounding edges and corners of stock, and sanding inside concave curves with spindle mounted

- Notes:
  - The sanding belt and the table are at right angles to each other, allowing it to be used to smooth and square up the edges of stock. Varying grades of belts can be mounted to either remove material or sand to a very smooth finish. With the belt removed and the spindle mounted, the sander can be used to smooth and shape the inside of curves.

- Use and Safety Tips:
  - Adjust belt so that it is centered on rollers, especially after changing belt.
  - Do not stand in kickback path.
  - Do not let others stand in kickback path.
  - Use belt-cleaning crepe bar after each job.

### 18-Gauge Brad Nailer

- Used for:
  - driving small nails ranging in length from 1" to 2", attaching wooden parts, holding wood parts together while glue dries, fast assembly of wooden parts, attaching Sintra or Gatorfoam exhibit panels to walls

- Notes:
  - The air-powered brad nailer has several advantages over conventional nails and screws. The brads have very small heads so the holes can be made almost invisible with putty. By adjusting the pressure on the compressor, brads can be driven below the surface to obviate the need for countersinking. Because it can be used one-handed, the nailer is very useful for assembling glued pieces without clamps. The brad nailer is very fast and speeds the production of exhibit furniture. Because the thin brads are easily removed, it is also useful for quickly making mock-ups and prototypes. It is also available in a 16-gauge size that uses longer and thicker nails and brads.

- Use and Safety Tips:
  - Place tip firmly on workpiece before pulling trigger.
  - Select appropriate length of nail or brad for work.
  - Make sure to match gauge of nail or brad to tool (16 gauge vs. 18 gauge).

### Compressor and Hose Reel

- Used for:
  - powering air tools such as the brad nailer and dusting off work

- Notes:
  - Air tools are a time-saving convenience in an exhibit workshop. With a trigger nozzle, the compressor can also be used to blow dust off constructed pieces before they are transported or painted. A retractable hose reel is useful for avoiding the tripping hazard of tangled hoses on the floor.

- Use and Safety Tips:
    - Adjust the pressure to suit the work being done.
    - Never point the trigger nozzle directly at a person.

### *Laminate Trimmer*

- Used for:

    - shaping edges of stock and assemblies, rounding over edges, flush trimming of edges

- Notes:

    - The laminate trimmer is a small, lightweight router. Originally developed for trimming the edges of laminate countertops, it can be held in one hand. It is very useful for putting a slight round-over on the edges of exhibit walls and cases, and for flush-trimming plywood facing. For thicker stock or heavy-duty work such as cutting a shaped edge, a full-size router is a better choice.

- Use and Safety Tips:

    - Frequently check tightness of foot plate.
    - Frequently check tightness of chuck.
    - Frequently check tightness of bearing on piloted bits.
    - Turn tool off and wait for bit to stop turning before laying tool on its side.

### *Random-Orbit Sander*

- Used for:

    - moderate to heavy sanding, finish sanding, rounding edges and corners of stock, finish removal

- Notes:

    - The random-orbit sander does not leave swirl marks in the surface being sanded. A wide variety of sandpaper grits are available and attach to the pad with either hook-and-loop fasteners or peel-and-stick adhesive. It is useful for the finish sanding of edges that have been shaped by the router or laminate trimmer, particularly in plywood.

- Use and Safety Tips:

    - Make sure the tool has completely stopped before setting it down.
    - Make sure the sander's built-in dust-collection bag is in place, or use a tool-triggered dust extractor.
    - Ventilate the work area when using the sander.
    - Replace sandpaper pads frequently.

### *Tool-Triggered Dust Extractor*

- Used for:

    - dust control for power tools such as the table saw, band saw, and belt/spindle sander, shop cleanup, and dust removal

- Notes:

    - If it is not possible to install a fixed dust-collection system in your workshop, a tool-triggered dust extractor can be used. The tool can be plugged into the unit and the unit plugged into the wall outlet so that it starts and stops when the tool does. Most power tools now have dust ports for attaching the hose, and a variety of adaptors are available.

- Use and Safety Tips:
  - Empty drum and clean filter frequently during heavy use.

### Cordless Drill

- Used for:
  - drilling and countersinking holes, driving screws
- Notes:
  - It is worth having two or more cordless drills so that one can be set up to drill holes and one to drive screws. The higher the voltage, the more powerful the drill. A twenty-volt drill will stand up to heavy use.
- Use and Safety Tips:
  - Select an appropriate clutch setting when driving screws so as not to overdrive.

### Clamps

- Used for:
  - holding work in place while glueing, fastening, or shaping
- Notes:
  - Trigger-operated quick clamps, which can be used one-handed, are very useful. Their soft rubber faces will not dent or mar the piece they are holding. They come in various sizes, based on the maximum width to which they can be opened. Spring clamps, C-clamps, and bar clamps are also useful.
- Use and Safety Tips:
  - A wall-mounted clamp rack will keep them easily accessible and out of the way.

### Hand Tools

- You will need a variety of hand tools, a few more of which can be purchased with each project that you do:
  - Screwdrivers
  - Staple puller
  - Tack puller
  - Handsaw
  - Measuring tape
  - Hook-end or zero-end stainless steel rulers
  - Bevel gauge
  - Adjustable square
  - Framing square
  - T-square
  - Long straightedge
  - Hex keys in metric and inch sizes

- ∘ Socket wrenches
- ∘ Torpedo and framing levels
- ∘ Hammers in several sizes
- ∘ Rubber mallet
- ∘ Staple gun

Other useful items of workshop equipment are:

- wheeled mobile bases for tools such as table saws, band saws, and scroll saws, especially in smaller shops;
- a fireproof metal cabinet for storing paint, solvents, and other flammable materials;
- a fireproof waste bin for disposing of oily and solvent-soaked materials;
- a vertical or horizontal rack for large sheets of plywood and other substrates; and
- a cabinet with bins of varying sizes to hold the multitude of screws, nails, other fasteners, and small parts that you will quickly begin to accumulate.

## Training

You may find among your staff or volunteers someone with the skills and experience to train and mentor your team in the workshop. If not, many community colleges and arts centers offer woodworking classes. You may also be able to bring an instructor to your shop for courses focused specifically on your needs. Depending on the skill level of your team, you can use a series of projects of gradually increasing complexity to build their knowledge and confidence. This kind of hands-on training not only builds your in-house capacity for fabrication but is also an excellent way to increase staff morale through team building and shared experience. By investing in training and development for your staff instead of turning to outside contractors and consultants, you can send an important message about how the institution values its employees.

## Safety

Health and safety are critical components of your workshop program. Before establishing an exhibit workshop, you should familiarize yourself with the relevant municipal, state/provincial, and federal regulations regarding health and safety. You should also review the scope of your workshop activities, and particularly the involvement of volunteers, with your insurer. As well as complying with regulations and health and safety standards, you will want to establish your own shop procedures. Here are some recommendations:

- Never work alone: always have two people in the shop.
- Always ask for an orientation before using a tool for the first time.
- Ask for help if you need it.
- Dress appropriately for working in the shop: safety shoes; no long or loose clothing or jewelry.
- Unplug power tools before adjusting or servicing.
- Always use appropriate personal protective equipment.
- Return tool/machine settings to the way you found them before leaving.
- Do not leave tools/machines partially adjusted: make sure the tool is safe for the next user.
- Report injuries and accidents as soon as possible, no matter how small.
- Report broken or out-of-order tools/machines as soon as possible.
- Put your tools away before leaving the shop for the day.
- Clean up your mess before leaving the shop for the day.

Table Saw

Panel Saw

Mitre Saw

Drill Press

Band Saw

Scroll Saw

Belt/Spindle Sander

18 Gauge Brad Nailer

Compressor and Hose Reel

**Figure 13.1** Exhibit workshop tools. Photos by author, courtesy of the Regional Municipality of Halton.

Laminate Trimmer

Random-Orbit Sander

Tool-Triggered Dust Extractor

Cordless Drill

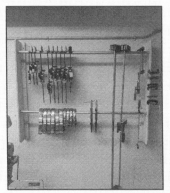
Clamps

Paint Cabinet and Waste Bin

Sheet Goods Rack

Parts and Fasteners Cabinet

**Figure 13.2** Exhibit workshop tools and equipment. Photos by author, courtesy of the Regional Municipality of Halton.

**Chapter Checklist**

1.  Establishing an exhibit workshop can lower project costs, build organizational capacity, and increase creative control of exhibit projects.
2.  Establishing an exhibit workshop represents an excellent opportunity to create community connections through a volunteer workforce.
3.  Establishing an exhibit workshop can build your staff morale and team cohesion.
4.  Your workshop must comply with all relevant health and safety regulations, and you should establish your own policies and procedures to ensure this.

# Chapter 14

*Exhibit Furniture*

Exhibits make use of a wide variety of constructed elements to contain and present artifacts. For the purposes of this book, we will refer to all of these as "exhibit furniture," including the actual furniture that visitors sit on while they are enjoying your exhibit. Exhibit furniture protects fragile artifacts from handling and adverse environmental conditions. Beyond preservation, exhibit furniture sets the artifacts off and transforms the materials and information you bring together for the exhibit into the "comprehensible three-dimensional journey" that designer Phillip Hughes referred to in chapter 10.

Along with protecting artifacts, thoughtfully placed exhibit furniture can create drama, reinforce storylines, draw attention to artifacts, and shape visitors' physical experience. At the same time, well-designed exhibit furniture should be a strong and silent partner, presenting the artifacts and shaping the experience without drawing too much attention to itself. Look for furniture with clean lines, a solid feeling, and simple detailing. Paint makes a better finish than varnished wood, and a satin or semigloss finish is better than gloss. Before purchasing or constructing exhibit furniture, you should review the materials and finishes to ensure that they do not pose any environmental risks to the artifacts they will house.

## Types of Furniture

Figures 14.1, 14.2, and 14.3 provide examples of some of the most commonly used types of exhibit furniture.

### *Plinths*

The most basic piece is the plinth, a pedestal or platform that raises an artifact off the floor. Placing an artifact on a plinth singles it out as being worthy of attention. A chair on the floor might just be a chair, but on a low plinth it suddenly becomes an artifact worthy of your attention. With a vitrine made of glass or Plexiglass on top of it, a plinth becomes an exhibit case. Plinths can also support flipbooks and other interactive devices.

Several plinths and vitrines of differing sizes can be grouped together to create a dense cluster that presents a number of artifacts in a grouping. Some types of artifacts, such as ship models, have exhibit cases that were created at the same time as the artifact. For them, a simple plinth can set the model at a suitable eye height.

### Dashboard Panels

"Dashboard" panels, also known as "reader boards," are typically placed in front of exhibit elements at an angle. They can also be combined with graphic panels to make complete units that can hold A/V or interactive units. As we saw in chapter 10, movable walls are an important part of making a gallery into an engaging visitor environment. Walls can be positioned to direct traffic by suggesting circulation paths to visitors. They can also hold graphic panels, A/V equipment, and wall-mounted cases.

Low plinth with chair       High plinth with vitrine       Plinth with flipbook

Plinths with vitrine and a "telephone booth" tall case       Cased artifact on plinth

Graphic panels with "dashboards"       Movable walls with wall-mounted cases

**Figure 14.1** Types of exhibit furniture.

## *Display Cases*

Display cases can be mounted on walls to free up floor space and to vary the visual pacing of the exhibit by placing groups of artifacts at different heights. Some wall-mounted cases are L-shaped, with a backboard fastened to a horizontal shelf and a vitrine making up the other two sides. Others are bins with angled tops into which artifacts can be placed. Artifacts can also be set on a wall-mounted shelf with a vitrine, and the whole assembly can be mounted on a backboard that extends beyond the vitrine for additional graphic emphasis.

In the late nineteenth and early twentieth centuries, museum exhibit furniture at larger institutions was often finely crafted from high-quality hardwoods such as oak and cherry using traditional furniture-making techniques. Tables that would not be out of place in a formal dining room were topped with vitrines made from elaborate wooden moldings and glass. Such cases were often used for the display of mineralogical or natural history specimens.

Other cases from this era stood on the floor and had a lighting "attic" set on top to supply illumination beyond the ambient gallery lighting. As case work got upgraded, these pieces of display furniture were handed down to other museums, and many are still in service. Museums also sometimes make use of late nineteenth- and early twentieth-century retail fixtures and furniture. Like the cases referred to above, they are often finely crafted from high-quality materials. Though no longer used by drug or department stores, they are often found at smaller community museums.

Some museums create walk-in, room-like spaces with glass fronts that resemble department-store windows. These spaces can contain large artifacts on the floor, plinths for smaller artifacts, and even very large artifacts such as vehicles. Costumes, clothing, and mannequins are often displayed in so-called "telephone booth" cases. These are tall cases with lighting at the top, typically with a pedestal at the bottom and glazing on three or four sides.

Some exhibit furniture provides contextual support for the material on display. Molded fiberglass "rocks" provide a base for a functioning aquarium. An exhibit about protest and social transformation uses cases made from cheap, disposable materials mounted on aluminum scaffolding to reinforce its message. Custom-made units on wheels can have graphics on the outside but open up when needed to reveal supplies, materials, and equipment for public programs that take place in the gallery.

If the budget permits, custom millwork and cases can be manufactured in almost any shape and material. Custom work is typically associated with long-term, "permanent" galleries or very high-value traveling exhibits. Sometimes, display cases will be built into the fabric of the building. These can range from trophy case–style installations in hallways to rooms large enough to walk into. Finally, exhibit furniture can also be found off the rack at furniture and decorating stores. Ready-to-use shelving, dressers, sideboards, and other pieces can be adapted for use in exhibits.

Wall-mounted off-the-rack cases

Wall-mounted bins

Wall-mounted shelf with vitrine and backboard

Vintage tables with vitrines

Vintage floor case with internal lighting attic

Vintage countertop case

Large "store window" with plinths and dashboards inside

"Telephone booth" case for clothing

**Figure 14.2** Types of exhibit furniture.

Faux rock base for aquarium

Inexpensive materials correspond to exhibit theme

Portable programming unit for use in galleries

Custom millwork benches with replica "suitcases" for interactive activity

Custom millwork and glazing

Millwork built into foyer of public building

Millwork combining display case and discovery drawers

Store-bought furniture used for visitor feedback station

**Figure 14.3** Types of exhibit furniture.

## Sources for Exhibit Furniture

Where does all this exhibit furniture come from? In order of cost from highest to lowest, here are some options:

- Custom Fabrication: Exhibit furniture can be made to order in many different materials, including wood, plastic, composites, and glass. The exhibit designer supplies shop drawings and specifications from which a fabricator makes the required elements.
- Purchase Off the Rack: Elements such as freestanding and wall-mounted display cases can be purchased ready-made in stock shapes and sizes from museum, library, and archive suppliers. You can also purchase modular display systems that include a variety of matching and compatible elements, such as walls, lighting, and associated hanging equipment from companies that supply trade fairs and consumer shows. Household furniture can also be repurposed for use in exhibits.
- Preowned: Many museum communities and networks maintain listservs where you can advertise to buy, sell, or trade exhibit furniture. Retail fixtures can sometimes be used, though care should be taken to make them suitable for museum use in both look and function. If you do purchase exhibit furniture from different places at different times, look for ways to unify the pieces through color and trim.
- Made In-House: If your institution has an in-house workshop or access to skilled volunteers who have their own tools and workspaces, you can also make your own exhibit furniture. Although it requires facilities, equipment, and training, this can be a very cost-effective option.

## Making Your Own Exhibit Furniture

As we saw in chapter 10, getting your exhibit off the walls of the gallery and out into the floor space creates a more interesting and effective visitor experience. In order to do this, you can use two basic pieces of exhibit furniture: walls and boxes. The illustrations and instructions that follow will show you how to build simple, sturdy examples that can be adapted for a wide variety of uses. Over the course of several exhibit projects, you can build up a good inventory of exhibit furniture pieces that can be used for many different exhibits. Because these pieces are freestanding and not built into the gallery, you will have maximum flexibility to arrange them to suit each new show. You can easily make scale representations of these pieces to use with your gallery model for exhibit development.

### Exhibit Walls

Figure 14.4 gives the dimensions and structure of a basic exhibit wall section. The entire wall is made from Baltic birch plywood. The ¾" plywood for the frame is ripped on the table saw, and the wall is skinned with ¼" Baltic birch. The frame and skins are fastened with carpenter's glue and air-gun brad nails. The dimensions have been chosen to make the most efficient use of 4' × 8' sheets of plywood. The leftover ¾" plywood strips can be used for the interior blocking and also for the exhibit box that we will talk about next. The walls are 47" wide so that the plywood skins can be put on oversized and trimmed to the exact shape of the framework with a router. The 78" height will fit comfortably under a standard 9' ceiling equipped with track lighting. Depending on how it is outfitted, a finished wall section will weigh from sixty to eighty pounds and can be comfortably carried by two people. Finished walls can be transported in the back of a cargo van and carried up narrow stairs and around corners.

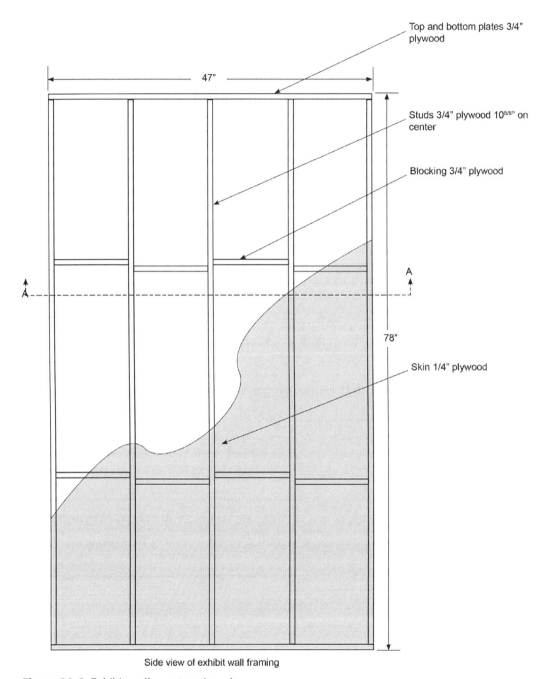

Top and bottom plates 3/4" plywood

47"

Studs 3/4" plywood 10$^{5/8"}$ on center

Blocking 3/4" plywood

A

78"

Skin 1/4" plywood

Side view of exhibit wall framing

**Figure 14.4** Exhibit wall construction plan.

The walls can be painted and/or covered with vinyl and graphic panels. Baseboards and moldings can be added to finish the tops and bottoms. Adjustable feet allow the walls to be leveled on uneven floors. If the ends of the walls are capped with a standard 2½" × ½" casing molding, graphics can be applied on a ⅛" Sintra sheet on each side and there will still be a small reveal that will cover the exposed edges of the Sintra. A single wall section is not freestanding on its own

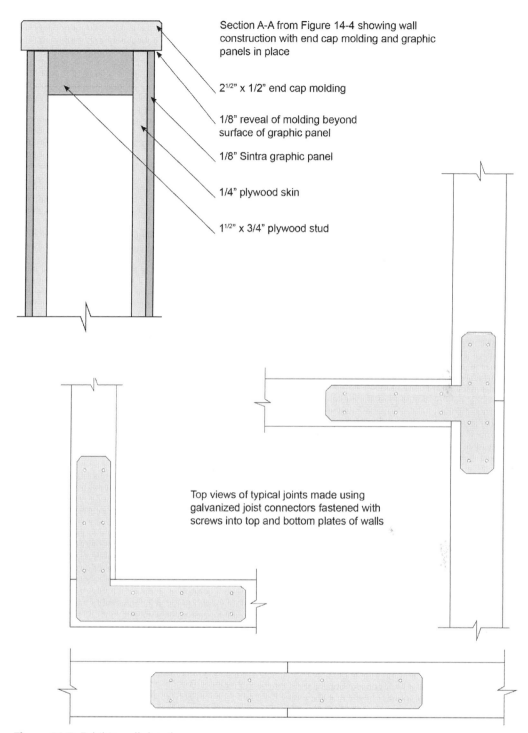

Section A-A from Figure 14-4 showing wall construction with end cap molding and graphic panels in place

2¹/²" x 1/2" end cap molding

1/8" reveal of molding beyond surface of graphic panel

1/8" Sintra graphic panel

1/4" plywood skin

1¹/²" x 3/4" plywood stud

Top views of typical joints made using galvanized joist connectors fastened with screws into top and bottom plates of walls

**Figure 14.5** Exhibit wall details.

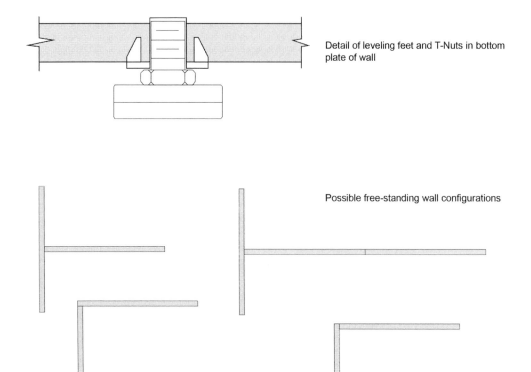

Detail of leveling feet and T-Nuts in bottom plate of wall

Possible free-standing wall configurations

**Figure 14.6** Exhibit wall details and configurations.

and must be joined to at least one other section. Walls can be joined into any number of configurations using galvanized joist connectors available from hardware stores and lumber yards.

Figures 14.7 and 14.8 show the assembly sequence for a typical wall section. Before the skins are applied, the basic framing can be adjusted as necessary to accommodate particular pieces of equipment. In figure 14.8, the wall is to have a flush-mounted video unit installed. The framing has been adapted to fit the back of the monitor, and PVC electrical conduit has been run to

Fabrication of the walls begins by ripping 3/4" ply

The strips are assembled with glue and brad nails

The finished frame of the wall with studs, plates and blocking

The plywood skins are cut slightly oversize on the panel saw so they can be trimmed flush after being fastened to the frame.

The skins are fastened with glue and brad nails

A flush-trim bit in the router

The bit trims the oversize sheet flush with the frame of the wall

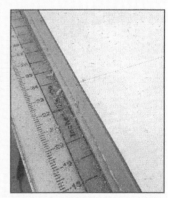
Trimming the skins this way makes a very clean edge

**Figure 14.7** Exhibit wall assembly.

take power cords. Because this particular exhibit will be traveling, the conduit has been run up and down to accommodate power supplied from the floor or the ceiling. If you need to attach a wall-mounted case or other piece of equipment, you can add solid blocking where the case will go so that it can be securely fastened.

The router (left) is trimming the skin flush with the panels. The laminate trimmer (right) is adding a slight round-over to the edges

After edge trimming the wall receives a thorough sanding

This wall has additional framing for an embedded video screen

The screen opening is cut to the edges of the frame

Conduit allows cables to be run inside the wall

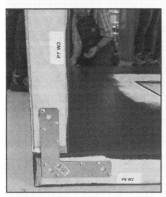

Top view of a corner showing the L bracket in place

The assembled walls can easily be lifted and moved

Two assembled walls before the screen is installed

**Figure 14.8** Exhibit wall assembly and installation.

### *Exhibit Boxes*

If you need an exhibit furniture element that is freestanding, consider making a box instead of a wall. Figure 14.9 gives the dimensions of an exhibit box. With the exception of some ¾" scrap plywood strips used to fasten the sides and ends, the box is made entirely of ½" Baltic birch plywood. The plywood is fastened at the corners, and the raw edges are covered by molding that also frames the graphic panels and covers the raw edges.

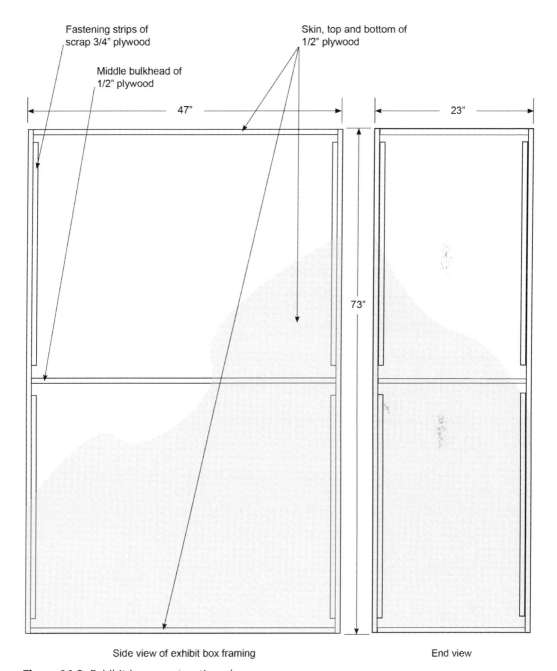

Side view of exhibit box framing    End view

**Figure 14.9** Exhibit box construction plan.

Because they are heavier than the wall sections, boxes are most useful if mounted on wheels. For a more casual or industrial look, the casters can be left exposed, as shown in figure 14.10. For a more finished look, they can be covered with plywood skirting that stops just short of the floor. The boxes can also be customized for a wide variety of uses. Wall-mounted cases and interactives can be attached to the outsides and lighting to the top or sides. Cases and interactive stations can also be set into the surface of the box.

Figure 14.11 shows how the boxes were used for an exhibit designed to be installed in a public concourse area. This exhibit consisted of graphics and interactives without artifacts. The graphics were mounted on 1/8" Sintra panels that were fastened to the boxes with air-gun brads.

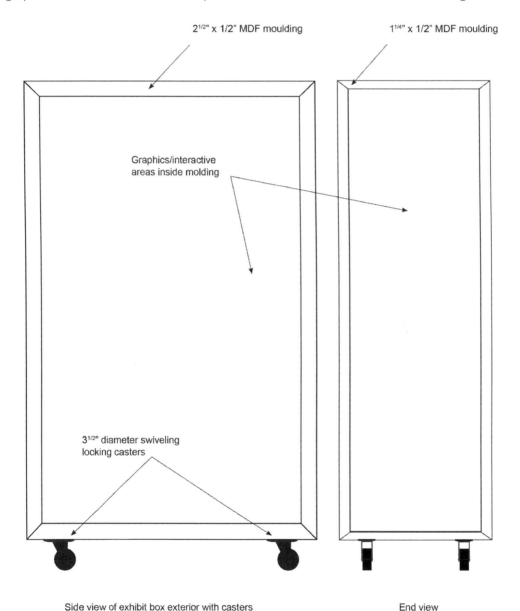

2$^{1/2}$" x 1/2" MDF moulding

1$^{1/4}$" x 1/2" MDF moulding

Graphics/interactive areas inside molding

3$^{1/2}$" diameter swiveling locking casters

Side view of exhibit box exterior with casters

End view

**Figure 14.10** Exhibit box details.

Interactive elements such as the comment desks were mounted on split battens attached to the box skin. Other interactives were mounted to the skin on cut-out panels. These could be removed to gain access to the inside of the box and the back of the panel so that the interactives could be mounted and serviced if necessary. The boxes featured dimensional letters on top cut from 2" thick Gatorfoam. With these removed, they could be rolled through a standard 80" high doorway and up the ramp and into a small truck.

Exhibit boxes used for a display in a public concourse area in combination with large wall graphics.

A simple interactive with strings to connect ideas and places

This interactive lets visitors record their choices

Determining the best angle for the comments desk

The finished comments desk

Completed comment cards are tucked behind elastic cords

**Figure 14.11** Exhibit boxes used in exhibit.

**Chapter Checklist**

1. Exhibit furniture serves to protect artifacts, but it also gives exhibits three-dimensional shape.
2. Good exhibit furniture should do its job quietly and present the artifacts without drawing attention to itself.
3. With a modest investment of time and materials, you can fabricate your own basic exhibit furniture.
4. If you build it yourself, you can also repair it and, more importantly, customize it or develop new pieces to meet your needs.
5. Over a number of exhibits, you can build up a good stock of furniture pieces that can be used again and again.

# Chapter 15

*Installation and Beyond*

It is finally almost done. The exhibit you have worked so hard on is ready to be installed. Hopefully any of the painting, renovation, or repair work that had to be done to the gallery space was completed on time and the space now ready to receive your exhibit.

**Tools and Equipment**

For installing an exhibit at your own institution, it is a good idea to set up a tool cart that can be loaded with all of the supplies and equipment you need. Having this right in the gallery with you can save a lot of running back and forth or up and down the stairs. For off-site installations, put one person in charge, develop a checklist, and pack the necessary equipment at least one day beforehand. This can avoid showing up at the installation site with a drill but not its battery charger, or having only square-drive screwdrivers for an exhibit that uses Phillips screws. Figure 15.1 shows a basic exhibit installation tool kit.

Because you have planned your schedule carefully, you will undoubtedly have left yourself several days to complete the installation. It will probably take longer than you think, and if you rush it and make mistakes, you can undo all of the rest of the good work you have put into the exhibit. Depending on how your galleries are set up, you may be working in public. This is not necessarily a bad thing, as visitors love to watch museum workers do stuff and it is definitely a teachable moment, but chatting with visitors and answering questions can slow you down. It can also spoil the surprise of the new exhibit, so you may want to block or drape the gallery entrance to give you some privacy. If you can't do that, you will at least want to use ropes and stanchions or tension barriers to block off a workspace so that nothing gets stepped on.

**Hanging and Mounting**

As we saw in the accessibility section of chapter 10, the aim for exhibit development is to make them as accessible as possible to as wide a range of audiences as possible. One of the easiest ways to improve the accessibility of your exhibit is to pay attention to the height at which the exhibit elements are mounted. Figure 15.2 provides some general guidelines. The next time you are visiting an exhibit, take a few moments to notice the height of text and graphic panels. Although these guidelines seem pretty obvious, they are not observed as often as they should be. Sometimes, the exhibit's developers have given in to the temptation to put in more content than they had room for, and so it ends up either down by the visitors' socks or up by their foreheads. In other cases, staff hang the exhibit so that it looks good to them without reference to the audience.

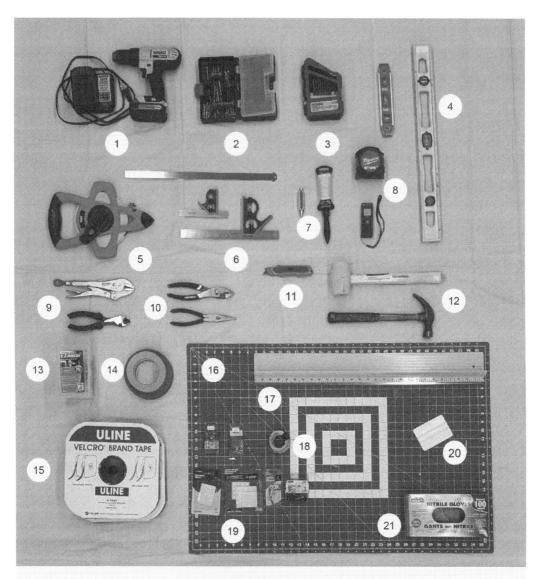

1. Drill, charger, spare battery
2. Driver bits
3. Drill bits
4. Levels
5. 100' measuring tape
6. Adjustable squares, ruler
7. Plumb bob
8. Measuring tape, laser measure
9. Vise grips, wire cutters
10. Pliers
11. Utility knife
12. Hammer, rubber mallet
13. Wall anchors
14. Masking tape, gaffer tape
15. Adhesive Velcro
16. Cutting mat
17. Cutting ruler
18. Picture wire
19. Picture hanging hardware
20. Vinyl squeegee
21. Gloves

**Figure 15.1** Exhibit installation tool kit.

For the first 12" off the floor, you should not have any exhibit elements at all. This is a very diffi-cult space in which to perceive content, and leaving it clear will also let the rest of the wall space "breathe" and not feel crowded. From 12" to 36" from the floor, you can use the space, but only for background graphics or colors. This area should not contain any content that visitors have to understand by reading. The area 36" to 66" from the floor is your main display space, the exhibit version of prime time in a television schedule. As you can see from the typical seated and stand-ing eye heights, this space covers the comfortable viewing zones for both. This is the place for labels, panels, and content that visitors have to think about.

As figure 15.2 shows, there is a very narrow zone of overlap between the seated and standing eye heights. The rule of thumb for hanging height is to have the vertical center of the panel, painting, or exhibit element located 57" to 61" from the floor. Note that this is irrespective of whether the ceiling is 9' or 25'. If you have separate labels that are not incorporated into your text panels, they should be placed in the lower part of this zone.

The next 12", from 66" to 78" above the floor, can be used for titles but should not contain any substantive content. From 78" to the ceiling is generally not used for exhibit elements, except in the case of a very large piece or graphic that is meant to be seen from a distance.

As you are hanging the panels, try to establish strong horizontal alignments, either by align-ing all of their tops or bottoms or all of the vertical centers. This will give the exhibit a sense of order and visual coherence. If you are using separate labels, mount them all at the same height. Nothing makes an exhibit look amateurish more than having small labels hopping up and down around the gallery walls. This is yet one more reason to group your exhibit elements into larger graphic panels in the design stage. A rotating laser construction level, which can be rented from a tool supplier or big-box home-improvement store, is a great help in establishing these alignments.

## Lighting

Like the exhibit furniture, the job of the exhibit lighting is to present the exhibit effectively without drawing undue attention to itself. Your exhibit will likely be installed in a gallery with track light-ing. If you do have the opportunity to install new lighting in a gallery, and the budget to support it, you can work with a consultant to design a custom solution, but for our purposes here we will assume that you have existing tracks and fixtures. There are two goals for lighting an exhibit: (1) to make the show look good; (2) to allow your visitors to find their way safely through the gallery.

You will probably have a predetermined number of track fixtures to work with, and chances are it will not be quite enough. If the gallery's electrical circuits have the capacity, you can add more fixtures. Otherwise, you will need to work with what you have. In order to match the available lighting with your exhibit, you can change the type of bulb in your fixtures. Most types of bulbs can be obtained in a variety of beam spreads, from narrow spot to wide flood. As you adjust the lighting, try to achieve an even, balanced look and avoid:

- Reflections;
- Uneven light levels on a single work, artifact, or case;
- Harsh, distinct spot-lit circles;

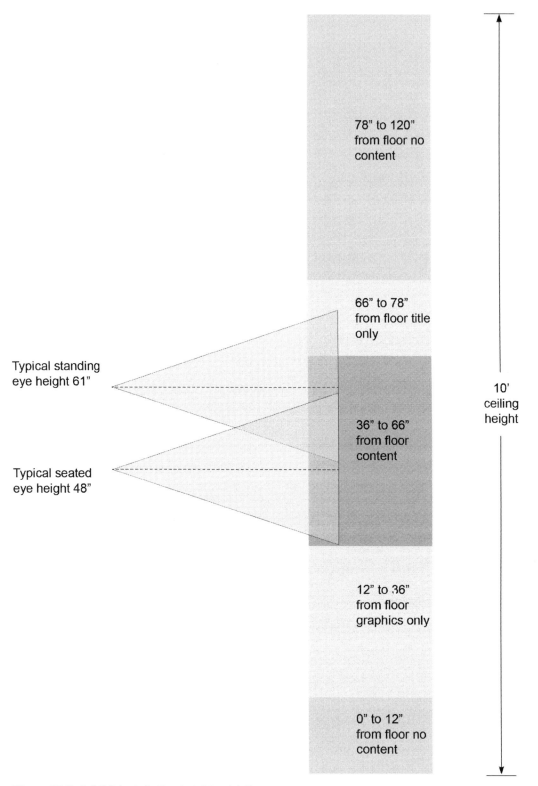

78" to 120"
from floor no
content

66" to 78"
from floor title
only

Typical standing
eye height 61"

36" to 66"
from floor
content

Typical seated
eye height 48"

10'
ceiling
height

12" to 36"
from floor
graphics only

0" to 12"
from floor no
content

**Figure 15.2** Exhibit installation height guidelines.

- Scalloping at top edges of panels and cases;
- Lights that point directly in visitor's eyes;
- Mixing different lighting types, such as incandescent, halogen, and LED, in the same exhibit; and
- Deep shadows that obscure adjacent labels or panels.

If you can control the ambient lighting in the gallery, aim for a presentation where overall lighting is slightly dimmer than the highlights on the artifacts and panels. This can provide dramatic emphasis and also assist with keeping the light levels on artifacts at acceptable levels. If the exhibit contains artifacts with light sensitivity, this should already have been identified during conservation review in the curatorial phase. Once the installation is complete, the level of light falling on the artifacts and panels should be confirmed with a light meter.

## Walk-Through and Punch List

If you have worked with a contracted service provider to design and/or fabricate your exhibit, a postinstallation walk-through should have been written into the request for proposals. From this, you will develop a punch list of work to be completed or corrected. Once all of the items on the punch list have been addressed to your satisfaction, the retainage portion of the contractor's fee can be released.

If you have designed and built the exhibit yourself, you still need to carry out a walk-through with all members of the project team to identify work that needs to be completed or corrected. The person who has been acting as your project manager should be responsible for seeing the punch list through to completion.

## Testing

The digital and interactive components of the exhibit should be tested after they are installed. Please note that this is not testing to see whether they are easy to use and instructions are clear. This should have been done during evaluation earlier in the project. This testing is to ensure that they are plugged into the correct circuits and are operating as intended. If these elements need to be turned on in the morning and off again at night, or periodically reset during the day, the front desk, floor, and maintenance staff should also be trained on how to use and troubleshoot them.

## Lessons Learned

Every exhibit development project is an adventure. It is an intense and creative process during which you will work hard, make decisions, and put your heart and soul into what you are creating. After the dust settles, it is a good idea to get your team back together and carry out an evaluation. Develop a form for staff to complete before the meeting, and then collate and anonymize the results. You can ask staff to rate the following on a scale of strongly disagree/disagree/neutral/agree/strongly agree/not applicable:

- Project objectives were clear and defined.
- My role during the content development stage was clear.
- My role during the design stage was clear.
- My role during the production and installation stages was clear.
- I felt that my ideas were acknowledged throughout the exhibition development process.

- I felt informed, as needed, throughout the project.
- I could spend enough time working on my deliverables for the project.
- I had enough resources to meet my deliverables for the project.
- I was involved at the correct times.
- Cross-departmental involvement and contributions were adequate.
- I was aware of the progress of the project.
- I could ask the project manager for help or information throughout the project.
- Overall, my work-life balance was not compromised throughout the project.
- The project objective was achieved.

With reference to the stages your institution uses to develop exhibits, you can also survey the staff regarding:

- What went well?
- What were some successes?
- What were some challenges during this project?
- What have we learned that can be used for future exhibition development projects?

## Archiving an Exhibit Project

If you have designed the exhibit digitally, you have will have developed a considerable body of files, images, and information during the project. Before you move on to other work, it is important to clean up and organize these records. Layout programs such as InDesign typically use low-resolution FPO images and maintain links to the original image files. If these links are not maintained, it can be difficult if not impossible to reprint graphics and panels later on. Once the final designs are approved, the source files for the images should be kept in the same location as when the panels were designed. If you archive your digital files carefully, paragraph and character styles, swatch palettes, graphics, and other design elements can be reused for subsequent projects.

Exhibit projects typically accumulate multiple versions of the same file, so it is a good idea to go through and purge all but the final version, together with images that did not end up being used. If images or materials were obtained from outside sources, it should be kept in the same folder as any applicable rights or permission agreements. Your objective should be to leave the project materials sufficiently organized so that someone who is not familiar with the project would be able to locate what they need.

## Chapter Checklist

1. Leave yourself enough time to do a careful and thorough installation. It is unprofessional and risky to be in the gallery at midnight before the next day's opening.
2. Hang and mount exhibit elements with accessibility in mind.
3. Carry out a walk-through with your staff and/or contractors and compile a punch list to make sure everything is complete and satisfactory.
4. Offer your staff a chance to review their work on the project and capture the lessons learned.
5. Carefully archive all of the project elements and clean up your files.
6. Finally, don't forget to enjoy the exhibit after it opens, and make sure that everyone waits a least one week before pointing out typos or other mistakes.

# Appendix 1
## Developing an Institutional Exhibit Plan

In addition to developing a plan for individual exhibits, a museum should have a multiyear institutional exhibit plan. Such a plan, which outlines what exhibits will happen and when, can confirm that exhibit projects are aligned with your institution's mission, mandate, and core documents. An institutional exhibit plan will ensure that your exhibits provide accurate information, are relevant to the community, communicate effectively, provide opportunities for learning, and safely display the artifacts in your collections. The document should include planning for the evaluation of exhibits as well as for inclusivity and accessibility. The creation of an institutional exhibit plan can be divided into three steps.

### Develop Your Process

In this step, the outline for the plan is developed in such a way as to ensure that it supports broader institutional goals and the processes for creating both the plan and a particular exhibit are defined. Gather and review your core organizational documents and summarize what guidance they provide for exhibit development. Does your institution have some or all of these documents? What do they say that might be relevant to an exhibit plan?

- Mission Statement
- Institutional Vision
- Strategic Plan
- Master Plan
- Collections Plan
- Interpretive Plan
- Interpretation and Education Policy
- Research Policy
- Exhibition Policy

Determine the approving authority for the exhibit plan and map the route to approval. Defining the approval process up front can increase institutional buy-in and avoid unpleasant surprises later on. Who approves what at your institution? Who will approve this plan? What are the stages in getting approval? Who needs to be on board for this to succeed? Who still needs to be convinced?

Recruit the team that will develop the plan, and write a scope of work that defines the overall objective and shows who will do what. Consider including some or all of the following on your team:

- Staff
- Volunteers

- Board Members
- Community Members
- Municipal Officials or Politicians

Determine the scope of your exhibits. Individual projects will vary, but it helps to define general categories of size and cost. Table A1.1 gives an example of an exhibit scope typology. In order to develop such a typology, you can use previous exhibits at your own institution to get a sense of typical sizes and complexity, and/or ask other museums what their typical figures are. The typology is only a guideline, but it is useful in determining the scope of projects during the planning process.

**Table A1.1** Exhibit Scope Typology

| Size | Scope | Typical Means of Expression | Typical Time Required |
|---|---|---|---|
| Extra-Small (XS) | A trophy case style wall-mounted display at a library or school | Graphics only, no artifacts, typically behind glass | Two months |
| Small (S) | Wall-mounted cases on floor, telephone booth style cases | Graphics and smaller artifacts inside cases | Four months |
| Medium (M) | Gallery of 200 to 500 square feet | Some or all of artifacts, media, graphics, interactives, online | Twelve months |
| Large (L) | Gallery of 500 to 1,000 square feet | Some or all of artifacts, media, graphics, interactives, online | Eighteen months |
| Extra Large (XL) | Gallery of 1,000 to 2,000 square feet | Some or all of artifacts, media, graphics, interactives, online | Twenty-four months |
| Extra Extra Large (XXL) | Gallery of more than 2,000 square feet | Some or all of artifacts, media, graphics, interactives, online | Thirty-six months |
| Digital Only (D) | Online exhibit and/or online component of physical exhibit | Web page, web site, app | Twelve months |

Outline the stages in your institution's exhibit development process. Depending on the size of your institution, the number of people involved in exhibit development, and the scope of the project, you may wish to modify the five basic stages shown in chapter 3.

**Create Your Product**

In this step, ideas for exhibits are gathered, evaluated, selected, and detailed. Table A1.2 gives an example of a proposal form that captures the big idea, intended audience, means of expression, learn-

**Table A1.2** Exhibit Proposal Form

| Exhibit Proposal Form |
|---|
| 1  What's the big idea of the exhibit? Can you put it into a single sentence? What's the exhibit all about? Why should a visitor see the exhibit? |
| 2  Who is the main audience for the exhibit? What do they already know about the topic? What do you think they might want to learn, and how? |
| 3  What will be in your exhibit? Artifacts? Pictures? Charts? Graphs? Text? Props? Stories? Will you tell the audience things? Will you ask the audience questions? |
| 4  What is the main thing you would like your visitors to understand after they visit your exhibit? What do you think they will remember most? How do you want them to feel after they have seen the exhibit? |

ing outcomes, and scope for each exhibit idea. The form you develop should ask for enough detail to understand the proposed exhibit but be general enough to appeal to nonspecialists and be written in plain language. The headings should also align with the exhibit brief used by your institution.

Gather exhibit ideas using the proposal form. Reach out as far as you can to gather proposals, and use the process to broaden your community engagement. If they have not been involved with exhibits before, consider holding a workshop about the exhibit development process to help them create a proposal. Using the proposal form makes exhibit development a true two-way street: the museum is accessible because proposals are welcome, but the proponents must show how the proposed exhibit helps to advance the museum's mission so they are not just tossing in random ideas or pet projects.

Review and rank the proposed exhibit ideas. Evaluate the proposals according to how well they align with the institution's core documents, how well they advance the mission, and how feasible they are to carry out. Select exhibit ideas for further development based on their ranking. Using the typology you developed (table A1.1), assign a scope to each exhibit. Develop the selected exhibit proposals by creating a brief (chapter 5) and a budget (chapter 9) for each one.

**Make Your Plan**

In this step, the content developed in step two and the process outlined in step one are combined, scheduled, and approved. Create an outline schedule that covers the whole term of your plan. Given the lead time required to develop some exhibits, three to five years is a good time frame to use. This is a high-level schedule so the exhibit projects are only broken down by year and quarter. After the institutional exhibit plan is approved, a more detailed schedule can be prepared for each project. You may wish to align the time frame of your plan with other relevant documents, such as the interval between reviews of your strategic plan or the term of council if you are a municipal museum.

Place your selected exhibits into the schedule using your exhibit development stages as milestones. Review the schedule and adjust as required. Read down the time columns and look for hard spots where projects overlap, conflict, or overextend your resources. Prepare the plan for approval. A suggested table of contents for an institutional exhibit plan is shown below.

1.  INTRODUCTION: Provide an executive summary of the plan, including any relevant background information, documents, and previous plans.

2. CORE ORGANIZATIONAL DOCUMENTS: List the core organizational documents that are relevant to the plan and summarize the pertinent section(s) of each. These could include a vision, mission statement, strategic plan, interpretive plan, collections plan, or similar documents.
3. EXHIBIT VISION AND STATEMENT OF CREATIVE APPROACH: Outline a broad vision for the character and scope of the exhibits in the plan. What is your institution's "house style" for exhibits? For example, your aim might be to develop traveling exhibits that can be easily set up and taken down by a maximum of two people, are suitable for display in nontraditional exhibit venues, and are secure enough to be left unattended. Or your exhibits might seek to present the past in the context of the present, linking artifacts and archival materials with contemporary issues.
4. EXHIBIT DEVELOPMENT AND APPROVAL PROCESS: Describe the exhibit development process and when approvals will be given. For example, using the stages in chapter 3, you might need to seek approval for the brief, schematic design, final design, and budget.
5. DEVELOPMENT OF THIS PLAN: Describe how the plan was initiated and developed, and by whom, and include consultations, focus groups, and surveys.
6. EXHIBIT TYPOLOGY: See table A1.1.
7. EXHIBIT BRIEF: Outline the structure of the brief you will be using to develop your exhibits.
8. SELECTION OF PROPOSED EXHIBIT TOPICS: Present all of the topics that were proposed during the consultation process and describe the criteria that were used to rank them and make a final selection.
9. SELECTED EXHIBITS: Provide a brief for each exhibit using the format above.
10. THREE-YEAR EXHIBIT SCHEDULE: See table A1.3.

**Table A1.3** Sample Institutional Exhibit Schedule

| | | Year One | | | | Year Two | | | | Year Three | | | |
|---|---|---|---|---|---|---|---|---|---|---|---|---|---|
| | | Q1 | Q2 | Q3 | Q4 | Q1 | Q2 | Q3 | Q4 | Q1 | Q2 | Q3 | Q4 |
| **Exhibit One** | | | | | | | | | | | | | |
| | Concept | ▓ | | | | | | | | | | | |
| | Design | | ▓ | ▓ | | | | | | | | | |
| | Fabrication | | | | ▓ | | | | | | | | |
| | Installation | | | | ▓ | | | | | | | | |
| **Exhibit Two** | | | | | | | | | | | | | |
| | Concept | | | ▓ | | | | | | | | | |
| | Design | | | | | | ▓ | | | | | | |
| | Fabrication | | | | | | | | ▓ | | | | |
| | Installation | | | | | | | | ▓ | | | | |
| **Exhibit Three** | | | | | | | | | | | | | |
| | Concept | | | | | | | | | ▓ | | | |
| | Design | | | | | | | | | ▓ | | | |
| | Fabrication | | | | | | | | | | | ▓ | |
| | Installation | | | | | | | | | | | | ▓ |

# *Appendix 2*
## Creating Traveling Exhibits

Once you have begun to create exhibits, you may consider sending them on the road to other institutions. Creating traveling exhibits can share your work with a wider audience, but it brings with it some additional challenges. Many exhibits could be put on a truck and transported to another venue, but the most successful traveling exhibits are those that are specifically designed to travel right from the beginning of their development process. And what do we mean by travel? Sharing an exhibit with the next museum down the road might require getting some staff together and renting a truck, but putting an exhibit on the road across the state, province, or country requires a more systematic approach. The following checklist identifies some of the special requirements that should be considered in developing a traveling exhibit.

### Concept

- Is your proposed topic of interest to a broader audience? Has this been evaluated through surveys, questionnaires, or expressions of interest? Can you obtain commitments to book the exhibit in advance?
- Is the concept suitable to be a traveling exhibit?
- What is the balance between two-dimensional and three-dimensional content? Sending exhibit cases and artifacts on the road is more complex and expensive than an exhibit composed mainly of graphic panels.
- Are there opportunities for borrowing institutions to add their own content to round out a core exhibit that your institution has created?

### Budget

- Traveling exhibits are more expensive to create because components must be designed to be taken apart and reassembled and because of the need for additional equipment such as shipping crates.
- The budget should include not only the initial cost of creating the exhibit but also the rental fees that will be charged and the length of time that will be required to recoup the investment.
- Because of their complexity, traveling exhibits will also require more staff time, both up front and to manage their circulation to different venues, than an in-house exhibit of the same size.

### Size

- What is the general size in square feet, allowing for circulation? How big a gallery will the borrower need to display it adequately?

- Is the size of the exhibit compatible with the galleries of the museums that you would like to receive it?
- Is there additional non-exhibit space required for the storage of crates and packing materials after it is installed? If so, how much?

## Configurations

- Can the exhibit be installed in varying configurations, or is there only one way to do it?
- Provide schematics of alternate arrangements and/or images of previous installations for prospective borrowers if that is an option.
- Must the exhibit be displayed in a gallery? On the walls only? On the walls and in the middle of the room? In the middle of the room only? In a concourse? In a hallway?

## Services

- Does it need electrical power? Is the power provided through wall outlets, floor outlets, and/or ceiling drops?
- How does the provision of power affect the suggested configurations? If it was originally designed to be powered from wall outlets, could it be powered from floor outlets only if that is what the borrower has available?

## Security

- Can it be displayed completely unattended, or does it need to be staffed when open?
- Will it need to be opened and closed each day, especially with regard to turning A/V and interactives on and off and restocking supplies such as handouts or program materials?
- Use secure one-way screws, bolts, mounting hardware, and arrangements, especially if it is to be displayed unattended.

## Spare Parts

- If there are moving parts and/or equipment, what is the procedure if they break? Borrower to replace? Lender to replace?
- Are spare parts readily available? If not, will items such as bulbs be provided to the borrower with exhibit?

## Durability

- Because you will not be seeing the exhibit every day at your own institution, the materials and finishes need to be more durable than they would be otherwise.
- Are the interactives simple and robust and easily repaired if they break?
- Are digital and A/V components simple and robust? Do they reset themselves to default/welcome screens if they are not used for a certain period of time or if a visitor bails out in midexperience?
- Are they self-booting?
- Do they have to be powered up all the time, or can they be on switched outlets?
- How often should the exhibit be returned to you for review and repair?

## Crates and Cases

- Will it use custom cases and crates, or can it use off-the-rack cases and crates in standard sizes?
- Pay attention to packed weights and consider how the exhibit will be loaded and unloaded. It may be easier for borrowers to work with three fifty-pound crates than one that weighs 150 pounds.
- Can cases and crates be incorporated into the exhibit as plinths, bases, or other elements so that they don't have to be stored separately?
- If not, can cases/crates break down to minimize storage requirements?
- Consider how the exhibit will be shipped when designing the crates, and familiarize yourself with the interior sizes of rental trucks and freight carriers. You will lower the shipping costs and make the exhibit more attractive to borrowers if the components fit efficiently into the vehicle.
- If components will be shipped on pallets instead of in packing crates, plan the shipping in terms of the standard pallet cube of 48" × 48" × 48".

## Load-In and Load-Out

- What are the dimensions of the largest packed element? What is the weight of the heaviest packed element?
- What is the minimum size of access doorways and hallways at the venues to which the exhibit will be going?
- What materials handling equipment is required to load and unload the exhibit: dolly, hand truck, pallet truck, forklift, loading dock, liftgate truck, truck with ramp?
- Is a member of your staff required to set up and take down the exhibit? Are their travel costs covered by the rental fee?

## Documentation

- Provide step-by-step illustrated setup and teardown instructions, keyed to crate numbers.
- Crate number one should always have all of the manuals, instructions, and forms required to start installation.

## Legalities

- The rental of the exhibit should be covered by a comprehensive contract that includes contact information, fees and fee deadlines, opening and closing schedule, installation requirements, special requirements for artifacts and A/V equipment, and indemnifications and procedures in case of loss or damage.

## Branding and Source Identification

- Will there be additional branding or identification required? That is, if it was developed by one museum but is on display at another, does the first museum need to be worked into the branding?
- Does your exhibit have a major sponsor? Were they given exclusive rights in exchange for their support? This may present an issue at other institutions with different sponsorship arrangements, so it is advisable to note any such restrictions in your promotional materials for the exhibit.

# Appendix 3
## Sample Request for Proposals

This request for proposals merges the exhibit proposed in chapters 4, 5, 7, and 8 with the (to the best of my knowledge) entirely fictitious Beaver Corners Historical Society and Community Museum. The institution and contact information are made up, but the language and project requirements represent a project where an outside firm is being hired to work with the museum to produce an exhibit. The issues addressed in this sample request for proposals are typical of those that should be addressed when hiring an exhibit consultant. This sample document is not intended to provide legal or contractual advice, and when you create an actual request for proposals for your own project, the document should be reviewed by your organization's legal counsel and governing authority before being issued.

\* \* \* \* \*

INTRODUCTION: The Beaver Corners Historical Society and Museum (hereafter the Project Owner) requires the services of an exhibit development contractor (hereafter the Contractor) to create a new long-term exhibit, tentatively titled *Wheels of Change: How the Automobile Shaped Our World*.

INSTITUTIONAL BACKGROUND: Industrialist and philanthropist Arthur Smith and his wife, Maureen, founded the Beaver Corners Historical Society and Museum in 1937. The mission statement of the BCHSM is "to acquire, preserve and exhibit such items from the past as can be used to interpret the history and development of Beaver Corners, together with such themes as may relate the history of Beaver Corners to the broader history of the United States." Lifelong residents of the Beaver Corners area, Mr. and Mrs. Smith were dedicated antiquarians and collectors. Inspired by the founding of Colonial Williamsburg and the burgeoning interest in early American history, they began collecting Americana and antiques in the early 1930s. In the late 1940s, with a group of like-minded friends and fellow collectors, they founded the Beaver Corners Historical Society. In the early 1960s, they raised funds and built the museum. Their collections became the basis of the museum's holdings, with their beloved 1918 Ford Model T the first artifact officially accessioned into the collection. Over the last five years, the museum building has undergone a major capital renovation. The scope of work for this project required the museum to be closed to the public for an extended period of time and the entire collection to be placed in storage. With the grand reopening planned within the next twelve-to-fourteen months, the organization is seeking an exhibit development contractor to create a signature exhibit for the reopening.

EXHIBIT PURPOSE: The purpose of the exhibit is to once again have the Smith's 1918 Model T on display in the museum. Unlike the previous pre-renovation exhibit, however, the intention behind this project is to create a full-fledged interpretive exhibit with the car as a focal point. The big idea behind the exhibit is that "the automobile was a disruptive technology that transformed the country's economy, industry, landscape and social structures," and the exhibit should embody and explore that idea.

EXHIBIT OBJECTIVE: See attached brief. As this will be the inaugural exhibit in the reopened museum, the scope, quality of execution, and positive reflection on the museum of the project are of paramount importance.

EXHIBIT COMPONENTS AND SCOPE OF WORK: As outlined in the attached brief, this exhibit will contain artifacts, archival material, audio-visual elements, and interactive experiences. The Contractor will design, supply, and/or install the elements of the exhibit specified below under Contractor Will Provide.

APPROVALS: The Contractor shall provide drawings, specifications, and, where relevant, mock-ups, of all exhibit components for approval by the Project Owner at the following stages:

- Concept;
- Schematic Design;
- Design Development;
- Final Design;
- The Contractor shall carry out a walk-through with the Project Owner following the completion of installation and no less than one week before the official opening to identify any remaining issues and determine how they are to be addressed; and
- The Contractor shall carry out a walk-through with the Project Owner no less than two weeks and no more than four weeks after the official opening to develop a final punch list and schedule for addressing all outstanding issues.

CONTRACTOR WILL PROVIDE:
- A detailed project schedule;
- Project management services to ensure that the exhibit is delivered on time and on budget;
- A detailed project budget within the limits outlined below, drafted in cooperation with museum staff;
- All required designs, drawings, and specifications;
- Installation of the completed exhibit;
- A written assurance that the physical elements, graphics, and the visitor experience of the finished exhibit conform to all relevant codes, standards, and guidelines, including those for accessibility;
- Attendance at all required project meetings; and
- Prompt response to all queries and issues.

MUSEUM WILL PROVIDE:
- All required research services, including image sourcing, acquisition, rights, and permissions;
- All required scanning and color-correction and retouching of images;
- All required exhibit text;
- All required artifacts and archival materials, either from its own collection or through loans;
- Fabrication of selected interactive elements to designs produced by the Contractor, with costs for the required materials to be included in this budget;

- Research, identification, sourcing, and management of all required in-loans of artifacts and archival materials;
- Upon receipt of suitable notice, access to collections and archival materials for the purposes of developing the exhibit;
- At its own cost, not included in the project budget below, all required cleaning, conservation, and/or restoration services required to prepare selected artifacts for display. The museum shall be the sole arbiter of whether or not such services are required, their extent, and how and by whom the work is to be performed;
- Attendance at all required project meetings; and
- Prompt response to all queries and issues.

BUDGET:
- The budget for this project is $115,000 (one hundred fifteen thousand dollars), inclusive of taxes, the Contractor's fee, all required disbursements, and a contingency of 20 percent of the total project cost (see attached);
- The fee charged by the Contractor for the services outlined above, exclusive of disbursements, shall amount to no more than 35 percent of the total project cost; and
- The Project Owner shall be responsible for all required repairs and alterations to the base building of the gallery, at its expense, exclusive of the project budget noted above.

PROJECT SCHEDULE:
- The contract for the work outlined in this request for proposals shall be awarded by ——;
- The exhibit shall be ready to open to the public no later than ——; and
- As part of its work for this project, the Contractor shall, with its proposal, prepare a detailed schedule showing all of the milestones, meetings, presentations, and other activities required to complete the project by ——.

PAYMENT SCHEDULE: The budget for this project shall be paid to the Contractor upon receipt of an invoice according to the following schedule:
- 10 percent of the total project cost upon receipt of a deposit invoice following the signing of a contract;
- 15 percent upon completion and approval of design development;
- 25 percent upon completion and approval of final design;
- 35 percent upon completion and approval of the preopening walk-through; and
- 15 percent upon completion of the items identified in the postopening punch list.

DELIVERABLES: The Contractor shall provide:
- Complete project documentation, including as-built drawings and specifications, records of materials and finishes used, and the sources of any spare parts that might be required to keep the exhibit operational.

OWNERSHIP OF WORK PRODUCT(S):
- All of the work product(s) prepared in the course of this project, including designs and creative work, will become the property of the Project Owner at the conclusion of the project; but
- Notwithstanding the above, the Contractor may request the right to use work carried out during the project for their own firm's portfolio and promotional purposes.

SUBMISSIONS IN RESPONSE TO THIS REQUEST FOR PROPOSALS TO INCLUDE:
- A statement of creative approach outlining how the Contractor will meet the requirements outlined above, particularly with regard to the exhibit objective;
- A summary of the Contractor's experience with exhibit development, particularly for projects of a budget, scope, and character similar to the work outlined above;
- A detailed budget;
- A detailed schedule;
- Professional resumes for all staff proposed for involvement in the project;
- A summary showing how many hours will be devoted to the project by the firm's principals, senior staff, and junior staff; and
- references for, and examples of, previous relevant work.

PROPOSAL COSTS:
- The Project Owner will not be responsible for any costs incurred in preparation of the proposals nor will any payment be made for any submissions in response to this request for proposals.

PROPOSAL EVALUATION CRITERIA:
- All proposals received in response to the request will be evaluated by the same criteria;
- Proposals will be evaluated on the degree to which they:

  ○ Meet the requirements outlined above, and
  ○ Will achieve the project objectives outlined above; and

- The Project Owner reserves the right to reject, without evaluation, any proposals deemed to be incomplete.

PROPOSAL SUBMISSION:
- Contractors should submit six (6) bound color copies of their proposal, together with a press-quality .pdf document corresponding to the hard copies;
- Proposals should be delivered to the offices of the Project Owner by 5 p.m. on ——; and
- The Project Owner reserves the right to reject, without evaluation, any proposals submitted after that time and date.

PROPOSAL ACCEPTANCE:
- The Project Owner is not necessarily obligated to accept either the lowest cost proposal nor any proposal submitted in response to this request;
- The successful Contractor will be notified by telephone with a follow-up email within one (1) week of the submission date; and
- Unsuccessful contractors will be notified by telephone with a follow-up email within two (2) weeks of the submission date.

FAILURE TO PERFORM:
- In the event that the Contractor, after signing the contract, fails to deliver on its obligations as outlined above and in the contract, the Project Owner shall be entitled to assess a financial penalty of up to 25 percent of the total value of the contract and/or at its sole discretion, and with one (1) week's written notice, terminate the contract.

CHANGES:
- Following the completion and approval of the final design for the project, changes proposed by the Project Owner shall be treated as additional items to the contract, and their cost negotiated with the Contractor; and
- Changes proposed by the Contractor shall be treated as items included within the contract, and their cost borne by the Contractor.

INSURANCE:
- For installation work undertaken on the Project Owner's premises, the Contractor shall name the Project Owner as an additional insured on a liability policy in the amount of two million dollars ($2,000,000) per occurrence.

INSTITUTIONAL CONTACT TO WHOM QUESTIONS SHOULD BE ADDRESSED:
- Questions concerning this request for proposals should be directed, by email only, to Mr. Charles W. Peale, Chief Curator, Beaver Corners Historical Society and Museum, cwpeale@ bchsm.org.

# Appendix 4
## Four Design Strategies

When you sit down to begin creating your first exhibit, it can be a bit overwhelming. After all, when you are writing a book you are only facing a blank sheet of paper that you have to fill with words. For an exhibit, you have a blank three-dimensional space that you have to fill with content. Where do you start? As you gain more experience with exhibit development, you will find your own tried-and-true, guaranteed-to-work design solutions. Until you get to that point, here are four good, solid tricks to get you started thinking like a designer. The next time you visit a museum or gallery, see how many of these strategies you can spot in action.

### Use Two-and-a-Half-Dimensional Graphics

A graphic panel is one-dimensional. An artifact is three-dimensional. In between is what a designer friend of mine calls "two-and-a-half-dimensional," which is really just a fancy way of saying "cutouts." By silhouetting an image and placing it just off a background (or "noncoplanar" as the same designer says); you give it dramatic emphasis. The top three images in figure A4.1 show how this can be applied. A piece of 1" × 6" poplar was given three ¼" dado grooves. Human figures were cropped out of historic black-and-white photographs and silhouetted in Photoshop. After being printed on adhesive vinyl, they were laminated onto ¼" Sintra and cut out to the edges of the photographs using a scroll saw. The finished figures were hot-glued into the dadoes and placed in front of a color background made from an enlarged postcard of the town showing a street view. Placed on the mantelpiece, the figures add interest to a part of the room in this historic house that otherwise would have been hard to program because it is too high for readable content.

The lower two images in figure A4.1 show the same technique on a grander scale. Colored engravings have been blown up to nearly life size and laminated onto ½" Plexiglass. They were then mounted on stand-offs to set them off from the wall and to create dramatic shadows that heighten their dramatic impact.

### Block the View

It may sound counterintuitive, but the last thing you want your visitors to see when they walk into the gallery is your exhibit. Ideally, their attention should be drawn to a title panel first, and it should be set up in such a way that they have to enter into the gallery to begin to view the exhibit. The example in figure A4.2 was developed for a very large gallery space. Covering more than six thousand square feet, it was a timber-frame building three stories high. The title graphic was first scanned at very high resolution from an out-of-copyright boating magazine. After it was adjusted and the text added, it was sent to a sign company for printing in color on vinyl mesh. The finished banner was 10' wide × 20' high.

The slotted base for the silhouetted figures

After being laminated onto 1/4" Sintra, the figures are cut to their final shapes on the scroll saw

The finished silhouetted figures in place in front of the background image

These almost life-size silhouetted figures were printed on vinyl and laminated onto 1/2" thick plexiglass

The shadows help to animate the figures

**Figure A4.1** Two-and-a-half-dimensional graphics.

The original magazine cover

The finished title graphic

The completed entrance banner. Printed on vinyl mesh, it measures 10' wide x 20' high.

**Figure A4.2** Exhibit entrance banner.

The perforations in the mesh were large enough that the graphic did not block the light but small enough that the image could still be readily understood from a normal viewing distance. Metal tubes were placed into pockets sewn into the banner at the top and bottom. It was suspended from thin, stainless-steel aircraft cable. Because the building opened directly to the outside, the lower end of the banner was anchored to the floor with more cable so that it would not sway in the wind.

### Silhouette an Image

Figure A4.3 shows how a historic photo can be incorporated into a graphic panel. In this case, it is a title panel created for the exhibit idea introduced in chapter 4 called *Wheels of Change*. Even though the exhibit features the Model T Ford, it would be giving too much away to show it on the title panel. At the same time, the big idea is larger than any one artifact. This photo, of a young boy viewing a model highway of the future created by General Motors in 1959, seemed to embody the idea of change and transformation, and so it was selected for use on the title panel. The original image is shown in the top left corner. In the top right corner, the background has been removed in Photoshop.

The original archival photo

The original photo has been sharpened, grayscaled and silhouetted

The silhouetted photo has been placed into an InDesign document the same size as the finished title panel and other elements have been added.

**Figure A4.3** Silhouetted image. Photo by author from the collections of The Henry Ford Museum, P1774.X.141.

The lower image shows the silhouetted photo incorporated into the new title panel. The title lettering has been rendered in a modern streamlined font from the same era as the image and placed immediately above the figures for maximum impact. The subtitle and introductory text have been set off to the right so that they will be read after the larger title text. They have been placed on a black background to the right of the original photo and separated from it by a graphic motif reminiscent of a highway centerline.

### Make It Big

In the example above, we saw how a large title banner could greet visitors to the exhibit and present a temporary obstacle that would draw them into the show to see more. The same principle of making things large enough to be noticeable can also be applied on a smaller scale. In the top left image in figure A4.4, a wall that once held a number of smaller images has been reformatted with three large panels. Each panel is the same size and similar in its basic graphic elements. Each has a full-bleed image in the background and a highlight bar of transparent color on the left-hand side that also contains the title. The number and placement of the images varies from panel to panel, but there is enough of a family resemblance to make them cohesive. The top right image shows part of a banner that was created to show through the entrance door to the gallery, which is located in a small historic cottage. On the mantelpiece are the silhouetted figures shown in figure A4.1. The back of the entrance banner can be seen in the lower image.

The wall in the lower image had two existing slant-top display cases, so the panels were kept the same size as the others but changed to landscape format to fit above the tops of the cases.

Smaller elements have been grouped into three large panels, each with a key color

A hanging banner in the doorway introduces the exhibit and directs visitors to the left

The back of the hanging banner can be seen to the left. Because of the display cases, these two graphic panels have been changed to landscape format and their widths matched to the cases below

**Figure A4.4** Large graphic panels.

Their layout differs somewhat because of the horizontal format, with the transparent color bars running across the panel, but the overall graphic treatment is similar enough that the exhibit panels still hold together.

By using these larger panels, the first thing the visitor sees when entering the gallery is a number of large, bright graphic panels with noticeable titles that introduce the themes of the exhibit. The impact is much stronger than it would be if each of the images and captions were a discreet item mounted to the wall without any background.

# Glossary

**Bleed** Extra image area added to a layout to allow for trimming.

**Cabinet of curiosities** Wide-ranging and eclectic Renaissance collections, primarily of natural history specimens (see *Wunderkammer*).

**Cantilever** An element projecting from a vertical surface without support.

**Casework** Any type of exhibit case.

**Center-punch** A mark made with a sharpened punch to locate a drilled hole.

**CMYK** The four colors used in process printing: cyan; magenta; yellow; key (black).

**Contingency** Funds set aside in a budget to allow for unexpected costs.

**Copy, body copy** Text; the main portion of the text.

**Critical success factor** An element that is absolutely necessary for a project to succeed.

**Crop mark** Small vertical and horizontal marks at the edges of a layout to show where it is to be trimmed.

**Cross-cut** Cutting across the grain of a piece of wood.

**Dado** A slot cut into a piece of stock, also known as a rebate or rabbet.

**Dashboard panel** A low text or graphic panel set in front of an exhibit, typically at a forty-five-degree angle.

**Design development** The phase after schematic design and before final design, where important elements are defined.

**Digital imaging** Creation of a digital image through photography or scanning.

**Dimensioned sketch** A drawing that is not to scale but has true dimensions noted.

**Endcap** A display element placed at the end of a wall or fixture.

**Executive summary** A short summary of the important points of a document.

**Exhibit furniture** Constructed elements used to present the artifacts, graphics, and other elements of an exhibit.

**FPO** For position only; low-resolution images used to create a design that will be substituted for high-resolution images before production.

**Greeking, greeked text** Non-English (typically Latin) text used as a placeholder in developing layouts.

**Imaging** See *Digital imaging*.

**Learning objectives** A statement of what exhibit visitors will know after having visited the exhibit.

**Millwork** Constructed elements, typically of wood, including cases, plinths, trim, and moldings.

**Miter** An angled cut, typically forty-five degrees, enabling two pieces to be joined at right angles to each other.

**Moiré** An undesirable pattern produced when the halftone dots in a printed image interfere with pixels during scanning.

**Plinth** A base or pedestal.

**Process color** See *CMYK*.

**Punch list** A document prepared near the end of the project listing work that is incomplete or incorrect that must be remedied before the project is completed.

**Retainage** A portion of the project fee withheld until the project is satisfactory and complete.

**Reveal** An exposed edge; for example, a molding that protrudes beyond a surface.

**RGB** A color model composed of red, green, and blue, used to render colors on a computer monitor.

**Rip** To cut a piece of wood with the grain.

**Safe zone** An area around the edges of a layout that contains background image or color but no content.

**Sans serif** Type without small lines at the end of characters, such as Helvetica.

**Schematic design** An initial design that defines the general scope and concept of a project.

**Serif** Type with small lines at the end of characters, such as Times New Roman.

**Shop drawings** Detailed design drawings used for fabrication of exhibit components.

**Spot color** A single premixed color applied at one time, as distinct from process color.

**Substrate** Any sheet material used to support graphics and images.

**Swatch** A small color sample.

**Taxonomic** Concerned with classification.

**Tombstone label** An exhibit label with only basic information, such as artist, title, medium, and date.

**Typology** Classification according to type.

**Universal design** Design principles that enable the widest possible spectrum of users.

**Vitrine** A glass or Plexiglass top for a display case.

**Wunderkammer** German for "wonder chamber," a cabinet of curiosities.

# Index

public programming: and integration with exhibit planning, 59; and physical design of exhibit, 60; sample ideas for, 60–61

raster image, 102

request for proposals: and exhibit brief, 42; outline for, 42–43; and scope of work, 42;

sample, 177–81
scale models of exhibits, 108–10
scanning images, 105–6
schedule, 23
schema, 24
scope creep, 24
stories, in exhibits, xix
streetscape exhibits, 4
styles, of exhibit, 3–4
supported interpretation, 5

text: amount, 70–71; audience for, 69; biases in, 65–66; editing, 71; institutional voice, 66–67; levels, 70; proofreading, 71–72; role in exhibits, 62; size and placement, 64; tips for writing, 72–74; writing directly in layouts, 67
tombstone label, 34, 116
traveling exhibit considerations, 173–75
typography: general rules, *100*; terminology, 99–101; universal design, 110–13

value engineering, in budget, 82
vector image, 102, 104
visitor's bill of rights, 13–14
visitor experience, xix, 16, 34; and interpretive planning, 55; and use of artifacts, 118
visitor motivations, 15, 18, 45

# About the Author

Drawing on more than three decades of work at cultural institutions in Canada and the United States, **John Summers** brings a wide variety of skills and perspectives to the planning and design of museum exhibits. His teaching and practice combine a curator's attention to detail and authenticity with an educator's sense of audience, a designer's eye for color and layout, a fabricator's knowledge of tools and materials, and a manager's ability to build and lead collaborative teams and keep on top of budgets and schedules.

He is currently manager of heritage services and curator for the regional municipality of Halton in Ontario, Canada, where he leads, develops, designs, and fabricates exhibit projects. He has taught students about museology, material culture studies, museums and technology, and exhibition design and planning for the Ontario Museum Association, the Fleming College Museum Management and Curatorship Program, the University of Victoria's Cultural Resource Management Program, and the University of Toronto's Faculty of Information, where he is an adjunct lecturer in the Museum Studies Program. He is course director for Exhibit Planning & Design, one of nine courses in the Ontario Museum Association's Certificate in Museum Studies.

After graduating from the University of Toronto's Master of Museum Studies Program, he worked for Heritage Toronto as supervisor of domestic interpretation at the Fort York National Historic Site, curator of The Marine Museum of Upper Canada, and curator of The Pier: Toronto's Waterfront Museum. During a decade in the United States, he was curator of the *Coronet* project at the International Yacht Restoration School in Newport, Rhode Island, and chief curator of the Antique Boat Museum in Clayton, New York. Returning to Canada, he served as general manager of the Canadian Canoe Museum in Peterborough, Ontario, before taking up his present position in 2014.